CHICKASAW BY BLOOD ENROLLMENT CARDS 1898-1914

VOLUME I

TRANSCRIBED BY

JEFF BOWEN

NATIVE STUDY
Gallipolis, Ohio
USA

Originally published:
Baltimore, Maryland
2009

Reprinted by:

Native Study LLC
Gallipolis, OH
www.nativestudy.com

Library of Congress Control Number: 2020915583

ISBN: 978-1-64968-039-6

Made in the United States of America.

Other Books and Series by Jeff Bowen

1901-1907 Native American Census Seneca, Eastern Shawnee, Miami, Modoc, Ottawa, Peoria, Quapaw, and Wyandotte Indians (Under Seneca School, Indian Territory)

1932 Census of The Standing Rock Sioux Reservation with Births And Deaths 1924-1932

Census of The Blackfeet, Montana, 1897- 1901 Expanded Edition

Eastern Cherokee by Blood, 1906-1910, Volumes I thru XIII

Choctaw of Mississippi Indian Census 1929-1932 with Births and Deaths 1924-1931 Volume I

Choctaw of Mississippi Indian Census 1933, 1934 & 1937, Supplemental Rolls to 1934 & 1935 with Births and Deaths 1932-1938, and Marriages 1936-1938 Volume II

Eastern Cherokee Census Cherokee, North Carolina 1930-1939 Census 1930-1931 with Births And Deaths 1924-1931 Taken By Agent L. W. Page Volume I

Eastern Cherokee Census Cherokee, North Carolina 1930-1939 Census 1932-1933 with Births And Deaths 1930-1932 Taken By Agent R. L. Spalsbury Volume II

Eastern Cherokee Census Cherokee, North Carolina 1930-1939 Census 1934-1937 with Births and Deaths 1925-1938 and Marriages 1936 & 1938 Taken by Agents R. L. Spalsbury And Harold W. Foght Volume III

Seminole of Florida Indian Census, 1930-1940 with Birth and Death Records, 1930-1938

Texas Cherokees 1820-1839 A Document For Litigation 1921

Choctaw By Blood Enrollment Cards 1898-1914 Volumes I thru XVII

Starr Roll 1894 (Cherokee Payment Rolls) Districts: Canadian, Cooweescoowee, and Delaware Volume One

Starr Roll 1894 (Cherokee Payment Rolls) Districts: Flint, Going Snake, and Illinois Volume Two

Starr Roll 1894 (Cherokee Payment Rolls) Districts: Saline, Sequoyah, and Tahlequah; Including Orphan Roll Volume Three

Other Books and Series by Jeff Bowen

Cherokee Intruder Cases Dockets of Hearings 1901-1909 Volumes I & II

Indian Wills, 1911-1921 Records of the Bureau of Indian Affairs
Books One thru Seven;

Native American Wills & Probate Records 1911-1921

Turtle Mountain Reservation Chippewa Indians 1932 Census with Births & Deaths, 1924-1932

This whole series is dedicated to my wife and best friend, Kathy.

ENROLLMENT CARDS FOR THE FIVE CIVILIZED TRIBES 1898-1914

On 93 rolls of this microfilm publication are reproduced the enrollment cards that were prepared by the staff of the Commission to the Five Civilized Tribes between 1898 and 1914. These records are part of Records of the Bureau of Indian Affairs, Record Group (RG) 75, and are housed in the Archives Branch of the Federal Archives and Records Center, Fort Worth, Tex. An act of Congress approved March 3, 1893 (27 Stat. 645), authorized the establishment of the Commission to negotiate agreements with the Cherokee, Choctaw, Chickasaw, Creek, and Seminole tribes providing for the dissolution of the tribal governments and the allotment of land to each tribal member. Senator Henry L. Dawes of Massachusetts was appointed Chairman of this Commission on November 1, 1893, after which it has commonly been referred to as the Dawes Commission. The Commission was authorized by an act of Congress approved June 28, 1898 (30 Stat. 495), to prepare citizenship (tribal membership) rolls for each tribe. These final rolls were the basis for allotment. Under this act, subsequent acts, and resulting agreements negotiated with each tribe, the Commission received applications for membership covering more than 250,000 people and enrolled more than 101,000. The tribal membership rolls were closed on March 4, 1907, by an act of Congress approved on April 26, 1906 (34 Stat. 370), although an additional 312 persons were enrolled under an act approved August 1, 1914. The Commission enrolled individuals as "citizens" of a tribe under the following categories: Citizens By Blood, Citizens by Marriage, New Born Citizens By Blood (enrolled under an act of Congress approved March 3, 1905), Minor Citizens By Blood (enrolled under an act of Congress approved April 26, 1906), Freedmen (former black slaves of Indians, later freed and admitted to tribal citizenship), New Born Freedmen, and Minor Freedmen. Delaware Indians adopted by the Cherokee tribe were enrolled as a separate group within the Cherokee. Within each enrollment category, the Commission generally maintained three types of cards: "Straight" cards for persons whose applications were approved, "D" cards for persons whose applications were considered doubtful and subject to question, and "R" cards for persons whose applications were rejected. Persons listed on "D" cards were subsequently transferred to either "Straight" or "R" cards depending on the Commission's decisions. All decisions of the Commission were sent to the Secretary of the Interior for final approval.

An enrollment card, sometimes referred to by the Commission as a "census card," records the information provided by individual applications submitted by members of the same family group or household and includes notation of the actions taken. The information given for each applicant includes name, roll number (individual's number if enrolled), age, sex, degree of Indian blood, relationship to the head of the family group, parents' names, and references to enrollment on earlier rolls used by the Commission for verification of eligibility. The card often includes references to kin-related enrollment cards and notations about births, deaths, changes in marital status, and actions taken by the Commission and the Secretary of the Interior. Within each enrollment category, the cards are arranged numerically by a "field" or "census card" number, which is separate from the roll number. The index to the final rolls, which is reproduced on roll 1 of this publication, provides the roll number for each person while the final rolls themselves provide the census card numbers for each enrollee. No indexes have been located for the majority of the "D" and "R" cards. There are a few Mississippi Choctaw "Identified" and "Field Cards" as well as some Chickasaw "Cancelled" that refer to person never finally enrolled.

National Archives and Records Administration
American Indians Catalogue, p. 41

INTRODUCTION

The following Introduction describes the considerations employed in transcribing the Chickasaw enrollment cards that comprise the basis for this series. The Chickasaw by Blood enrollment cards, sometimes called "census cards" by the Dawes Commission, were pre-printed cards or loose sheets of paper labeled **Chickasaw Nation. Chickasaw Roll (Not Including Freedmen) with Residence County**. The heading **Post Office** appeared on the left side of each card, and **Card No., Field No.** on the right. The cards were further broken down into the categories *Dawes No., Name, Relationship to Person First Named, Age, Sex, Blood, Tribal Enrollment (Year, Town, Page), Name of Father, Year, Town, Name of Mother, Year, Town*, as well as *Tribal Enrollments of Parents*. For whatever reason, no card numbers were recorded in the corresponding field on any of the cards.

This and subsequent volumes have been transcribed from National Archives microfilm series M-1186: Roll 67, 1-662 and Roll 68, 663-1424. The page format of this transcription does not follow the microfilm exactly, owing to the space restrictions of the book format, but I have endeavored to include all categories of information supplied in the original. Also, the Dawes Roll No. has been relegated to the Notes area of each transcribed page. The notes section also contains information such as, Other name listings, Transfers to different cards, Birth dates, Death dates, listings on various payrolls with years, even sometimes a mention of a spouse in the doubtful category with card number, spouse possibly from another tribe, or a marriage license and certificate that was on file along with location. Sometimes the notes contain revealing information such as the following, "5/31/99. It is reported that Wm. Washington has this woman on his place and had parties to marry and they have never lived together—Investigate." Interestingly, this tidbit was found not under the representation of Wm. Washington but under that of Head of Household "Frank Osavior." Finally, the category "County" indicates the status of Non-Citizen, ethnicity, or Creek Roll, Cherokee Roll, Chocktaw Roll, etc.

Jeff Bowen
Gallipolis, OH
NativeStudy.com

RESIDENCE: Tishomingo **COUNTY** **CARD NO.**
POST OFFICE: Connerville, Ind. Ter. **FIELD NO.**

	NAME	RELATIONSHIP TO PERSON FIRST NAMED	AGE	SEX	BLOOD	TRIBAL ENROLLMENT YEAR	COUNTY	PAGE
1	Alexander, Gipson		26	M	Full	1897	Tishomingo	37

TRIBAL ENROLLMENT OF PARENTS

	NAME OF FATHER	YEAR	COUNTY	NAME OF MOTHER	YEAR	COUNTY
1	Pierce Alexander	Dead	Chickasaw roll	Lucy Alexander	Dead	Chickasaw Roll

(NOTES)

Sept. 27/98.

RESIDENCE: Pontotoc **COUNTY** **CARD NO.**
POST OFFICE: Purcell, Ind. Ter. **FIELD NO.**

	NAME	RELATIONSHIP TO PERSON FIRST NAMED	AGE	SEX	BLOOD	TRIBAL ENROLLMENT YEAR	COUNTY	PAGE
1	Johnston, Lawrence Lister		42	M	1/8	1897	Pontotoc	64
2	" Georgianna	Wife	36	F	I.W.	1897	"	81
3	" Willie	Son	16	M	1/16	1897	"	64
4	" Dellena	Dau	14	F	1/16	1897	"	64
5	" Maggie May	"	11	"	1/16	1897	"	64
6	" Annie	"	9	"	116	1897	"	64

TRIBAL ENROLLMENT OF PARENTS

	NAME OF FATHER	YEAR	COUNTY	NAME OF MOTHER	YEAR	COUNTY
1	Thos. B. Johnston (I.W.)	Dead	Pontotoc	Lizzie Johnston	Dead	Pontotoc
2	Benj. Barnett	"	Non-Citizen	Mary Barnett		Non-Citizen
3	No. 1			No. 2		
4	No. 1			No. 2		
5	No. 1			No. 2		
6	No. 1			No. 2		

(NOTES)

No. 2 on Chickasaw roll as Georianna Johnston *(No. 2 Dawes' Roll No. I.W. 32)*
No. 5 " " " " Maggie "
No. 1 " " " " L.L. "
No. 4 is now the wife of Fred A. Autry. Evidence of marriage filed October 25, 1902.
See also evidence of Fred A. Autry taken Oct. 22, 1902.

Sept. 27/98.

RESIDENCE: Pickens **COUNTY**					**CARD NO.**		
POST OFFICE: Lock, Ind. Ter.					**FIELD NO.**		
	NAME	**RELATIONSHIP TO PERSON FIRST NAMED**	**AGE**	**SEX**	**BLOOD**	**TRIBAL ENROLLMENT**		
						YEAR	**COUNTY**	**PAGE**
1	Lewis, Polly		49	F	Full	1897	Pickens	25
2	Kaney, Lafayette	G.Son	15	M	"	1897	"	25

TRIBAL ENROLLMENT OF PARENTS

	NAME OF FATHER	**YEAR**	**COUNTY**	**NAME OF MOTHER**	**YEAR**	**COUNTY**
1	Sha-pe-ya-ke	Dead	Chickasaw roll	Co-ik-ke	Dead	Chickasaw roll
2	Harmon Kaney	1897	Pickens	Sophie Hunter	"	Pickens

(NOTES)

No. 2 on Chickasaw roll as Lafeate

Sept. 27/98.

RESIDENCE: Tishomingo **COUNTY**					**CARD NO.**		
POST OFFICE: Tishomingo, Ind. Ter.					**FIELD NO.**		
	NAME	**RELATIONSHIP TO PERSON FIRST NAMED**	**AGE**	**SEX**	**BLOOD**	**TRIBAL ENROLLMENT**		
						YEAR	**COUNTY**	**PAGE**
1	Burris, Lemuel Colbert		27	M	1/2	1897	Tishomingo	38
2	" Zula	Wife	26	F	I.W.			--
3	" George Washington	Bro	26	M	1/2	1897	"	40
4	" Lemuel Colbert	Son	4mo	"	1/4			
5	" Emily	Dau	1mo	F	1/4			

TRIBAL ENROLLMENT OF PARENTS

	NAME OF FATHER	**YEAR**	**COUNTY**	**NAME OF MOTHER**	**YEAR**	**COUNTY**
1	Colbert A. Burris	1897	Pontotoc	Laura A. Burris (I.W.)	1897	Pontotoc
2	James McClatchy		Non-Citizen	Lucy McClatchy		Non-Citizen
3	Colbert A. Burris	1897	Pontotoc	Laura A. Burris	1897	Pontotoc
4	No. 1			No. 2		
5	No. 1			No. 2		

(NOTES)

No. 1 on Chickasaw roll as L.C. Burssi

No. 2 Marriage license and certificate to be supplied. Received Sept. 27/98. *(No. 2 Dawes' Roll No. I.W. 31)*

No. 3 on Chickasaw roll as G.W. Burris

No 1 and 2 as to evidence of marriage of parents see Card No. 44

No. 5 Enrolled Jany 11, 1901.

No. 1 Died Oct. 9, 1901. Proof of death filed Nov. 8, 1902.

No. 4 Enrolled Nov. 3/99.

(Another notation illegible, too light)

Sept. 27/98.

RESIDENCE: Tishomingo COUNTY					CARD NO.			
POST OFFICE: Dougherty, Ind. Ter.					FIELD NO.			
	NAME	RELATION-SHIP TO PERSON FIRST NAMED	AGE	SEX	BLOOD	TRIBAL ENROLLMENT		
						YEAR	COUNTY	PAGE
1	Hays, Thomas		32	M	1/2			
2	" Rose	Wife	21	F	I.W.			
3	" Annetta	Dau	2	"	1/4			
4	" Jennetta	"	8mos	"	1/4			
5	" Benton Orthella	Son	3mos	M	1/4			

TRIBAL ENROLLMENT OF PARENTS

	NAME OF FATHER	YEAR	COUNTY	NAME OF MOTHER	YEAR	COUNTY
1	Alexander Hays	Dead	Choctaw roll	Jennie Hays	Dead	Chickasaw roll
2	B.T. Elkin		Non-Citizen	Tempey Elkin		Non citizn
3	No. 1			No. 2		
4	No. 1			No. 2		
5	No. 1			No. 2		

(NOTES)

Nos 1 and 3 on Choctaw Census Record No. 2, Page 258; transferred to Chick roll by Dawes Com.
No. 2 " " Intermarried Roll, " 47 " " " " " " "
No. 4 affidavit of attending physician to be supplied – Received Oct. 5/98.
No. 1 on Choctaw Roll 1896 Chickasaw District No. 6161 as Thomas Hayes
No. 2 " " " 1896 " " " 14667 as Rose "
No. 3 " " " 1896 " " " 6170 as Annetta Hays
No. 5 Enrolled May 24, 1900.

Sept. 27/98.

RESIDENCE: Pickens COUNTY					CARD NO.			
POST OFFICE: Bradley, Ind. Ter.					FIELD NO.			
	NAME	RELATION-SHIP TO PERSON FIRST NAMED	AGE	SEX	BLOOD	TRIBAL ENROLLMENT		
						YEAR	COUNTY	PAGE
1	Bradley, Frank Colbert		17	M	1/8	1897	Pickens	93
2	" Clara Hicks	Sister	15	F	1/8	1897	"	93
3	" Earnest	Bro	13	M	1/8	1897	"	93
4	" Nellie	Sister	11	F	1/8	1897	"	P.R.#2 40
5	" Holmes	Bro	8	M	1/8	1897	"	93
6	" Winter P.	Father	47	M	I.W.			

	TRIBAL ENROLLMENT OF PARENTS					
	NAME OF FATHER	YEAR	COUNTY	NAME OF MOTHER	YEAR	COUNTY
1	Winter P. Bradley		White man	Texanna Bradley	Dead	Pickens
2	" " "		" "	" "	"	"
3	" " "		" "	" "	"	"
4	" " "		" "	" "	"	"
5	" " "		" "	" "	"	"
6	Pressley Bradley	Dead	Non-Citizen	Francis Bradley	Dead	Non-Citizen

(NOTES)

No. 1 admitted by U.S. Court, Ardmore, I.T. March 12, 1898 case #811
No 1 to 6 incl. admitted by Com in 96 Case No. 18
No. 6 transferred from Chickasaw Card #C-5 July 15, 1904.

Sept. 26/98.

RESIDENCE: Tishomingo COUNTY						CARD NO.		
POST OFFICE: Davis, Ind. Ter.						FIELD NO.		
	NAME	RELATION-SHIP TO PERSON FIRST NAMED	AGE	SEX	BLOOD	TRIBAL ENROLLMENT YEAR	COUNTY	PAGE
1	Guy, William Malcolm		53	M	1/8	1897	Tishomingo	31
2	" Maggie J.	Wife	20	F	I.W.	1897	"	83
3	" Serena Josephine	Dau	7	F	1/16	1897	Tishomingo	31
4	" Angeline Elizabeth	"	5	F	1/16	1897	"	31

	TRIBAL ENROLLMENT OF PARENTS					
	NAME OF FATHER	YEAR	COUNTY	NAME OF MOTHER	YEAR	COUNTY
1	Wm M. Guy	Dead	Non-Citizen	Jan McGee Guy	Dead	Chickasaw Roll
2	Lindsey	Dead	Non-Citizen	Pam Lindsey		
3	No. 1			Maggie J. Guy		white woman
4	No. 1			" " "		" "

(NOTES)

No. 1 on Chickasaw roll as William Guy *(No. 2 Dawes' Roll No. I.W. 186)*
No. 3 " " " " Serena "
No. 4 " " " " Angeline "
No. 1 husband of Maggie J. Guy, Chickasaw Card No. D.79
No. 2 transferred from Chickasaw Card D.79
See decision.

Sept. 26/98.

RESIDENCE: Panola COUNTY					CARD NO.		
POST OFFICE: Meade, Ind. Ter.					FIELD NO.		
NAME	RELATION-SHIP TO PERSON FIRST NAMED	AGE	SEX	BLOOD	TRIBAL ENROLLMENT		
					YEAR	COUNTY	PAGE
1 Godfrey, Wesley Calhoun		23	M	Full	1897	Panola	2
2 " Louisa	Dau	3	F	1/2	1897	"	2

TRIBAL ENROLLMENT OF PARENTS

	NAME OF FATHER	YEAR	COUNTY	NAME OF MOTHER	YEAR	COUNTY
1	Johnson Calhoun	Dead	Chickasaw roll	Emily Calhoun	Dead	Chickasaw roll
2	No. 1			Nellie Godfrey		Non-Citizen

(NOTES)

No. 1 Member of Company "M". Roosevelt's Rough Riders
No. 2 on Chickasaw roll as Louisa Calhoun
No. 1 Died about Feb. 27, 1901; Proof of death filed Nov. 8, 1902.

Sept. 26/98.

RESIDENCE: Pickens COUNTY					CARD NO.		
POST OFFICE: Kingston, Ind. Ter.					FIELD NO.		
NAME	RELATION-SHIP TO PERSON FIRST NAMED	AGE	SEX	BLOOD	TRIBAL ENROLLMENT		
					YEAR	COUNTY	PAGE
1 Sealy, Dave		38	M	Full	1897	Pickens	22
2 " Julie	Wife	25	F	I.W.	1897	"	79
3 " Annie	Dau	7	F	1/2	1897	"	22
4 " Wilburn	Son	3	M	1/2	1897	"	22
5 " Limond	"	1mo	"	1/2			
6 " Ely	Son	4mo	M	1/2			

TRIBAL ENROLLMENT OF PARENTS

	NAME OF FATHER	YEAR	COUNTY	NAME OF MOTHER	YEAR	COUNTY
1	Stephen Sealy	Dead	Chickasaw Roll	Phoebi Sealy	1897	Pickens
2	William Thomason	"	Non-Citizen	Cyntha Thomason	Dead	Non-Citizen
3	No. 1			No. 2		
4	No. 1			No. 2		
5	No. 1			No. 2		
6	No. 1			No. 2		

(NOTES)

No. 2 on Chickasaw roll as Julia Sealy
No. 5 affidavit of attending physician to be supplied. Received Oct. 10/98.
No. 6 Enrolled June 14, 1901.
No. 4 Died May 1, 1902. Proof of death filed Nov. 7, 1902 Sept. 26/98.

RESIDENCE: Tishomingo COUNTY					CARD NO.		
POST OFFICE: Mill Creek, Ind. Ter.					FIELD NO.		
NAME	RELATION-SHIP TO PERSON FIRST NAMED	AGE	SEX	BLOOD	TRIBAL ENROLLMENT		
					YEAR	COUNTY	PAGE
1 Browning, Annie		30	F	Full	1897	Tishomingo	29
2 " Josiah	Son	7	M	1/2	1897	"	29
3 " Albert	Son	4	M	1/2	1897	"	29
4 " Lovie Ann	Dau	2	F	1/2	1897	"	29
5 " William H.	Son	1mo	M	1/2	New born	"	29
6 " Bula B.	Dau	6mo	F	1/2			
7 " Samuel Winston	Husb	45	M	I.W.			

TRIBAL ENROLLMENT OF PARENTS

	NAME OF FATHER	YEAR	COUNTY	NAME OF MOTHER	YEAR	COUNTY
1	Walton Hall	Dead	Chickasaw Roll	Malinda Hall	Dead	Chickasaw Roll
2	Samuel W. Browning (I.W.)		White man	No. 1		
3	" " "		" "	No. 1		
4	" " "		" "	No. 1		
5	" " "		" "	No. 1		
6	" " "		" "	No. 1		
7	Wm. Henry Browning		Non-Citizen	Lucy Browning	Dead	Non-Citizen

(NOTES)

No. 1 on Chickasaw Roll as Anna Browning, wife of Samuel Winston Browning
Chickasaw Card No. #D78.
No. 2 on Chickasaw roll as Joe Browning
No. 4 " " " " Lower "
No. 5 Enrolled June 8, 1900
No. 1 Died April 10, 1902; broof of death filed Aug. 16, 1902
No. 6 Born Feby 13, 1902; enrolled Aug. 28, 1902 Sept. 26/98.
No. 3 is a male; change made under Dept *(illegible word)* of March 9, 1904
No. 7 transferred from Chickasaw card #D78. See decision of March 5, 1904. March 3, 1904

RESIDENCE: Tishomingo COUNTY					CARD NO.		
POST OFFICE: Tishomingo, Ind. Ter.					FIELD NO.		
NAME	RELATION-SHIP TO PERSON FIRST NAMED	AGE	SEX	BLOOD	TRIBAL ENROLLMENT		
					YEAR	COUNTY	PAGE
1 Brown, Cyrus Harris		32	M	1/8	1897	Tishomingo	37
2 " Ida Belle	Wife	24	F	I.W.	1897	"	79
3 " William Josiah	Son	8	M	1/16	1897	"	37

4	" James Lewis	"	6	"	1/16	1897	"	38
5	" Guy	"	4	"	1/16	1897	"	38
6	" Virginia Catherine	Dau	2	"	1/16	1897	"	38
7	" Ethel	"	2mos	"	1/16			
8	" Cyrus Harris	Son	2wks	M	1/16			

Tribal Enrollment of Parents

	Name of Father	Year	County	Name of Mother	Year	County
1	Josiah Brown	1897	Tishomingo	Frances V. Brown	Dead	Non-Citizen
2	W.A. Anderson	"	Non-Citizen	Mary M. Anderson	"	" "
3	No. 1			No. 2		
4	No. 1			No. 2		
5	No. 1			No. 2		
6	No. 1			No. 2		
7	No. 1			No. 2		
8	No. 1			No. 2		

(Notes)

No. 1 on Chickasaw roll as C.H. Brown
No. 2 " " " " I.B. " *(No. 2 Dawes' Roll No. 125)*
No. 3 " " " " W.J. "
No. 4 " " " " J.L. "
No. 6 " " " " Kate " *(No. 6 Dawes' Roll No. 4123)*
No. 6 Proof of birth received and filed Nov. 7, 1902.
No. 7 Affidavit of attending physician to be supplied. Received Sept. 06/98.
No. 8 Enrolled Sept. 11, 1901. Sept. 26/98.

Residence: Tishomingo **County** **Card No.**
Post Office: Tishomingo, Ind. Ter. **Field No.**

	Name	Relationship to Person First Named	Age	Sex	Blood	Tribal Enrollment Year	County	Page
1	Brown, Josiah		63	M	1/4	1897	Tishomingo	37
2	" Martha Josephine	Wife	42	F	I.W.	1897	"	79

Tribal Enrollment of Parents

	Name of Father	Year	County	Name of Mother	Year	County
1	Louis L. Brown	Dead	Non-Citizen	Catherine Brown	Dead	Chickasaw roll
2	Jacob Roberts	"	" "	Margaret M. Roberts	"	Non-Citizen

(Notes)

No. 1 On Chickasaw roll as Joe Brown, Sr.
No. 2 " " " " N.J. "

Sept. 26/98.

RESIDENCE: Tishomingo **COUNTY**					**CARD NO.**			
POST OFFICE: Palmer, Ind. Ter.					**FIELD NO.**			
	NAME	**RELATIONSHIP TO PERSON FIRST NAMED**	**AGE**	**SEX**	**BLOOD**	**TRIBAL ENROLLMENT**		
						YEAR	**COUNTY**	**PAGE**
1	Palmer, Thomas L.		38	M	I.W.	1897	Pontotoc	80
2	" Rhoda	Wife	38	F	Full	1897	"	48
3	" Joseph	Son	9	M	1/2	1897	"	48
4	" Lafayette	"	1	M	1/2	1897	"	48
5	" Elizabeth M.	Dau	5wks	F	1/2			

TRIBAL ENROLLMENT OF PARENTS

	NAME OF FATHER	**YEAR**	**COUNTY**	**NAME OF MOTHER**	**YEAR**	**COUNTY**
1	Joe Palmer	Dead	Non-Citizen	Jane Palmer	Dead	Non-Citizen
2	Amos McGee	"	Chickasaw Roll	Lottie McGee	"	Chickasaw roll
3	No. 1			No. 2		
4	No. 1			No. 2		
5	No. 1			No. 2		

(NOTES)

No. 1 on Chickasaw Roll as Bud Palmer *(No. 1 Dawes' Roll No. I.W. 29)*
No. 4 " " " " Lafeate "
Elizabeth M. Palmer born Dec. 8/99, on Card D.309
No. 5 born December 8, 1899; transferred to the card February 1, 1902.

P.O. Sulphur, I.T. 11/6/02 Sept. 26/98.

RESIDENCE: Tishomingo **COUNTY**					**CARD NO.**			
POST OFFICE: Sulphur, Ind. Ter.					**FIELD NO.**			
	NAME	**RELATIONSHIP TO PERSON FIRST NAMED**	**AGE**	**SEX**	**BLOOD**	**TRIBAL ENROLLMENT**		
						YEAR	**COUNTY**	**PAGE**
1	McCarty, William		34	M	1/4	1897	Tishomingo	29
2	" Sampie	Wife	27	F	I.W.	1897	"	79
3	" Mary Elizabeth	Dau	9	"	1/8	1897	"	29
4	" Nettie	"	7	"	1/8	1897	"	29
5	" James William	Son	5	M	1/8	1897	"	29
6	" Claudie Eugene	"	1	"	1/8			
7	" Jennie Lou Mittie	Dau	1mo	F	1/8			
8	" Jefferson Odie L.	Son	3wks	M	1/8			

	TRIBAL ENROLLMENT OF PARENTS					
	NAME OF FATHER	YEAR	COUNTY	NAME OF MOTHER	YEAR	COUNTY
1	Jim McCarty	Dead	Non-Citizen	Mary McCarty	Dead	Chickasaw Roll
2	Jeff Moss		" "	Sarah Moss	"	Non-Citizen
3	No. 1			No. 2		
4	No. 1			No. 2		
5	No. 1			No. 2		
6	No. 1			No. 2		
7	No. 1			No. 2		
8	No. 1			No. 2		

(NOTES)

No. 2 on Chickasaw roll as Samp. McCarty
No. 3 " " " " Mary L. "
No. 5 " " " " Jas. "
No. 6 Affidavit of midwife to be supplied. Received Oct. 31/98.
No. 7 Enrolled June 7, 1900.
No. 8 Born Sept. 23, 1902. Enrolled Oct. 15. 1902. *(No. 8 Dawes' Roll No. 4422)*

Sept. 26/98.

RESIDENCE: Choctaw Nation, (3rd Dist.) ***COUNTY*** ***CARD NO.***
POST OFFICE: Stringlown, I.T. ***FIELD NO.***

	NAME	RELATION-SHIP TO PERSON FIRST NAMED	AGE	SEX	BLOOD	TRIBAL ENROLLMENT		
						YEAR	COUNTY	PAGE
1	Bond, Mary		49	F	1/2			
2	" Cornelius	Son	18	M	1/4			
3	" Eliza	Dau	14	F	1/4			
4	" Sallie Ann	"	11	"	1/4			
5	" Emeline	"	8	"	1/4			
6	" Esther	"	5	"	1/4			

	TRIBAL ENROLLMENT OF PARENTS					
	NAME OF FATHER	YEAR	COUNTY	NAME OF MOTHER	YEAR	COUNTY
1	Alexander Billie	Dead	Choctaw roll	Ah-lawecha Billie	Dead	Chickasaw Roll
2	Jesse Bond		Jack Fork County Choctaw roll	No. 1		
3	" "		" "	No. 1		
4	" "		" "	No. 1		
5	" "		" "	No. 1		
6	" "		" "	No. 1		

(NOTES)

All on Choctaw Census Record No. 2, Page 76; transferred to Chickasaw roll by Dawes Com.
No. 1 is wife of No. 1 on Choctaw roll card #1900
No. 1 on Choctaw Roll 1896, Jack Fork County, No. 1873
No. 2 " " " 1896, " " " " 1874
No. 3 " " " 1896, " " " " 1875
No. 4 " " " 1896. " " " " 1876 as Sally Ann Bond
No. 5 " " " 1896, " " " " 1877
No. 6 " " " 1896, " " " " 1878

Sept. 26/98.

RESIDENCE: Choctaw Nation (3rd Dist.) COUNTY CARD NO.
POST OFFICE: Stringlown, Ind. Ter. FIELD NO.

	NAME	RELATIONSHIP TO PERSON FIRST NAMED	AGE	SEX	BLOOD	TRIBAL ENROLLMENT YEAR	COUNTY	PAGE
1	Bond, Henry J.		26	M	1/4			

TRIBAL ENROLLMENT OF PARENTS

	NAME OF FATHER	YEAR	COUNTY	NAME OF MOTHER	YEAR	COUNTY
1	Jesse Bond		Jack Fork County Choctaw Roll	Mary Bond		Chick residing in Choctaw 3rd Dist.

(NOTES)

On Choctaw Census Record No. 2, Page 76; transferred to Chickasaw roll by Dawes Com.
Husband of Lizzie Bond, Choctaw Roll, Card No. 291.
Also on Choctaw Roll 1896, Jack Fork County, No. 1879, as Henry Bond.

Sept. 26/98.

RESIDENCE: Tishomingo COUNTY CARD NO.
POST OFFICE: Davis. Ind. Ter. FIELD NO.

	NAME	RELATIONSHIP TO PERSON FIRST NAMED	AGE	SEX	BLOOD	TRIBAL ENROLLMENT YEAR	COUNTY	PAGE
1	Harris, Henderson		25	M	1/2	1893	Pontotoc	P.R.#7 118
2	" Irene	Wife	29	F	I.W.			

TRIBAL ENROLLMENT OF PARENTS

	NAME OF FATHER	YEAR	COUNTY	NAME OF MOTHER	YEAR	COUNTY
1	Culberson Harris	Dead	Tishomingo	Viney Harris	Dead	Tishomingo
2	Winton W. Miller		Non-Citizen	Margaret E. Miller		Non-Citizen

(NOTES)

Husband of Irene Harris, Chickasaw Card No. D.77 *(No. 1 Dawes' Roll No. 4421)*

Also on Page 49, 1896 Roll, Pontotoc County *(No. 2 Dawes' Roll No. I.W. 282)*
No. 2 transferred from Chickasaw Card #D.77. See decision of March 5, 1904. March 23, 1904.

Sept. 26/98.

RESIDENCE: Choctaw Nation	COUNTY	CARD NO.
POST OFFICE: San Bois, Ind. Ter.		FIELD NO.

	NAME	RELATIONSHIP TO PERSON FIRST NAMED	AGE	SEX	BLOOD	TRIBAL ENROLLMENT YEAR	COUNTY	PAGE
1	Cooper, Norris		25	M	1/2			
2	" Frances	Wife	19	F	I.W.			
3	" Maude	Dau	1	"	1/4			

TRIBAL ENROLLMENT OF PARENTS

	NAME OF FATHER	YEAR	COUNTY	NAME OF MOTHER	YEAR	COUNTY
1	Henry Cooper	Dead	Choctaw roll	Becky Cooper	1897	Chick residing in Choctaw Na. 1st Dist.
2	John Banks	"	Non-Citizen	Mary Banks		Non-Citizen
3	No. 1			No. 2		

(NOTES)

No. 1 on Choctaw Census Record No. 2, Page 84, transferred to Chickasaw roll by Dawes Com.
No. 2 " " Intermarried Roll " 12 " " " " " " "
No. 1 on Choctaw Roll 1896, Sans Bois County, No. 2093
No. 2 " " " 1896 " " " " 14371 as Francis Cooper.

Sept. 26/98.

RESIDENCE: Choctaw Nation	COUNTY	CARD NO.
POST OFFICE: San Bois, Ind. Ter.		FIELD NO.

	NAME	RELATIONSHIP TO PERSON FIRST NAMED	AGE	SEX	BLOOD	TRIBAL ENROLLMENT YEAR	COUNTY	PAGE
1	Cooper, Becky		50	F	1/2			
2	" Robert	Son	19	M	1/4			
3	" Mary	Dau	14	F	1/4			
4	" Frances	"	12	"	1/4			
5	Bohannan, Silas W.	Grandson	2mo	M	1/8			

TRIBAL ENROLLMENT OF PARENTS

	NAME OF FATHER	YEAR	COUNTY	NAME OF MOTHER	YEAR	COUNTY
1	Coley	Dead	Choctaw roll	Rhoda Coley	Dead	Chickasaw roll
2	Henry Cooper	"	" "	No. 1		
3	" "	"	" "	No. 1		

4	" "	"	" "	No. 1		
5	Joseph Bohanan		" "	No. 3		

(NOTES)

Nos. 1, 3 and 4 on Choctaw Census Record No. 2, Page 84, transferred to Chickasaw roll by Dawes Com.
No. 2 " " " " No. 2, " 83, " " " " " " "
No. 1 at present the wife of Isreal Cooper, Choctaw roll Card No. 289
No. 4 on Choctaw roll as Frances Cooper
No. 3 is the wife of Joseph Bohanan on Choctaw Card #2838.
No. 1 on Choctaw Roll 1896 Sans Bois County, No. 2075 as Beckie Cooper
No. 2 " " " 1896 " " " " 2071
No. 3 " " " 1896 " " " " 2080
No. 4 " " " 1896 " " " " 2081 as Francis Cooper
No. 5 Enrolled November 21, 1900
No. 4 Died November 13, 1899. Evidence of death filed April 3, 1901.
No. 2 is now the husband of Sarah A. Mason a non-citizen
Evidence of marriage filed Mar. 6/01.
Evidence of marriage of No. 3 to be supplied; -
Filed Feby. 13, 1901.

Sept. 26/98.

RESIDENCE: Choctaw Nation (1st Dist.) ***COUNTY*** ***CARD NO.***
POST OFFICE: Alderson, Ind. Ter. ***FIELD NO.***

	NAME	RELATIONSHIP TO PERSON FIRST NAMED	AGE	SEX	BLOOD	TRIBAL ENROLLMENT YEAR	COUNTY	PAGE
1	McBee, Millie		42	F	Full	1897	Chickasaw residing in Choctaw N. 1st Dist.	68
2	Worcester, Arlington Telle	Bro	6	M	"	1897	" " " "	68

TRIBAL ENROLLMENT OF PARENTS

	NAME OF FATHER	YEAR	COUNTY	NAME OF MOTHER	YEAR	COUNTY
1	Nicholas Worcester	Dead	Chickasaw Roll	Tel-lo-neck-ka	Dead	Chickasaw Roll
2	" "	"	" "	Sil-le-a	"	" "

(NOTES)

No. 2 on Chickasaw Roll as Arlington T. Worcester *(No. 1 Dawes' Roll No. 4770)*
Sept. 12-99 No. 1 Married since above enrollment to William Impson, Choctaw

Sept. 26/98.

RESIDENCE: Choctaw Nation		**COUNTY**			**CARD NO.**				
POST OFFICE: Cartersville, Ind. Ter.					**FIELD NO.**				

	NAME	RELATION-SHIP TO PERSON FIRST NAMED	AGE	SEX	BLOOD	TRIBAL ENROLLMENT YEAR	COUNTY	PAGE
1	Hickman, Eugene A.		36	M	I.W.			
2	" Lucy	Wife	31	F	1/8			
3	" Chester	Son	12	M	1/16			
4	" Gertie	Dau	10	F	1/16			
5	" Manie	"	8	"	1/16			
6	" Willis	"	4	"	1/16			
7	" Hester	"	2	"	1/16			
8	" Lucy	"	4mos	"	1/16			
9	" Edwin L.	Nephew	19	M	1/4			
10	" Frankie	"	15	"	1/4			

TRIBAL ENROLLMENT OF PARENTS

	NAME OF FATHER	YEAR	COUNTY	NAME OF MOTHER	YEAR	COUNTY
1	Lad Hickman	Dead	Non-Citizen	Josephine Hickman		Non-Citizen
2	Peter McKinney	"	Choctaw roll	Jincey McKinney	Dead	Chickasaw Roll
3	No. 1			No. 2		
4	No. 1			No. 2		
5	No. 1			No. 2		
6	No. 1			No. 2		
7	No. 1			No. 2		
8	No. 1			No. 2		
9	Frank Hickman	Dead	Non-Citizen	Serena Hickman	Dead	Chickasaw Roll
10	" "	"	" "	" "	"	" "

(NOTES)

No. 1 on Choctaw Intermarried Roll, Page 40, transferred to Chickasaw roll by Dawes Com.
All others " " Census Record, No. 2 Page 218 " " " " " " "
No. 8 Affidavit of attending physician to be supplied. Received Nov. 7/98.
No. 1 on Choctaw Roll 1896, Sans Bois County No. 14593 as E.A. Hickman
All others (except No. 8) on Choctaw Roll 1896, Sans Bois County, No. 5, 5112 to 5119 inclusive
See list of names and numbers hereto attached.

Sept. 26/98.

RESIDENCE: Choctaw Nation **COUNTY** **CARD NO.**
POST OFFICE: Garland, Ind. Ter. **FIELD NO.**

	NAME	RELATIONSHIP TO PERSON FIRST NAMED	AGE	SEX	BLOOD	TRIBAL ENROLLMENT		
						YEAR	COUNTY	PAGE
1	Folsom, Frank		34	M	1/4			

TRIBAL ENROLLMENT OF PARENTS

	NAME OF FATHER	YEAR	COUNTY	NAME OF MOTHER	YEAR	COUNTY
1	Willie Folsom	Dead	Choctaw roll	Sim-cha-che	Dead	Chickasaw roll

(NOTES)

Husband of Charlotte Folsom, Choctaw roll, Card No. 288
On Choctaw Census Record No. 2, San Bois Co., Page 164, transferred to Chickasaw roll by Dawes Com.
Also on Choctaw roll, 1896, Sans Bois County, No. 3857.

Sept. 26/98.

RESIDENCE: Pickens **COUNTY** **CARD NO.**
POST OFFICE: Ara, Ind. Ter. **FIELD NO.**

	NAME	RELATIONSHIP TO PERSON FIRST NAMED	AGE	SEX	BLOOD	TRIBAL ENROLLMENT		
						YEAR	COUNTY	PAGE
1	Pickens, Edmon		8	M	1/2	1897	Tishomingo	31

TRIBAL ENROLLMENT OF PARENTS

	NAME OF FATHER	YEAR	COUNTY	NAME OF MOTHER	YEAR	COUNTY
1	Ed Pickens	Dead	Panola	Fannie Grove Marker		Non-Citizen

(NOTES)

On Chickasaw roll as Edmon Jr.
Mother Fannie Grove Pickens got a divorce from Ed Pickens and married G.G. Marker, Non-Citizen.

Sept. 26/98.

RESIDENCE: Choctaw Nation **COUNTY** **CARD NO.**
POST OFFICE: San Bois, Ind. Ter. **FIELD NO.**

	NAME	RELATIONSHIP TO PERSON FIRST NAMED	AGE	SEX	BLOOD	TRIBAL ENROLLMENT		
						YEAR	COUNTY	PAGE
1	Folsom, Elias		28	M	1/4			
2	" Edler	Wife	22	F	I.W.			
3	" Irene	Dau	2	"	1/8			
4	" Willis	Son	2mo	M	1/8			
5	" Vera	Dau	6wks	F	1/8			
6	" Dennis	Son	1mo	M	1/8			

TRIBAL ENROLLMENT OF PARENTS						
	NAME OF FATHER	YEAR	COUNTY	NAME OF MOTHER	YEAR	COUNTY
1	Willis Folsom	Dead	Choctaw roll	Sim-e-cha-che	Dead	Chickasaw roll
2	Matt Wade		Non-Citizen	Mary Wade		Non-Citizen
3	No. 1			No. 2		
4	No. 1			No. 2		
5	No. 1			Delena Folsom		Non-Citizen
6	No. 1			" "		" "

(NOTES)

Marriage certificate to be supplied.
Nos. 1 and 3 on Choctaw Census Record No. 2, Page163, transferred to Chickasaw roll by Dawes Com.
No. 2 " " Intermarried roll " 28 " " " " " " "
No. 2 on Choctaw roll as Edlin Folsom
No. 2 is dead and No. 1 was married Feby. 1st, 1900 to Delena Priest, a Non-Citizen
Evidence of marriage filed April 10, 1900
No. 4 Affidavit of attending physician to be supplied.
No. 4 Evidence of birth received and filed Sept. 6, 1902.
No. 1 on Choctaw Roll, 1896, Sans Bois County, No. 3829
No. 2 " " " 1896 " " " " 14509 as Edler Folsom
No. 3 " " " 1896 " " " " 3830.
Evidence of marriage between Nos. 1 and 2 received and filed March 29, 1902.
No. 5 Enrolled Dec. 26, 1900.
No. 6 Born July 10, 1902; enrolled Aug. 7, 1902.

Sept. 26/98.

RESIDENCE: Choctaw Nation COUNTY						CARD NO.		
POST OFFICE: Burgevin, Ind. Ter.						FIELD NO.		
	NAME	RELATION-SHIP TO PERSON FIRST NAMED	AGE	SEX	BLOOD	TRIBAL ENROLLMENT		
						YEAR	COUNTY	PAGE
1	McDaniel, Mary		43	F	1/4			
2	" Thomas	Son	22	M	1/8			
3	" Marvin	"	15	M	1/8			
4	" James	"	12	"	1/8			
5	" Mitchell	"	8	"	1/8			
6	" Ruth	Dau	7	F	1/8			
7	" Lula	"	4	"	1/8			
8	McCurtain, Ben	Nephew	22	M				
9	" Randolph	Son of No. 8	3mo	M				

TRIBAL ENROLLMENT OF PARENTS						
	NAME OF FATHER	YEAR	COUNTY	NAME OF MOTHER	YEAR	COUNTY
1	Willis Folsom	Dau[sic]	Choctaw roll	Sin-e-cha-che	Dead	Chickasaw roll
2	Ed McDaniel		Choctaw residing in Chickasaw Dist.	No. 1		
3	" "		" "	No. 1		
4	" "		" "	No. 1		
5	" "		" "	No. 1		
6	" "		" "	No. 1		
7	" "		" "	No. 1		
8	Green McCurtain		Choctaw Roll	Rhoda Fulsom	Dead	Chickasaw roll
9	No. 8			Clara McCurtain		Non-Citizen

(NOTES)

All on Choctaw Census Record No. 2, Page 361, transferred to Chickasaw roll by Dawes Com.
No. 8 " " " " No. 2, " 360 " " " " " " "
No. 1 on Choctaw Roll 1896, Skullyville County, No. 9035
No. 2 " " " 1896 " " " 9036
No. 3 " " " 1896 " " " 9037
No. 4 " " " 1896 " " " 9038
No. 5 " " " 1896 " " " 9039
No. 6 " " " 1896 " " " 9040
No. 7 " " " 1896 " " " 9041
No. 8 " " " 1896 " " " 9000

Husband of No. 1 and father of her children is Ed. McDaniel on Choctaw card #287

No. 8 husband of No. 1 on Chickasaw card #D.366 9/16/02.
No. 9 Born June 14, 1902, enrolled Sept. 11, 1902.
No. 2 is now the husband of Katie Folsom on Choctaw card #2786. March 7, 1902.
No. 3 is now the husband of Cammie McDaniel on Chick. Card #D.370. Sept. 23, 1902.
Post Office address of above now Cowlington, I.T.
No. 8 is now the husband of Clara McCurtaiss – Non-Citizen. Evidence of marriage filed Sept. 11, 1902.

Sept. 26/98.

RESIDENCE: Tishomingo COUNTY					CARD NO.			
POST OFFICE: Tishomingo, Ind. Ter.					FIELD NO.			
	NAME	RELATION-SHIP TO PERSON FIRST NAMED	AGE	SEX	BLOOD	TRIBAL ENROLLMENT		
						YEAR	COUNTY	PAGE
1	Kemp, Joel Carr		41	M	1/4	1897	Tishomingo	34

TRIBAL ENROLLMENT OF PARENTS						
	NAME OF FATHER	YEAR	COUNTY	NAME OF MOTHER	YEAR	COUNTY
1	Joel Kemp	Dead	Chickasaw Roll	Maria Kemp	Dead	Chickasaw Roll

(NOTES)

On Chickasaw roll as J.C. Kemp.
Husband of Elizabeth Minerva Kemp, Choctaw roll Card No. 286. Sept. 26/98.

RESIDENCE: Choctaw Nation (1st Dist.) **COUNTY** **CARD NO.**
POST OFFICE: Cowlington, Ind. Ter. **FIELD NO.**

	NAME	RELATIONSHIP TO PERSON FIRST NAMED	AGE	SEX	BLOOD	TRIBAL ENROLLMENT YEAR	COUNTY	PAGE
1	Folsom, Nathan		23	M	1/4			

TRIBAL ENROLLMENT OF PARENTS

	NAME OF FATHER	YEAR	COUNTY	NAME OF MOTHER	YEAR	COUNTY
1	Walker Folsom		San Bois County Choctaw roll	Hettie Folsom	Dead	Chickasaw roll

(NOTES)

On Choctaw Census Record No. 2, Page 163; transferred to Chickasaw roll by Dawes Com.
Also on Choctaw roll, 1896, Sans Bois County, No. 3822, as Nathan Folsum.

Sept. 26/98.

RESIDENCE: Choctaw Nation (3rd Dist.) **COUNTY** **CARD NO.**
POST OFFICE: Folsom, Ind. Ter. **FIELD NO.**

	NAME	RELATIONSHIP TO PERSON FIRST NAMED	AGE	SEX	BLOOD	TRIBAL ENROLLMENT YEAR	COUNTY	PAGE
1	Conway, Elizabeth J		56	F	I.W.			

TRIBAL ENROLLMENT OF PARENTS

	NAME OF FATHER	YEAR	COUNTY	NAME OF MOTHER	YEAR	COUNTY
1	Hardin Perkins	Dead	Non-Citizen	Katie Perkins	Dead	Non-Citizen

(NOTES)

Not on Chickasaw roll. *(No. 1 Dawes' Roll No. I.W. 470)*

Dec. 2 – 99: Docket shows this woman to have been rejected by Com in 1896, from which there was no appeal. Denied by Dawes Commission in 1896 both as a citizen by blood and by intermarriage; see Chickasaw 1896 Case #242.

Sept. 26/98.

RESIDENCE: Tishomingo **COUNTY** **CARD NO.**
POST OFFICE: Tishomingo, Ind. Ter. **FIELD NO.**

	NAME	RELATIONSHIP TO PERSON FIRST NAMED	AGE	SEX	BLOOD	TRIBAL ENROLLMENT YEAR	COUNTY	PAGE
1	Wolfe, Harriett		15	F		1897	Tishomingo	32
2	" Mattie	Sister	12	"	1/2	1897	"	32
3	" Frances	"	9	"	1/2	1897	"	32

	TRIBAL ENROLLMENT OF PARENTS					
	NAME OF FATHER	YEAR	COUNTY	NAME OF MOTHER	YEAR	COUNTY
1	Jim Wolfe	Dead	Tishomingo	Esther McLish		Cherokee Indian
2	" "	"	"	" "		" "
3	" "	"	"	" "		" "

(NOTES)

No. 1 transferred to Chickasaw Card No. 1492 at Durant, I.T. ?/15/99
No. 3 on Chickasaw roll as Francis Wolfe
Mother, Esther McLish, widow of Jim Wolfe. She was never on Cherokee rolls, although her parents were Cherokee Indians.

Sept. 26/98.

RESIDENCE:	Choctaw Nation (1st Dist.)	COUNTY		CARD NO.	
POST OFFICE:	Stigler, Ind. Ter.			FIELD NO.	

	NAME	RELATION-SHIP TO PERSON FIRST NAMED	AGE	SEX	BLOOD	TRIBAL ENROLLMENT		
						YEAR	COUNTY	PAGE
1	Coleman, Arian		28	F	1/4			
2	" Bertha Marie	Dau	4	"	1/8			
3	" Bessie Neva	"	1	"	1/8			
4	" Ola Gladys	Dau	4mo	"	1/8			

	TRIBAL ENROLLMENT OF PARENTS					
	NAME OF FATHER	YEAR	COUNTY	NAME OF MOTHER	YEAR	COUNTY
1	Walker Folsom		San Bois County Choctaw roll	Hettie Folsom	Dead	Chickasaw roll
2	Henry L. Coleman		Non-Citizen	No. 1		
3	" " "		" "	No. 1		
4	" " "		" "	No. 1		

(NOTES)

All on Choctaw Census Record No. 2, Page 86; transferred to Chickasaw roll by Dawes Com.
No. 1 On Choctaw roll as Aaron Coleman
No. 2 " " " " Marie "
No. 3 " " " " Bessie "
No. 1 on Choctaw roll, 1896, Sans Bois County, No. 2128
No. 2 " " " 1896 " " " No. 2129 as Marie Coleman
No. 4 Enrolled May 24, 1900.

Sept. 26/98.

RESIDENCE: Tishomingo COUNTY		CARD NO.						
POST OFFICE: Nebo, Ind. Ter.		FIELD NO.						
	NAME	RELATION-SHIP TO PERSON FIRST NAMED	AGE	SEX	BLOOD	TRIBAL ENROLLMENT YEAR	COUNTY	PAGE
1	Sharp, Sallie		34	F	1/2	1897	Tishomingo	32
2	James, Lucy	Dau	9	"	1/2	1897	"	32
3	Sharp, Mary Gladys	"	1mo	F	1/4			

TRIBAL ENROLLMENT OF PARENTS

	NAME OF FATHER	YEAR	COUNTY	NAME OF MOTHER	YEAR	COUNTY
1	Ed. Colbert	Dead	Choctaw roll	Elsie Colbert	Dead	Chickasaw roll
2	Joe James	"	Tishomingo	No. 1		
3	J.M. Sharp		Non-Citizen	No. 1		

(NOTES)

Nos. 1-2 Also on 1897 roll, Page 92, as Tishomingo Co.
No. 1 on 1897 roll as Celey James
No. 2 " 1897 " " Lou "
No. 1 is now the wife of J.M. Sharp – Non-Citizen. Evidence of marriage filed May 19, 1902.
No. 3 Born April 26, 1902; enrolled May 24, 1902.

P.O. Chickasaw, I.T. Sept. 26/98.

RESIDENCE: Tishomingo COUNTY		CARD NO.						
POST OFFICE: Mill Creek, Ind. Ter.		FIELD NO.						
	NAME	RELATION-SHIP TO PERSON FIRST NAMED	AGE	SEX	BLOOD	TRIBAL ENROLLMENT YEAR	COUNTY	PAGE
1	Chummuttie, Tennessee		42	F	Full	1897	Tishomingo	27
2	Greenwood, Susie	Dau	21	"	"	1897	"	27
3	" George	Son of No. 2	8mo	M	"			

TRIBAL ENROLLMENT OF PARENTS

	NAME OF FATHER	YEAR	COUNTY	NAME OF MOTHER	YEAR	COUNTY
1	Ah-ho-ka-tubby	Dead	Chickasaw roll	Mollish	Dead	Chickasaw roll
2	Chummuttie	"	" "	No. 1		
3	Simeon Greenwood	1897	Tishomingo	No. 2		

(NOTES)

No. 1 on Chickasaw roll Chummettie
No. 2 is now the wife of Simeon Greenwood on Chickasaw card #74; affidavit of Simeon Greenwood filed April 7, 1902.
No. 3 Born March 9, 1902; enrolled Nov. 10, 1902. *(No. 3 Dawes' Roll No. 4420)* Sept. 26/98.

RESIDENCE: Tishomingo **COUNTY** **CARD NO.**
POST OFFICE: Mill Creek, Ind. Ter. **FIELD NO.**

	NAME	RELATIONSHIP TO PERSON FIRST NAMED	AGE	SEX	BLOOD	TRIBAL ENROLLMENT YEAR	COUNTY	PAGE
1	Lewis, Lena		48	F	3/4	1897	Tishomingo	30

TRIBAL ENROLLMENT OF PARENTS

	NAME OF FATHER	YEAR	COUNTY	NAME OF MOTHER	YEAR	COUNTY
1	Blunt Lewis	Dead	Chickasaw roll	Jennis Lewis	Dead	Chickasaw roll

(NOTES)

Sept. 26/98.

RESIDENCE: Tishomingo **COUNTY** **CARD NO.**
POST OFFICE: Mill Creek, Ind. Ter. **FIELD NO.**

	NAME	RELATIONSHIP TO PERSON FIRST NAMED	AGE	SEX	BLOOD	TRIBAL ENROLLMENT YEAR	COUNTY	PAGE
1	Lewis, Sholika		78	F	Full	1897	Tishomingo	28
2	" Hepsie	Sister	65	"	"	1897	"	28

TRIBAL ENROLLMENT OF PARENTS

	NAME OF FATHER	YEAR	COUNTY	NAME OF MOTHER	YEAR	COUNTY
1	To-ko-thlon-che	Dead	Chickasaw roll	Ma-ko-e-cha	Dead	Chickasaw roll
2	"	"	" "	"	"	" "

(NOTES)

No. 2 On Chickasaw roll as Eplia

Sept. 26/98.

RESIDENCE: Tishomingo **COUNTY** **CARD NO.**
POST OFFICE: Mill Creek, Ind. Ter. **FIELD NO.**

	NAME	RELATIONSHIP TO PERSON FIRST NAMED	AGE	SEX	BLOOD	TRIBAL ENROLLMENT YEAR	COUNTY	PAGE
1	Lewis, Benjamin		70	M	Full	1897	Tishomingo	31
2	Brown, Susan	Wife	80	F	"	1897	"	31
3	Scott, Louisa	Niece in law	60	"	1/2	1897	"	31
4	McLane, Tom	Gr Nephew in law	24	M	1/4	1897	"	31

TRIBAL ENROLLMENT OF PARENTS

	NAME OF FATHER	YEAR	COUNTY	NAME OF MOTHER	YEAR	COUNTY
1	To-ko-thlon-ke	Dead	Chickasaw Roll	Ma-ko-e-cha	Dead	Chickasaw Roll
2	Tish-o-ham-bey	"	" "	To-yah-he-na	"	" "

3	William Scott	"	Creek Citz.	Oth-to-hi-ye	"	"	"
4	Labon McLane	"	Choctaw roll	No. 3			

(NOTES)

No. 1 on Chickasaw roll as Benj. Lewis
No. 3 " " " " Louisa "
No. 4 Died April 6, 1899; Proof of death filed Nov. 18, 1902.

P.O. Marlow, I.T. Sept. 26/98.

RESIDENCE:	Choctaw Nation (1st District)		***COUNTY***		***CARD NO.***				
POST OFFICE:	Stigler, Ind. Ter.				***FIELD NO.***				
	NAME	**RELATIONSHIP TO PERSON FIRST NAMED**	**AGE**	**SEX**	**BLOOD**	**TRIBAL ENROLLMENT**			
						YEAR	**COUNTY**	**PAGE**	
1	Coleman, Sarah Gaddy		17	F	1/8				
2	" Riley Buford	Son	5mo	M	1/16				
3	Garry, Lillie	Sister	15	F	1/8				
4	Coleman, Donie B.	dau	3mo	"	1/16				
5	" Ruby Almedia	"	3w	"	1/16				

TRIBAL ENROLLMENT OF PARENTS

	NAME OF FATHER	**YEAR**	**COUNTY**	**NAME OF MOTHER**	**YEAR**	**COUNTY**
1	Arch Gaddy	Dead	Non-Citizen	Adeline Gaddy	Dead	Chickasaw roll
2	Riley L. Coleman		" "	No. 1		
3	Arch Gaddy	Dead	" "	Adeline Gaddy	Dead	Chickasaw roll
4	Riley Coleman		" "	No. 1		
5	Riley L. Coleman		" "	No. 1		

(NOTES)

Nos 1 and 3 on Choctaw Census Record No. 2, Page 197; transferred to Chickasaw roll by Dawes Com.
No. 1 on Choctaw roll as Sarah Gaddy
No. 1 on Choctaw Roll 1896 Sans Bois County, No. 4633 as Sarah Gaddy
No. 2 Affidavit of attending physician to be supplied. Received Oct. 11/98.
No. 3 on Choctaw Roll 1896 Sans Bois County, No. 4655 as Aley Gaddy.
No. 4 Born Sept 6/99. Affidavit irregular and returned for correction and filed Feby 24, 1900.
No. 5 Enrolled January 16, 1901.

Sept. 26/98.

RESIDENCE: Choctaw Nation (1st District)	COUNTY	CARD NO.
POST OFFICE: Cowlington, Ind. Ter.		FIELD NO.

	NAME	RELATIONSHIP TO PERSON FIRST NAMED	AGE	SEX	BLOOD	TRIBAL ENROLLMENT YEAR	COUNTY	PAGE
1	Folsom, Walter W.		21	M	1/4			
2	" Leora	Wife	19	F	I.W.			
3	" Lloyd Ray	Son	3wks	M	1/8			
4	" Olen William	Son	1mo	M	1/8			

TRIBAL ENROLLMENT OF PARENTS

	NAME OF FATHER	YEAR	COUNTY	NAME OF MOTHER	YEAR	COUNTY
1	Walker Folsom		Sans Bois County Choctaw Roll	Hettie Folsom	Dead	Chickasaw Roll
2	F.M. Greenlee		Non-Citizen	V.E. Greenlee		Non-Citizen
3	No. 1			No. 2		
4	No. 1			No. 2		

(NOTES)

No. 1 On Choctaw Census Record No. 2, Page 164; transferred to Chickasaw by Dawes Com.
No. 1 on Choctaw roll as Walter Folsom.
Married under U.S. Law in Choctaw Nation
No. 1 on Choctaw roll, 1896, Sans Bois County, No. 3880, as Walter Folsum.
No. 3 enrolled Nov. 18/98.
No. 4 Enrolled June 3, 1901.

Sept 26/98.

RESIDENCE: Tishomingo COUNTY		CARD NO.
POST OFFICE: Tishomingo, Ind. Ter.		FIELD NO.

	NAME	RELATIONSHIP TO PERSON FIRST NAMED	AGE	SEX	BLOOD	TRIBAL ENROLLMENT YEAR	COUNTY	PAGE
1	Rennie, William		35	M	1/16	1897	Tishomingo	38
2	" Mary Ellen	Wife	34	F	1/4	1897	"	38
3	" Mary Adeline	Dau	14	"	1/8	1897	"	38
4	" Jessie D.	"	11	"	1/8	1897	"	38
5	" Nora	"	9	"	1/8	1897	"	38
6	" Cecil C.	Son	7	M	1/8	1897	"	38
7	" Claude C.	"	7	"	1/8	1897	"	38

TRIBAL ENROLLMENT OF PARENTS

	NAME OF FATHER	YEAR	COUNTY	NAME OF MOTHER	YEAR	COUNTY
1	Alexander Rennie I.W.	1897	Pickens	Mary M. Rennie	1897	Pickens
2	Michael Campbell	Dead	Non-Citizen	Adelaide Bond	1897	Pontotoc

3	No. 1			No. 2		
4	No. 1			No. 2		
5	No. 1			No. 2		
6	No. 1			No. 2		
7	No. 1			No. 2		

(NOTES)

No. 1 descendant of John McLish
No. 1 Enrolled Nov. 25/98.
No. 2 on Chickasaw roll as M.E. Rennie
No. 3 " " " " May "
No. 4 " " " " Jessie "
No. 6 " " " " Cecil "
No. 7 " " " " Claude "

Sept. 26/98.

RESIDENCE: Tishomingo **COUNTY** **CARD NO.**
POST OFFICE: Mill Creek, Ind. Ter. **FIELD NO.**

	NAME	RELATION-SHIP TO PERSON FIRST NAMED	AGE	SEX	BLOOD	TRIBAL ENROLLMENT YEAR	COUNTY	PAGE
1	Brown, Douglas Cooper		22	M	1/2	1897	Tishomingo	27

	NAME OF FATHER	YEAR	COUNTY	NAME OF MOTHER	YEAR	COUNTY
1	Wm Brown	Dead	Pickens	Martha Brown	Dead	Pickens

(NOTES)

On Chickasaw roll as Doug Brown.

Sept. 26/98.

RESIDENCE: Tishomingo **COUNTY** **CARD NO.**
POST OFFICE: Mill Creek, Ind. Ter. **FIELD NO.**

	NAME	RELATION-SHIP TO PERSON FIRST NAMED	AGE	SEX	BLOOD	TRIBAL ENROLLMENT YEAR	COUNTY	PAGE
1	Harris, James W.		34	M	3/4	1897	Tishomingo	27
2	" Tennie	Wife	32	F	1/2	1897	"	27
3	" William	Son	13	M	5/8	1897	"	27
4	" Lucretia	Dau	11	F	5/8	1897	"	27
5	" Bertie	"	9	"	5/8	1897	"	27
6	" John	Son	6	M	5/8	1897	"	27
7	" Hettie	Dau	4	F	5/8	1897	"	27
8	" Amanda	"	2	F	5/8	1897	"	87

TRIBAL ENROLLMENT OF PARENTS						
	NAME OF FATHER	YEAR	COUNTY	NAME OF MOTHER	YEAR	COUNTY
1	Cyrus Harris	Dead	Chickasaw Roll	Hettie Harris	1897	Tishomingo
2	William Brown		" "	Elizabeth Brown	Dead	Chickasaw roll
3	No. 1			No. 2		
4	No. 1			No. 2		
5	No. 1			No. 2		
6	No. 1			No. 2		
7	No. 1			No. 2		
8	No. 1			No. 2		

(NOTES)

No. 1 on Chickasaw roll as James M. Harris *(No. 8 Dawes' Roll No. 4565)*
No. 7 " " " " Hattie "
Rec'd notice of death of No. 2 which occurred Feby. 21/98. Same is hereto attached marked "Copy".
No. 1 Died October 23, 1900. Proof of death filed January 29, 1901.

No 3 P.O. Sulphur, I.T. Sept. 26/98.

RESIDENCE: Choctaw Nation (1st District) ***COUNTY*** ***CARD NO.***
POST OFFICE: Stigler, Ind. Ter. ***FIELD NO.***

	NAME	RELATION-SHIP TO PERSON FIRST NAMED	AGE	SEX	BLOOD	TRIBAL ENROLLMENT		
						YEAR	COUNTY	PAGE
1	Stigler, Joseph S.		37	M	I.W.			
2	" Mary	Wife	29	F	3/4			
3	" Edward Buckley	Son	10	M	3/8			
4	" Willie Grady	"	6	"	3/8			
5	" Hettie Lee	Dau	4	F	3/8			

TRIBAL ENROLLMENT OF PARENTS						
	NAME OF FATHER	YEAR	COUNTY	NAME OF MOTHER	YEAR	COUNTY
1	Edward Stigler		Non-Citizen	Adeline Stidler	Dead	Non-Citizen
2	Walker Folsom		San Bois County Choctaw roll	Hettie Folsom	"	Chickasaw roll
3	No. 1			No. 2		
4	No. 1			No. 2		
5	No. 1			No. 2		

(NOTES)

No. 1 on Choct. Int. Roll, Page 96, transferred to Chickasaw roll by Dawes Com.
All others " " Census Record #2, Page 417, " " " " " " "
No. 1 on Choctaw roll as J.S. Stigler, 1896 Sans Bois Co, No. 15017
No. 3 " " " " Edward " 1896 " " " " 11103

No. 4 " " " " Willie " 1896 " " " " 11104
No. 5 " " " " Lela H. " 1896 " " " " 11105
No. 2 " " " " Mary " 1896 " " " " 11102

Sept. 26/98.

RESIDENCE: Tishomingo ***COUNTY*** ***CARD NO.***
POST OFFICE: Vaughan, Ind. Ter. ***FIELD NO.***

	NAME	RELATION-SHIP TO PERSON FIRST NAMED	AGE	SEX	BLOOD	TRIBAL ENROLLMENT		
						YEAR	COUNTY	PAGE
1	Kinney, John H.		47	M	I.W.	1897	Pickens	79
2	" Minnie	Wife	37	F	1/2	1897	Tishomingo	29
3	" James	Son	20	M	1/4	1897	"	29
4	" Amanda	Dau	16	F	1/4	1897	"	29
5	" Levi	Son	14	M	1/4	1897	"	29
6	" Osceola	"	12	M	1/4	1897	"	29
7	" Lillie	Dau	9	F	1/4	1897	"	29
8	" Jesse	Son	8	M	1/4	1897	"	29
9	" Ida	Dau	4	F	1/4	1897	"	29
10	" Ludie	Son	10mo	M	1/4			
11	Polk, Oscar Alinton	Son of No. 4	2mos	M	1/8			

TRIBAL ENROLLMENT OF PARENTS

	NAME OF FATHER	YEAR	COUNTY	NAME OF MOTHER	YEAR	COUNTY
1	Patrick Kinney	Dead	Non-Citizen	Margaret Kinney	Dead	Non-Citizen
2	Cyrus Harris	Dead	Chickasaw Roll	Nancy Harris	"	Chickasaw roll
3	No. 1			No. 2		
4	No. 1			No. 2		
5	No. 1			No. 2		
6	No. 1			No. 2		
7	No. 1			No. 2		
8	No. 1			No. 2		
9	No. 1			No. 2		
10	No. 1			No. 2		
11	Henry T. Polk		Non-Citizen	No. 4		

(NOTES)

No. 1 Certified copy of marriage record to be supplied – Received Sept. 26/98 *(No. 1 Dawes' Roll No. I.W. 318)*
No. 6 on Chickasaw roll as Oscola Kinney
No. 8 " " " " Jessie "
No. 10 Affidavit of attending physician to be supplied *(No. 10 Dawes' Roll No. ?449)*

No. 4 is now the wife of Henry T. Polk, Non-Citizen, Evidence of marriage filed Nov. 6, 1902.
No. 11 Born Sept. 9, 1902; Enrolled Nov. 6, 1902.

P.O. Suplhur, I.T. 11/30/02

Sept. 26/98.

RESIDENCE: Choctaw Nation (1st Dist.) **COUNTY** **CARD NO.**
POST OFFICE: Garland, Ind. Ter. **FIELD NO.**

	NAME	RELATION-SHIP TO PERSON FIRST NAMED	AGE	SEX	BLOOD	TRIBAL ENROLLMENT		
						YEAR	COUNTY	PAGE
1	Folsom, Arnold		54	M	3/4			
2	" Lizzie	Wife	30	F	I.W.			
3	" Clarence	Son	8	M	3/8			
4	" Cleveland	"	6	"	3/8			
5	" Prudence	Dau	3	F	3/8			
6	" Lela	"	"	"	3/8			
7	" Lewis F.	Son	1mo	M	3/8			

TRIBAL ENROLLMENT OF PARENTS

	NAME OF FATHER	YEAR	COUNTY	NAME OF MOTHER	YEAR	COUNTY
1	Willis Folsom	Dead	Choctaw roll	Winnie Folsom	Dead	Chickasaw roll
2	Lewis	"	Non-Citizen	Mary Lewis	"	Non-Citizen
3	No. 1			No. 2		
4	No. 1			No. 2		
5	No. 1			No. 2		
6	No. 1			No. 2		
7	No. 1			No. 2		

(NOTES)

No. 2 on Choctaw Int. roll, Page 28, transferred to Chickasaw roll by Dawes Com.
All others " " Census Record No. 2, Page 164 transferred to Chickasaw roll by Dawes Com
No. 2 marriage certificate to be supplies
No. 6 on Choctaw roll as Leyca Folsom
No. 1 on Choctaw Roll 1896 Sans Bois County, No. 3868.
No. 2 " " " " " " " " 14507
No. 3 " " " " " " " " 3872
No. 4 " " " " " " " " 3873
No. 5 " " " " " " " " 3874
No. 7 born Nov. 14, 1899; transferred to this card Feb. 1, 1902.
Lewis F. son of Nos 1-2, born Nov. 14/99 on Card No. D.300.

Sept. 26/99.

RESIDENCE: Choctaw Nation ***COUNTY*** ***CARD NO.***
POST OFFICE: Hartshorn, Ind. Ter. ***FIELD NO.***

	Name	Relationship to Person First Named	Age	Sex	Blood	Tribal Enrollment Year	Tribal Enrollment County	Tribal Enrollment Page
1	Brennan, Nannie E.		39	F	I.W.	1896	Choc. Dist.	82

	Name of Father	Year	County	Name of Mother	Year	County
1	Alex. Hamilton	Dead	Non-Citizen	Lutitia Hamilton	Dead	Non-Citizen

(NOTES)

No. 1 on 1896 Roll as Nanny McCoy

No. 1 in 18974 married James McCoy, who is identified on 1878 Chickasaw Annuity Roll, Panola County. Was divorced from him and in 1875 married Harris McCann, a Choctaw by blood. After his death, No. 1 successivily[sic] married George Johnson, James Brown and Thomas Brennan, all of whom were non citizens, white men. *(The rest illegible, too light)*

Sept. 26/98.

RESIDENCE: Tishomingo ***COUNTY*** ***CARD NO.***
POST OFFICE: Buckhorn, Ind. Ter. ***FIELD NO.***

	Name	Relationship to Person First Named	Age	Sex	Blood	Tribal Enrollment Year	Tribal Enrollment County	Tribal Enrollment Page
1	Lowrance, Willis B.		68	M	I.W.	1897	Tishomingo	89
2	" Mary Easter	Wife	46	F	1/8	1897	"	28
~~3~~	~~" Robert H.~~	~~Son~~	~~20~~	~~M~~	~~1/16~~	~~1897~~	~~"~~	~~28~~
4	" Oscar K.	"	15	"	1/16	1897	"	28
5	" Charles Orrick	"	2	"	1/16	1897	"	29

TRIBAL ENROLLMENT OF PARENTS

	Name of Father	Year	County	Name of Mother	Year	County
1	John Lowrance	Dead	Non-Citizen	Eleanor Lowrance	Dead	Non-Citizen
2	Peter Fletcher	"	Chickasaw Roll	Mary Ester Flercher (I.W.)	"	Chickasaw roll
~~3~~	~~No. 1~~			~~No. 2~~		
4	No. 1			No. 2		
5	No. 1			No. 2		

(NOTES)

No. 2 on Chickasaw Roll as May A. Lowrance *(No. 1 Dawes' Roll No. 429)*
No. 3 " " " " Robt. A. Lowrance
Mo. 4 " " " " Oscar "
No. 5 " " " " Charley "
No. 2 Died May 23, 1900; Proof of death filed Oct. 25, 1902.
No. 3 3/20/90. Married and transferred to Card No. 1377.

Sept. 26/98.

RESIDENCE: Tishomingo COUNTY					CARD NO.		
POST OFFICE: Tishomingo, Ind. Ter.					FIELD NO.		
NAME	RELATIONSHIP TO PERSON FIRST NAMED	AGE	SEX	BLOOD	TRIBAL ENROLLMENT		
					YEAR	COUNTY	PAGE
1 Brailey, Nettie		20	F	1/2	1897	Tishomingo	38
2 Harris, Mary	Sister	18	"	1/2	1897	"	38
3 " Helen	"	16	"	1/2	1897	"	38
4 " Tommie	"	14	"	1/2	1897	"	38
5 " Lucy	"	8	"	1/2	1897	"	38

TRIBAL ENROLLMENT OF PARENTS

NAME OF FATHER	YEAR	COUNTY	NAME OF MOTHER	YEAR	COUNTY
1 R.W. Harris		Choctaw residing in Chickasaw Dist.	Lucy Harris	Dead	Tishomingo
2 " " "		" " "	" "	"	"
3 " " "		" " "	" "	"	"
4 " " "		" " "	" "	"	"
5 " " "		" " "	" "	"	"

(NOTES)

Nos. 1-5 inclusive are children of R.M. Harris on Choctaw card #281. *(No. 1 Dawes' Roll No. 4118)*
No. 2 on Chickasaw roll as Mamie
No. 3 Died Oct. 11, 1899; proof of death filed June 9, 1902.
No. 1 is wife of Z.A. *(Last name and two other entries illegible, too light)*

Sept. 26/98.

RESIDENCE: Pickens COUNTY					CARD NO.		
POST OFFICE: Marietta, Ind. Ter.					FIELD NO.		
NAME	RELATIONSHIP TO PERSON FIRST NAMED	AGE	SEX	BLOOD	TRIBAL ENROLLMENT		
					YEAR	COUNTY	PAGE
1 Vail, Willie		22	M	1/4	1897	Pickens	26
2 " Vergie	Dau	2mo	F	1/8			

TRIBAL ENROLLMENT OF PARENTS

NAME OF FATHER	YEAR	COUNTY	NAME OF MOTHER	YEAR	COUNTY
1 Vail	Dead	Non-Citizen	Jinsey Colbert Vail	Dead	Chickasaw Roll
2 No. 1			Rebecca Vail		Non-Citizen

(NOTES)

No. 1 is now the husband of Rebecca Vail, Non-Citizen. Evidence of marriage filed Oct. 29, 1902.
No. 2 born Aug. 16, 1902. Enrolled Oct. 29, 1902.

Sept. 26/98.

RESIDENCE: Pickens ***COUNTY*** ***CARD NO.***
POST OFFICE: Ardmore, Ind. Ter. ***FIELD NO.***

	NAME	RELATION-SHIP TO PERSON FIRST NAMED	AGE	SEX	BLOOD	TRIBAL ENROLLMENT		
						YEAR	COUNTY	PAGE
1	Lester, E.W.		56	M	I.W.			

TRIBAL ENROLLMENT OF PARENTS

	NAME OF FATHER	YEAR	COUNTY	NAME OF MOTHER	YEAR	COUNTY
1	E.W. Lester	Dead	Non-Citizen	America Lester	Dead	Non-Citizen

(NOTES)

Admitted by Dawes Commission Case No. 234, and no appeal taken.
Marriage license and certificate on file in office of Dawes Com. Muskogee
No. 1 was formerly the husband of Ella Lester on Chickasaw card #502

Sept. 24/98.

RESIDENCE: Pickens ***COUNTY*** ***CARD NO.***
POST OFFICE: Ardmore, Ind. Ter. ***FIELD NO.***

	NAME	RELATION-SHIP TO PERSON FIRST NAMED	AGE	SEX	BLOOD	TRIBAL ENROLLMENT		
						YEAR	COUNTY	PAGE
1	Keel, Guy		28	M	Full	1897	Pickens	9
2	" Lula	Wife	20	F	1/16	1897	"	9
3	" Overton	Son	2	M	1/2	~~1897~~	"	~~85~~
4	" William Simon	"	7mos	"	1/2			
5	" Cecil	Dau	6mo	F	1/2			
6	" Lewis Colbert	Son	?	M	1/2			

TRIBAL ENROLLMENT OF PARENTS

	NAME OF FATHER	YEAR	COUNTY	NAME OF MOTHER	YEAR	COUNTY
1	Johnson Keel	Dead	Pickens	Winona Keel	1897	Pickens
2	W.A. Potts		Non-Citizen	Sophia Potts	Dead	"
3	No. 1			No. 2		
4	No. 1			No. 2		
5	No. 1			No. 2		
6	No. 1			No. 2		

(NOTES)

No. 3 Proof of birth received and filed Oct. 14, 1902. *(No. 3 Dawes' Roll No. 4117)*
No. 5 Enrolled May 24, 1900.
No. 5 Died Aug. 30, 1900. Evidence of death filed Sept. 5, 1901.
No. 6 Enrolled July 16, 1901.

P.O. Oakland, I.T. Sept. 24/98.

RESIDENCE: Pickens COUNTY					CARD NO.		
POST OFFICE: Ardmore, Ind. Ter.					FIELD NO.		
	NAME	RELATION-SHIP TO PERSON FIRST NAMED	AGE	SEX	BLOOD	TRIBAL ENROLLMENT		
						YEAR	COUNTY	PAGE
1	Colbert, Henrietta		35	F	I.W.	1897	Pickens	78
2	" Czarina M.	Dau	14mo	"	none	1897	"	86
3	" Walter Cevera	Son	9Day	M	"			
4	Juzan, Alexia	Dau	11	F	1/16	1897	Pickens	16

TRIBAL ENROLLMENT OF PARENTS

	NAME OF FATHER	YEAR	COUNTY	NAME OF MOTHER	YEAR	COUNTY
1	Charlie Hume	Dead	Non-Citizen	Mary E. Huna		Non-Citizen
2	Walter Colbert		Choctaw residing in Chickasaw District	No. 1		
3	" "		" "	No. 1		
4	Alex Juzan	Dead	Pickens	No. 1		

(NOTES)

No. 1 wife of Walter Colbert, Choctaw Card No. 279 - widow of Alex Juzan, 1/8 Chickasaw Indian
No. 2 also on 1897 Roll, Page 93, as Czarina Colbert *(No. 1 Dawes' Roll No. 124)*
No. 2 and 3 transferred to Choctaw card #279 with their father, Feb. 4, 1902.
No. 3 Affidavit of attending physician to be supplied. Received Sept. 26/98.
No. 4 on Chickasaw roll as Alevia Juzan.
No. 4 Died May 22, 1901. Proof of death filed Nov. 1, 1902.
See affidavit of J.N. Dickerson, Jas. Yarbrough and J.N. White filed March 24, 1903.

Sept. 24/98.

RESIDENCE: Tishomingo COUNTY					CARD NO.		
POST OFFICE: Mill Creek, Ind. Ter.					FIELD NO.		
	NAME	RELATION-SHIP TO PERSON FIRST NAMED	AGE	SEX	BLOOD	TRIBAL ENROLLMENT		
						YEAR	COUNTY	PAGE
1	Penner, Felix		39	M	I.W.	1897	Tishomingo	79
2	" Amanda	Wife	45	F	1/2	1897	"	30
3	" Charley	Son	6	M	1/4	1897	"	30
4	" Cyrus	"	4	"	1/4	1897	"	30

TRIBAL ENROLLMENT OF PARENTS

	NAME OF FATHER	YEAR	COUNTY	NAME OF MOTHER	YEAR	COUNTY
1	Augustus Penner		Non-Citizen	Pauline Penner	Dead	Non-Citizen
2	Cyrus Harris	Dead	Tishomingo	Nancy Harris	"	Tishomingo
3	No. 1			No. 2		
4	No. 1			No. 2		

(NOTES)

No. 2 on Chickasaw roll as Amanda Penna *(No. 1 Dawes' Roll No. 28)*
No. 3 " " " " Charley Penna
No. 4 " " " " Cyrus "

Sept. 24/98.

RESIDENCE: Pickens COUNTY					CARD NO.		
POST OFFICE: Cheek, Ind. Ter.					FIELD NO.		
NAME	RELATION-SHIP TO PERSON FIRST NAMED	AGE	SEX	BLOOD	TRIBAL ENROLLMENT		
					YEAR	COUNTY	PAGE
1 Hare, Samuel J.		28	M	1/4	1897	Pickens	19
2 " Laura J.	Wife	29	F	I.W.			

TRIBAL ENROLLMENT OF PARENTS

	NAME OF FATHER	YEAR	COUNTY	NAME OF MOTHER	YEAR	COUNTY
1	F.M. Hare		Cherokee Citz.	Sarah Hare	1897	Pickens
2	Benj. Wells	Dead	Non Citz.	Maria J. Wells	Dead	Non Citz.

(NOTES)

On Chickasaw roll as Samuel I. Hare.
No. 2 enrolled Aug. 31/99. *(No. 2 Dawes' Roll No. 123)*
Certified copy of divorce proceedings between No. 2 and her former husband filed Feby 25, 1903.

P.O. Mannsville, I.T. Sept. 24/98.

RESIDENCE: Pickens COUNTY					CARD NO.		
POST OFFICE: Woodford, Ind. Ter.					FIELD NO.		
NAME	RELATION-SHIP TO PERSON FIRST NAMED	AGE	SEX	BLOOD	TRIBAL ENROLLMENT		
					YEAR	COUNTY	PAGE
1 Abram, Amanda		32	F	1/4	1897	Pickens	16
2 " Riva Ann	Dau	8	F	1/8	1897	"	16
3 " Tom Garritt	Son	5	M	1/8	1897	"	16
4 " Vina Maude	Dau	4	F	1/8	1897	"	16
5 " Bula May	"	1	"	1/8			
6 " Elward	Son	4mo	M	1/8			

TRIBAL ENROLLMENT OF PARENTS

	NAME OF FATHER	YEAR	COUNTY	NAME OF MOTHER	YEAR	COUNTY
1	Steve Stephenson	Dead	Chick Freedman	Mollie Mollardy	Dead	Chickasaw roll
2	Edward Abram		" "	No. 1		

3	" "		" "	No. 1		
4	" "		" "	No. 1		
5	" "		" "	No. 1		
6	" "		" "	No. 1		

(NOTES)

Abram, Edward husband of No. 1 appears on Chickasaw Freedman Card #699.
No. 2 on Chickasaw roll as Arivan
No. 3 " " " " Tom
No. 4 " " " " *(illegible name)*
No. 5 Died August 18, 1900; Evidence of death filed July 7, 1902.
No. 6 enrolled Dec. 13/99.

P.O. Milo, I.T. Sept. 24/98.

RESIDENCE: Pickens **COUNTY** **CARD NO.**
POST OFFICE: Ardmore, Ind. Ter. **FIELD NO.**

	NAME	RELATION-SHIP TO PERSON FIRST NAMED	AGE	SEX	BLOOD	TRIBAL ENROLLMENT		
						YEAR	COUNTY	PAGE
1	Thomas, Charles W.		39	M	I.W.	1897	Pickens	78??
2	" Minnie	Wife	34	F	1/16	1897	"	12
3	McCauley, Peachie	StepDau	12	"	5/32	1897	"	12
4	" Susie	" "	10	"	5/32	1897	"	12
5	" Junie	" "	8	"	5/32	1897	"	12
6	" Wm Walkins	" Son	7	M	5/32	1897	"	12
7	Thomas, Russell Gardner	Son	2wks	"	1/32			
8	" Charles Cruce	Son	1mo	M	1/32			

TRIBAL ENROLLMENT OF PARENTS

	NAME OF FATHER	YEAR	COUNTY	NAME OF MOTHER	YEAR	COUNTY
1	C.D. Thomas	Dead	Non-Citizen	Margaret Thomas	Dead	Non-Citizen
2	A. Nichols	1897	Pickens	Susan Nichols	1897	Pickens
3	C.T. McCauley	Dead	Chickasaw Roll	No. 2		
4	" " "	"	" "	No. 2		
5	" " "	"	" "	No. 2		
6	" " "	"	" "	No. 2		
7	No. 1			No. 2		
8	No. 1			No. 2		

(NOTES)

Marriage license and certificate on file in office of Dawes Com. Muskogee, Ind. Ter.
No. 1 on Chickasaw roll as Charley Thomas *(No. 1 Dawes' Roll No. 122)*
No. 3 " " " " Richie McCauley

No. 5 " " " " Jennie "
No. 6 " " " " William "
No. 7 Enrolled Nov. 25/98.
No. 8 Born Nov. 2, 1901; - Enrolled Nov. 29, 1901.

See Choctaw case 1896 #1397 Sept. 24/98.

RESIDENCE: Pickens **COUNTY** **CARD NO.**
POST OFFICE: Eastman, Ind. Ter. **FIELD NO.**

	NAME	RELATIONSHIP TO PERSON FIRST NAMED	AGE	SEX	BLOOD	TRIBAL ENROLLMENT YEAR	COUNTY	PAGE
1	Osavior. Frank		26	M	1/2	1893	Pickens	PR#2 P170
2	" Dollie	Wife	20	F	I.W.			

TRIBAL ENROLLMENT OF PARENTS

	NAME OF FATHER	YEAR	COUNTY	NAME OF MOTHER	YEAR	COUNTY
1	Osavior Duroderigo	Dead	Mexican	O-nah-he	Dead	Chickasaw Roll
2	R.H. Stapleton	"	Non-Citizen	Mary Stapleton		Non-Citizen

(NOTES)

No. 1 on Chickasaw roll as Osovior. On Chickasaw Intermarried roll by mistake. *(No. 1 Dawes' Roll No. 4416)*
Dec. 2 - 99: See testimony taken in this case. *(No. 2 Dawes' Roll No. 369)*
No. 1 on 1893 Payroll #2, page 170 and Franklin *(illegible word)*
5/31/99 It is reported that Wm Washington has this woman on his place and had parties to marry and they have never lived together - Investigate

Sept. 24/98.

RESIDENCE: Pickens **COUNTY** **CARD NO.**
POST OFFICE: Marietta **FIELD NO.**

	NAME	RELATIONSHIP TO PERSON FIRST NAMED	AGE	SEX	BLOOD	TRIBAL ENROLLMENT YEAR	COUNTY	PAGE
1	Black, Sam		30	M	I.W.	1897	Pickens	77
2	" Ida	Wife	24	F	1/16	1897	"	13
3	" Overton	Son	5	M	1/32	1897	"	13
4	" John Dechard	"	3	"	1/32	1897	"	13
5	" Sophia Ellen	Dau	1 1/2	F	1/32	1897	"	96
6	" Annie Lee	"	1wk	F	1/32			
7	" Camelia	Dau	2mo	F	1/32			
8	" Henretta[sic]	Dau	2wks	F	1/32			

TRIBAL ENROLLMENT OF PARENTS						
	NAME OF FATHER	YEAR	COUNTY	NAME OF MOTHER	YEAR	COUNTY
1	Sam Black	Dead	Non-Citizen	Sophie A. Black		Non-Citizen
2	Wm.H. Morris I.W.	"	Pickens	Annie Morris	Dead	Pickens
3	No. 1			No. 2		
4	No. 1			No. 2		
5	No. 1			No. 2		
6	No. 1			No. 2		
7	No. 1			No. 2		
8	No. 1			No. 2		

(NOTES)

(No. 1 Dawes' Roll No. I.W. 27)

No. 4 on Chickasaw Roll as John Black
No. 5 " " " " Sophia E. "
No. 6 Enrolled Nov. 21/98.
No. 7 Enrolled May 24, 1900.
No. 8 born Nov. 29, 1901; Enrolled Dec. 14, 1901.

Sept. 23/98.

RESIDENCE: Pickens **COUNTY** **CARD NO.**
POST OFFICE: Marietta, Ind. Ter. **FIELD NO.**

	NAME	RELATION-SHIP TO PERSON FIRST NAMED	AGE	SEX	BLOOD	TRIBAL ENROLLMENT		
						YEAR	COUNTY	PAGE
1	Jordan, Jesse L.		28	M	I.W.	1897	Pickens	77
2	" Mollie	Wife	25	F	1/8	1897	"	12
3	" Martha	Dau	5	F	1/16	1897	"	12
4	" Anneta	"	6mos	"	1/16			

TRIBAL ENROLLMENT OF PARENTS						
	NAME OF FATHER	YEAR	COUNTY	NAME OF MOTHER	YEAR	COUNTY
1	Jos. H. Jordan	Dead	Non-Citizen	Sally Jordan	Dead	Non-Citizen
2	Overton Love	1897	Pickens	Martha Love	"	Pickens
3	No. 1			No. 2		
4	No. 1			No. 2		

(NOTES)

(No. 1 Dawes' Roll No. I.W. 121)

No. 1 on Chickasaw roll as Jessie Jordan
No. 2 " " " " Mollie Jourdan

Sept. 23/98.

RESIDENCE: Pickens ***COUNTY***					***CARD NO.***			
POST OFFICE: Mansville, Ind. Ter.					***FIELD NO.***			

	NAME	RELATION-SHIP TO PERSON FIRST NAMED	AGE	SEX	BLOOD	TRIBAL ENROLLMENT		
						YEAR	COUNTY	PAGE
1	Nichols, Stanwaite		30	M	1/16	1897	Pickens	14
2	" Maggie B.	Wife	23	F	I.W.			
3	" Lena	Dau	2 1/2	"	1/32	1897	Pickens	14
4	" Jewel	"	5mo	"	1/32			

TRIBAL ENROLLMENT OF PARENTS

	NAME OF FATHER	YEAR	COUNTY	NAME OF MOTHER	YEAR	COUNTY
1	A. Nichols		Non-Citizen	Susan M. Nichols	1897	Pickens
2	L.G. Copeland		" "	Betty Copeland		Non-Citizen
3	No. 1			No. 2		
4	No. 1			No. 2		

(NOTES)

No. 1 on Chickasaw roll as Wait Nichols.
No. 1 also on 1896 Choctaw Roll, Page 249, No. 9847 as Waitie Nicholas.
Nos 1 and 2 married in Choctaw Nation under Choctaw law.
No. 2 also on 1896 Choctaw Roll, Page 396, No. 14905, as Maggie Nicholas.
Dec. 6/99. See if she was not denied by Commission in 1896. Case No. 225.
No. 2 was denied by Dawes Commission in 1896 in Chickasaw case #255 as M. Brenda Nichols: no appeal. --
No. 3 also on 1896 Choctaw Roll, Page 249, No. 9848 as Lena Nicholas.
No. 4 Affidavit of physician to be supplied. Received Oct. 31/98.

No. 2 enrolled Oct. 5/98.
all others Sept. 23/98.

P.O. Ardmore, I.T. 11/5/02

RESIDENCE: Pickens ***COUNTY***					***CARD NO.***			
POST OFFICE: Earl, Ind. Ter.					***FIELD NO.***			

	NAME	RELATION-SHIP TO PERSON FIRST NAMED	AGE	SEX	BLOOD	TRIBAL ENROLLMENT		
						YEAR	COUNTY	PAGE
1	Thomas, Isaac Alva		2	M	1/16			
2	Belk, Belle	Mother	29	F	I.W.			

TRIBAL ENROLLMENT OF PARENTS

	NAME OF FATHER	YEAR	COUNTY	NAME OF MOTHER	YEAR	COUNTY
1	Isaac Thomas	Dead	Tishomingo	Belle Belk		white woman
2	Marion Hampton		Non-Citizen	Fannie Hampton	Dead	Non-Citizen

(NOTES)

Mother, Belle Belk, on Chickasaw roll card No. D.70. *(No. 1 Dawes' Roll No. 4115)*
Affidavit of attending physician to be supplied. Received Sept. 27/98. *(No. 2 Dawes' Roll No. I.W. 592)*
Father of No. 1 on 1893 Payroll No. *(illegible)*

No. 2 formerly wife of Isaac Thomas, a recognized, enrolled citizen by blood of the Chickasaw Nation who was identified in 1893 Chickasaw Leases Dist. Payment Roll No. 1, page 132.
No. 2 now is the wife of George Belk, a white man.
No. 2 originally listed for enrollment on Chickasaw card #D.70.
transferred to this card May 15, 1903. See decision of Feb. 3, 1903.

P.O. Oconee, I.T. Sept. 23/98 Sept. 23/98.

RESIDENCE: Pontotoc ***COUNTY*** ***CARD NO.***
POST OFFICE: Minco, Ind. Ter. ***FIELD NO.***

	NAME	RELATION-SHIP TO PERSON FIRST NAMED	AGE	SEX	BLOOD	TRIBAL ENROLLMENT		
						YEAR	COUNTY	PAGE
1	Davis, John		37	M	I.W.	1897	Pontotoc	81
2	" Julia	Wife	27	F	3/4	1897	"	65
3	" Dora Stella	Dau	6	"	3/8	1897	"	65
4	" James Russell	Son	4	M	3/8	1897	"	65
5	" Nora Belle	Dau	2	F	3/8	1897	"	65
6	" Benjamin	Son	1wk	M	3/8			
7	" John Henry	Son	2wks	"	3/8			

TRIBAL ENROLLMENT OF PARENTS

	NAME OF FATHER	YEAR	COUNTY	NAME OF MOTHER	YEAR	COUNTY
1	John Davis	Dead	Non-Citizen	Elizabeth Davis	Dead	Non-Citizen
2	Creek Toms	"	Chickasaw roll	Becky Toms	"	Chickasaw Roll
3	No. 1			No. 2		
4	No. 1			No. 2		
5	No. 1			No. 2		
6	No. 1			No. 2		
7	No. 1			No. 2		

(NOTES)

No. 3 on Chickasaw Roll as D.S. Davis
No. 4 " " " " James R. "
No. 5 " " " " Nora B. "
No. 6 enrolled Oct. 21/98.
No. 7 Born April 8, 1902; enrolled April 24, 1902.

Sept. 23/98.

RESIDENCE: Pickens **COUNTY** **CARD NO.**
POST OFFICE: Ardmore, Ind. Ter. **FIELD NO.**

	NAME	RELATION-SHIP TO PERSON FIRST NAMED	AGE	SEX	BLOOD	TRIBAL ENROLLMENT		
						YEAR	COUNTY	PAGE
1	Bonner, Zadok Augustus		48	M	I.W.	1897	Pickens	87
2	" Iszoda	Wife	22	F	1/2	1897	"	19
3	" Flora	Dau	8mo	"	1/4			
4	" Whitmel Francis	Son	1mo	M	1/4			

TRIBAL ENROLLMENT OF PARENTS

	NAME OF FATHER	YEAR	COUNTY	NAME OF MOTHER	YEAR	COUNTY
1	Wm. F. Bonner	Dead	Non-Citizen	Susan E. Bonner		Non-Citizen
2	Francis Hare		Cherokee Citz.	Sarah Hare	1897	Pickens
3	No. 1			No. 2		
4	No. 1			No. 2		

(NOTES)

No. 1 on Chickasaw roll as Z.A. Bonner.
No. 2 " " " " Zoda Hare.
No. 3 enrolled Nov. 3/99.
No. 4 enrolled December 10, 1900.

P.O. Mannsville, I.T. 11/7/02. Sept. 23/98.

RESIDENCE: Pickens **COUNTY** **CARD NO.**
POST OFFICE: Ardmore, Ind. Ter. **FIELD NO.**

	NAME	RELATION-SHIP TO PERSON FIRST NAMED	AGE	SEX	BLOOD	TRIBAL ENROLLMENT		
						YEAR	COUNTY	PAGE
1	Turman, Louis N.		38	M	I.W.	1897	Pickens	79
2	" Vinnie Ream	Wife	24	F	1/8	1897	"	23
3	" Annie Ream	Dau	5	"	1/16	1897	"	23
4	" Vinnie Hoxie	"	15mos	"	1/16	1897	"	23
5	" Louis Brudinot	Son	2mo	M	1/16			

TRIBAL ENROLLMENT OF PARENTS

	NAME OF FATHER	YEAR	COUNTY	NAME OF MOTHER	YEAR	COUNTY
1	Thos. J. Turman	Dead	Non-Citizen	Martha E. Turman	Dead	Non-Citizen
2	Robt. L. Ream I.W.	"	Chick residing in Choctaw Nat. 1st Dist	Annie Guy Ream	1897	Pontotoc
3	No. 1			No. 2		
4	No. 1			No. 2		

5	No. 1			No. 2		

(NOTES)

No. 1 on Chickasaw roll as Louis M. Turman *(No. 1 Dawes' Roll No. I.W. 120)*
No. 2 " " " " Vinnie Beam Furman
No. 3 " " " " Annie R. "
No. 4 Died April 24, 1902; Proof of death filed Nov. 8, 1902.
No. 5 Enrolled June 23, 1900

Sept. 23/98.

RESIDENCE: Pickens ***COUNTY***					***CARD NO.***			
POST OFFICE: Atlee - Ind. Ter.					***FIELD NO.***			
	NAME	**RELATION-SHIP TO PERSON FIRST NAMED**	**AGE**	**SEX**	**BLOOD**	**TRIBAL ENROLLMENT**		
						YEAR	**COUNTY**	**PAGE**
1	Ball, Myrtle Virginia		11	F	1/8	1897	Pickens	31
2	" Ada Clifford	Sister	9	"	1/8	1897	"	31

TRIBAL ENROLLMENT OF PARENTS

	NAME OF FATHER	**YEAR**	**COUNTY**	**NAME OF MOTHER**	**YEAR**	**COUNTY**
1	M.F. Ball		white man	Lucy O. Anglen	1897	Pickens
2	" " "		" "	" " "	1897	"

(NOTES)

No. 1 on Chickasaw roll as Myrtle V. Ball
No. 2 " " " " Ada C. "
Nos. 1 and 2 are children of Lucy Obedient Anglin, on Chickasaw Care #599 and Millard F. Ball on Chickasaw card #D.208.

Sept. 23/98.

RESIDENCE: Pickens ***COUNTY***					***CARD NO.***			
POST OFFICE: Pike, Ind. Ter.					***FIELD NO.***			
	NAME	**RELATION-SHIP TO PERSON FIRST NAMED**	**AGE**	**SEX**	**BLOOD**	**TRIBAL ENROLLMENT**		
						YEAR	**COUNTY**	**PAGE**
1	Anglin, Lucy Obedient		32	F	1/4	1897	Pickens	31
2	" Albert Thomas	Son	6	M	1/8	1897	"	31
3	" Annie May	Dau	4	F	1/8	1897	"	31
4	" Lillie Rhoda	"	2	"	1/8	1897	"	86
5	" Sydney C.	Son	4mo	M	1/8			

TRIBAL ENROLLMENT OF PARENTS

	NAME OF FATHER	**YEAR**	**COUNTY**	**NAME OF MOTHER**	**YEAR**	**COUNTY**
1	W.T. Box	Dead	Non-Citizen	Rhoda Fulsom Box	Dead	Chickasaw Rolls

2	W.A. Anglin		" "	No. 1		
3	" " "		" "	No. 1		
4	" " "		" "	No. 1		
5	" " "		" "	No. 1		

(NOTES)

Nos. 1 and 3 admitted by Commission 1896 in Chickasaw case #280.
No. 1 is mother of children on Chickasaw card #600.
No. 1 was first married to Millard F. Ball on Chickasaw card #D.208.
No. 1 on Chickasaw Roll as Lucy Anglin
No. 2 " " " " Albert P. "
No. 3 " " " " Mary A. "
No. 4 " " " " Rhoda L. "
No. 4 Proof of birth received and filed Sept. 19, 1902.
No. 5 enrolled Dec. 13/99.

P.O. address: Burneyville, I.T. May 24, 1902. Sept. 23/98.

RESIDENCE: Pickens ***COUNTY*** ***CARD NO.***
POST OFFICE: Ardmore, Ind. Ter. ***FIELD NO.***

	NAME	RELATIONSHIP TO PERSON FIRST NAMED	AGE	SEX	BLOOD	TRIBAL ENROLLMENT		
						YEAR	COUNTY	PAGE
1	Law, Margaret Elizabeth		16	F	1/8	1897	Pickens	16

TRIBAL ENROLLMENT OF PARENTS

	NAME OF FATHER	YEAR	COUNTY	NAME OF MOTHER	YEAR	COUNTY
1	Adolphus H. Law	1897	Pickens	Margaret Elizabeth Law	Dead	Pickens

(NOTES)

On Chickasaw roll as Elizabeth Law.
Admitted by Dawes Com. Case No. 70, and no appeal taken
Father, Adolphus H. Law, on Chickasaw Card No. D.69
No. 1 is also enrolled as No. 3 on Chickasaw Court Card #C.122.

Sept. 23/98.

CANCELLED stamped across the card

RESIDENCE: Pickens ***COUNTY*** ***CARD NO.***
POST OFFICE: Keller, Ind. Ter. ***FIELD NO.***

	NAME	RELATIONSHIP TO PERSON FIRST NAMED	AGE	SEX	BLOOD	TRIBAL ENROLLMENT		
						YEAR	COUNTY	PAGE
1	Robison, Hattie Adeline		17	F	1/4	1897	Pickens	14
2	" Addie L.	Dau	7mos	"	1/8			

3	" Altai E.	Dau	2mo	F	1/8			
4	" *(Illegible)*	Son	1mo	M	1/8			

TRIBAL ENROLLMENT OF PARENTS

	Name of Father	Year	County	Name of Mother	Year	County
1	Joe Hollis	Dead	Non-Citizen	Susan McDonell	1897	Pickens
2	W.F. Robison		" "	No. 1		
3	" " "		" "	No. 1		
4	" " "		" "	No. 1		

(NOTES)

No. 1 on Chickasaw roll as Hattie Robison.
No. 2 affidavit of attending physician to be supplied. Received Oct. 5/98.
No. 3 Enrolled May 24, 1900.
No. 4 Born April 30, 1902; Enrolled May 20, 1902.

P.O. Sneed, I.T. Sept. 23/98.

RESIDENCE: Pickens ***COUNTY*** ***CARD NO.***
POST OFFICE: Wheeler, Ind. Ter. ***FIELD NO.***

	Name	Relationship to Person First Named	Age	Sex	Blood	Tribal Enrollment		
						Year	County	Page
1	McDonell, Susan		42	F	1/2	1897	Pickens	14
2	Sealy, Josephine	Dau	14	"	1/2	1897	"	14
3	McDonell, Norval	Son	8	M	1/4	1897	"	14
4	" Cleveland	"	7	M	1/4	1897	"	14
5	" Isaac	"	4	M	1/4	1897	"	14
6	" Eliza Jane	Dau	4	F	1/4	1897	"	14
7	" Nona	"	2	"	1/4	1897	"	14
8	" Nicodemus	Son	8mos	M	1/4			
9	" Josephus	Son	3wks	M	1/4			

TRIBAL ENROLLMENT OF PARENTS

	Name of Father	Year	County	Name of Mother	Year	County
1	George Johnson	Dead	Chickasaw Roll	Lucy Johnson	Dead	Chickasaw Roll
2	George Sealy		" "	No. 1		
3	W.R. McDonell		Non-Citizen	No. 1		
4	" " "		" "	No. 1		
5	" " "		" "	No. 1		
6	" " "		" "	No. 1		
7	" " "		" "	No. 1		
8	" " "		" "	No. 1		

9	" " "		" "	No. 1		

(NOTES)

No. 6 on Chickasaw roll as Lizzie
No. 7 " " " " Hannie
Josephus McDonell on Card No. D.310.
No. 9 born December 23, 1899; transferred to this card February 1, 1902.

Sept. 23/98.

RESIDENCE: Pickens ***COUNTY*** ***CARD NO.***
POST OFFICE: Hewitt, Ind. Ter. ***FIELD NO.***

	NAME	RELATION-SHIP TO PERSON FIRST NAMED	AGE	SEX	BLOOD	TRIBAL ENROLLMENT		
						YEAR	COUNTY	PAGE
1	Worsham, John Farley		43	M	I.W.	1897	Pickens	78
2	" Lucretia	Wife	38	F	Full	1897	"	17
3	" Richard	Son	14	M	1/2	1897	"	17
4	" Samuel	"	12	"	1/2	1897	"	17
5	" Mattie	Dau	10	F	1/2	1897	"	17
6	" Jewel	"	9	"	1/2	1897	"	17
7	" Birdie Guy	"	7	"	1/2	1897	"	17
8	Mobley, Tennie	"	16	"	1/2	1897	"	17
9	" Helen Louise	Grand Daughter	2mo	F	1/4			
10	" Gerald Farley	Son of No. 8	2mo	M	1/4			

TRIBAL ENROLLMENT OF PARENTS

	NAME OF FATHER	YEAR	COUNTY	NAME OF MOTHER	YEAR	COUNTY
1	Samuel Worsham	Dead	Non-Citizen	Martha Worsham	Dead	Non-Citizen
2	Cornelius McGee	"	Chickasaw Roll	Liza McGee	"	Chickasaw Roll
3	No. 1			No. 2		
4	No. 1			No. 2		
5	No. 1			No. 2		
6	No. 1			No. 2		
7	No. 1			No. 2		
8	No. 1			No. 2		
9	B.E. Mobley		Non-Citizen	No. 8		
10	" " "		" "	No. 8		

(NOTES)

Certified copies of marriage license and certificate to be supplied. Received Sept. 28/98.
No. 1 on Chickasaw roll as Farley Worsham *(No. 1 Dawes' Roll No. 317)*
No. 2 " " " " Loucrita "

No. 4 " " " " Sam "
No. 7 " " " " Birdie "
No. 8 " " " " Tennie Worsham; wife of Robert Cox, U.S. Citizen, who has abandoned her
No. 8 is now the wife of Benj. E. Mobly. Evidence of marriage filed May 1, 1901.
No. 9 Enrolled May 11, 1901.
No. 10. Born May 20, 1902. Enrolled July 14, 1902.

P.O. Ardmore, I.T. 1/9/03 Sept. 23/98.

Residence: Pickens ***County*** ***Card No.***
Post Office: Ardmore, Ind. Ter. ***Field No.***

	Name	Relationship to Person First Named	Age	Sex	Blood	Tribal Enrollment		
						Year	County	Page
1	Gaddis, William Manuel		28	M	1/16	1897	Pickens	22
2	" John Dewey	Son	2mo	M	1/32			
3	" William B.	Son	2wks	M	1/32			
4	" Georgia	Wife	29	F	I.W.			

Tribal Enrollment of Parents

	Name of Father	Year	County	Name of Mother	Year	County
1	Bill Gaddis	Dead	Non-Citizen	Melvina Love Gaddis	Dead	Chickasaw Roll
2	No. 1			Georgia A. Gaddis		non citz.
3	No. 1			" " "		" "
4	N.A. Eddington		Non Citz.	Sarah Eddington	D'd	Non Citz

(Notes)

No. 4 transferred from *(the remainder is illegible, too light)*
on Chickasaw roll as William Gaddis
Georgia Gaddis, wife of No. 1 on Chickasaw card D.320.
No. 2 Enrolled June 25, 1900.
No. 3 Born May 29, 1902; enrolled June 11, 1902.

P.O. Commanche, I.T. 6/11/02. Sept. 23/98.
P.O. Loco, I.T. 2/3-04

Residence: Pickens ***County*** ***Card No.***
Post Office: Ardmore, Ind. Ter. ***Field No.***

	Name	Relationship to Person First Named	Age	Sex	Blood	Tribal Enrollment		
						Year	County	Page
1	Johnson, Laura L.		21	F	1/32	1897	Pickens	12
2	" Ben	Son	2	M	1/64	1897	"	12

3	" William A.	"	2	m	1/64			

Tribal Enrollment of Parents

	Name of Father	Year	County	Name of Mother	Year	County
1	John Criner	1897	Pickens	Mollie Criner	Dead	Non-Citizen
2	Sam Johnson		Non-Citizen	No. 1		
3	" "		" "	No. 1		

(Notes)

No. 1 on Chickasaw roll as Laura Criner
No. 2 " " " " Ben "
No. 3 Enrolled Sept. 26, 1900.

Sept. 23/98.

Residence: Pickens ***County*** ***Card No.***
Post Office: Ardmore, Ind. Ter. ***Field No.***

	Name	Relationship to Person First Named	Age	Sex	Blood	Tribal Enrollment Year	Tribal Enrollment County	Tribal Enrollment Page
1	Criner, John	Named	47	M	1/16	1897	Pickens	13
2	" Franklin	Son	16	"	1/32	1897	"	13
3	" John Adolphus	Son	6	"	1/32	1897	"	13
4	" Joe William	"	5	"	1/32	1897	"	13
5	" Frank	"	3	"	1/32	1897	"	13
6	" Alva	"	2	"	1/32	1897	"	13
7	" Buck	"	2wks	"	1/32			
8	" Charles Cook	"	1mo	"	1/32			
9	" Etta	Wife	33	F	I.W.	1897	Pickens	78

Tribal Enrollment of Parents

	Name of Father	Year	County	Name of Mother	Year	County
1	George Criner	Dead	Chickasaw Roll	Matilda Love Criner	Dead	Chickasaw Roll
2	No. 1			Mollie Criner	"	Non-Citizen
3	No. 1			Etta Criner		white woman
4	No. 1			" "		" "
5	No. 1			" "		" "
6	No. 1			" "		" "
7	No. 1			" "		" "
8	No. 1			" "		" "
9	Pete Baugh		Non-Citizen	Ann Baugh		Non-Citizen

(Notes)

No. 1 husband of Etta Criner. Chickasaw card No. D.67
No. 2 on Chickasaw roll as Bob Criner

No. 3 " " " " Dolphus "
No. 4 " " " " Joe "
No. 8 Enrolled January 3, 1901.
No. 9 transferred from Chickasaw Card #D.67 *(No. 9 Dawes' Roll No. I.W. 135)*

Sept. 23/98.

Residence: Pickens ***County*** ***Card No.***
Post Office: Overbrook, Ind. Ter. ***Field No.***

	Name	Relationship to Person First Named	Age	Sex	Blood	Tribal Enrollment		
						Year	County	Page
1	Criner, George	Named	25	M	1/8	1897	Pickens	13
2	" Minnie	Wife	24	F	I.W.	"	"	78
3	" Norma	Dau	2mos	"	1/16			
4	" Hazel	Dau	2mo	F	1/16			

Tribal Enrollment of Parents

	Name of Father	Year	County	Name of Mother	Year	County
1	John Criner	1897	Pickens	Mollie Criner	Dead	Non-Citizen
2	Joe McAlester		Non-Citizen	Kate McAlester		" "
3	No. 1			No. 2		
4	No. 1			No. 2		

(Notes)

No. 4 born Oct. 13, 1901: Enrolled Dec. 3, 1901 *(No. 2 Dawes' Roll No. I.W. 24)*
No. 4 Died Aug. 25, 1902. Proof of death filed Nov. 4, 1902.

Sept. 23/98.

Residence: Pickens ***County*** ***Card No.***
Post Office: Ardmore, Ind. Ter. ***Field No.***

	Name	Relationship to Person First Named	Age	Sex	Blood	Tribal Enrollment		
						Year	County	Page
1	Chase, Abel D. Sr.	Named	72	M	I.W.	1897	Pickens	77
2	" Nancy	Wife	56	F	3/4	1897	"	12
3	Blake, Callie	Dau	15	"	3/8	1897	"	12

Tribal Enrollment of Parents

	Name of Father	Year	County	Name of Mother	Year	County
1	Abel D. Chase	Dead	Non-Citizen	Emma Chase	Dead	Non-Citizen
2	James McCoy	"	Chickasaw Roll	Sibby McCoy	"	Chickasaw Roll
3	No. 1			No. 2		

(NOTES)

No. 1 On Chickasaw Roll as Abel D. Chase *(No. 1 Dawes' Roll No. 119)*
No. 1 Admitted by Dawes Com. Case No. 245.
No. 3 is now the wife of John Y. Blake on Choctaw card #509. Evidence of marriage requested April 25, 1902. Received and filed May 3, 1902.
Affidavit of Minerva J. Graham as to marriage between Nos. 1 and 2 filed Nov. 13, 1902.
John Y.F. Blake husband of No. 3 now on Chickasaw card #18?? *(difficult to read)*

Sept. 23/98.

RESIDENCE: Pickens COUNTY		CARD NO.					
POST OFFICE: Berwyn, Ind. Ter.		FIELD NO.					
NAME	RELATION-SHIP TO PERSON FIRST NAMED	AGE	SEX	BLOOD	TRIBAL ENROLLMENT YEAR	COUNTY	PAGE
1 Colbert, Ed. F.		34	M	1/4	1897	Pickens	20
2 Taylor, Lena	Wife	31	F	I.W.	1897	"	77

TRIBAL ENROLLMENT OF PARENTS

	NAME OF FATHER	YEAR	COUNTY	NAME OF MOTHER	YEAR	COUNTY
1	Sam Colbert	Dead	Chickasaw Roll	Mary Colbert	Dead	Panola
2	John Hereford	"	Non-Citizen	Tibbie Hereford	"	Non-Citizen

(NOTES)

No. 1 on Chickasaw roll as E.F. Colbert
No. 2 was divorced from No. 1 July 8, 1902, and is now married to Joseph Taylor - a Non-Citizen, white man. July 18, 1901.

P.O. No. 2 Ardmore, I.T. c/o Thompson and Broom

Sept. 23/98.

RESIDENCE: Pickens COUNTY		CARD NO.					
POST OFFICE: Ardmore, Ind. Ter.		FIELD NO.					
NAME	RELATION-SHIP TO PERSON FIRST NAMED	AGE	SEX	BLOOD	TRIBAL ENROLLMENT YEAR	COUNTY	PAGE
1 Norris, Tom		50	M	I.W.	1897	Pickens	78
2 " Josephine	Wife	28	F	1/64	1897	"	16
3 " Minnie	Dau	11	"	1/128	1897	"	16
4 " Maude	"	9	"	1/128	1897	"	16
5 " Myrtie	"	6	"	1/128	1897	"	16
6 " T.	Son	2	M	1/128	1897	"	16

TRIBAL ENROLLMENT OF PARENTS						
	NAME OF FATHER	YEAR	COUNTY	NAME OF MOTHER	YEAR	COUNTY
1	James Norris	Dead	Non-Citizen	Margaret A.L. Norris	Dead	Non-Citizen
2	James Easton (I.W.)	1897	Tishomingo	Margaret Easton	"	Tishomingo
3	No. 1			No. 2		
4	No. 1			No. 2		
5	No. 1			No. 2		
6	No. 1			No. 2		

(NOTES)

No. 1 See decision of June 13, 04 *(No. 1 Dawes' Roll No. 388)*
No. 2 on Chickasaw roll as Josie Norris
No. 5 Died May 20, 1901: Proof of death filed Nov. 3, 1902.
See testimony of No. 1 taken Oct. 30, 1902.
Certificate of Clerk of Court Van Zandt Co, Texas relative to record of divorce proceedings between V.I. Norris and Thomas Norris filed Feby 21, 1900

P.O. Baum, I.T. 10/30/02

Sept. 23/98.

RESIDENCE: COUNTY							CARD NO.	
POST OFFICE:							FIELD NO.	
	NAME	RELATION-SHIP TO PERSON FIRST NAMED	AGE	SEX	BLOOD	TRIBAL ENROLLMENT		
						YEAR	COUNTY	PAGE
1	Cox, William R.		63	M	I.W.	1893	Pickens	
2	Cox, Ada E		11	F	1/4	1897	Pickens	14

TRIBAL ENROLLMENT OF PARENTS						
	NAME OF FATHER	YEAR	COUNTY	NAME OF MOTHER	YEAR	COUNTY
1	Wm Cox	Dead	Non-Citizen	Mary Cox	Dead	Non-Citizen
2	Wm R. Cox		white man	Susan McDaniel	1897	Pickens

(NOTES)

No. 2 on Chickasaw roll as Ida Cox
No. 2 also on Chickasaw roll as Ada Cox Page 17
No. 2 is daughter of William R. Cox on Chickasaw #D.209
No. 1 transferred from Chickasaw card #D.209 Oct. 31, 1902
No. 1 was formerly husband of Susan McDaniel on Chickasaw Card *(illegible)*

Sept. 23/98.

RESIDENCE: Pickens COUNTY					CARD NO.		
POST OFFICE: Pike, Ind. Ter.					FIELD NO.		
NAME	RELATION-SHIP TO PERSON FIRST NAMED	AGE	SEX	BLOOD	TRIBAL ENROLLMENT		
					YEAR	COUNTY	PAGE
1 Troop, Laura May		21	F	1/8	1897	Pickens	16
2 " Myrtle Jane	Dau	3	"	1/16	1897	"	16
3 " Cecil Gordon	Son	16 mo	M	1/16	1897	"	86
4 " Newel	"	1 wk	"	1/16			
5 " Addie Jewel	Dau	3 mo	F	1/16			
6 " Jesse L.	Husband	31	M	I.W.			

TRIBAL ENROLLMENT OF PARENTS

NAME OF FATHER	YEAR	COUNTY	NAME OF MOTHER	YEAR	COUNTY
1 John Parker	Dead	Pickens	Mattie Grundy	1897	Pickens
2 Jesse L. Troop		white man	No. 1		
3 " " "		" "	No. 1		
4 " " "		" "	No. 1		
5 " " "		" "	No. 1		
6 Franklin Troop			Mahala Jane Troop		

(NOTES)

No. 1 Wife of Jesse L. Troop, Chickasaw Card No. D.65
No. 1 died April 26, 1900; Proof of death filed Oct. 2, 1902
No. 1 on Chickasaw roll as Laura Troop
No. 2 " " " " Myrtle "
No. 2 Died June 25, 1899; proof of death filed Oct. 31, 1902
No. 3 Proof of birth received and filed Oct. 2, 1902 *(No. 3 Dawes' Roll No. 4114)*
No. 4 born October 13/98. Enrolled Oct. 17/98
No. 4 Died July 2, 1899; proof of death filed Oct. 31, 1902
No. 5 Enrolled June 26, 1900
No. 5 Died Oct. 13, 1900; proof of death filed Oct. 31, 1902
No. 6 transferred from Chick card #C.162 July 30, 1906. See decision of July 14, 1906.
No. 1 Hereon dismissed under order of The Commission to The Five Civilized Tribes March 31 - 1905

Sept. 23/98.

RESIDENCE: Pickens COUNTY					CARD NO.		
POST OFFICE: Dougherty, Ind. Ter					FIELD NO.		
NAME	RELATION-SHIP TO PERSON FIRST NAMED	AGE	SEX	BLOOD	TRIBAL ENROLLMENT		
					YEAR	COUNTY	PAGE
1 Adkins, L.P.		46	M	I.W.			

2	" Harvey G.	Son	18	M	1/4	1897	Pickens	16
3	" Israel Earnest	"	17	"	1/4	1897	"	16
4	" Charles Richard	"	14	"	1/4	1897	"	16
5	" Edna Ellen	Dau	8	F	1/4	1897	"	16
6	" Evelina	"	4	"	1/4	1897	"	16

TRIBAL ENROLLMENT OF PARENTS

	NAME OF FATHER	YEAR	COUNTY	NAME OF MOTHER	YEAR	COUNTY
1	H.G. Adkins	Dead	Non-Citizen	Elander Adkins		Non-Citizen
2	No. 1			Frances Willis	1897	Pickens
3	No. 1			" "	1897	"
4	No. 1			" "	1897	"
5	No. 1			" "	1897	"
6	No. 1			" "	1897	"

(NOTES)

No. 2 on Chickasaw roll as Harvey Atkins *(No. 1 Dawes' Roll No. I.W. 281)*
No. 3 " " " " Isreal "
No. 4 " " " " Charles "
No. 5 " " " " Edna "

Sept. 23/98.

RESIDENCE: Pickens ***COUNTY***					***CARD NO.***			
POST OFFICE: Dougherty, Ind. Ter.					***FIELD NO.***			
	NAME	RELATION-SHIP TO PERSON FIRST NAMED	AGE	SEX	BLOOD	TRIBAL ENROLLMENT		
						YEAR	COUNTY	PAGE
1	Willis, Frances		37	F	1/2	1897	Pickens	32
2	" Floradel	Dau	2	"	1/4	1897	"	32
3	" Archie Leonard	Son	10mo	M	1/4			

TRIBAL ENROLLMENT OF PARENTS

	NAME OF FATHER	YEAR	COUNTY	NAME OF MOTHER	YEAR	COUNTY
1	Bill Williams	Dead	Choctaw roll	Missie Williams	Dead	Chickasaw roll
2	Jacob L. Willis		Non-Citizen	No. 1		
3	" " "		" "	No. 1		

(NOTES)

No. 2 on Chickasaw roll as Flordelio
No. 3 Affidavit of attending physician to be supplied. Received Oct. 5/98.

P.O. Durwood, I.T. Sept. 23/98.

RESIDENCE: Pickens *COUNTY* *CARD NO.*
POST OFFICE: Ardmore, Ind. Ter. *FIELD NO.*

	NAME	RELATIONSHIP TO PERSON FIRST NAMED	AGE	SEX	BLOOD	TRIBAL ENROLLMENT		
						YEAR	COUNTY	PAGE
1	Maupin, Laurina P.		27	F	1/16	1897	Pickens	17
2	" Charles Stuart	Hus	35	M	I.W.	1897	"	78

TRIBAL ENROLLMENT OF PARENTS

	NAME OF FATHER	YEAR	COUNTY	NAME OF MOTHER	YEAR	COUNTY
1	Charles Laflon		Choctaw roll	Mary A. Laflon	Dead	Chickasaw Roll
2	Milton Maupin	Dead	Non-Citizen	Melinda Maupin	Dead	Non-Citizen

(NOTES)

Nos 1 & 2 Admitted by Dawes Com. Case No. 74, and no appeal taken. *(No. 2 Dawes' Roll No. I.W. 230)*
on Chickasaw Roll as Lorena Maupin.
Wife of C.S. Maupin, Chickasaw Card No. D.63
No. 2 transferred from Chickasaw card #?. 63. See decision of March 5, 1904

Sept. 22/98.

RESIDENCE: Pickens *COUNTY* *CARD NO.*
POST OFFICE: Ardmore, Ind. Ter. *FIELD NO.*

	NAME	RELATIONSHIP TO PERSON FIRST NAMED	AGE	SEX	BLOOD	TRIBAL ENROLLMENT		
						YEAR	COUNTY	PAGE
1	Ebisch, Christian Frederick		32	M	I.W.	1897	Pickens	77
2	" Mattie	wife	22	F	3/4	1897	"	22
3	" Wagoner	son	4	M	3/8	1897	"	22
4	" C.A. Frederick	"	2	"	3/8	1897	"	22
5	" May	Dau	4 mo	F	3/8			
6	" Liddia	Dau	3 wk	F	3/8			
7	" W.F. Ernest	Son	1 mo	M	3/8			

TRIBAL ENROLLMENT OF PARENTS

	NAME OF FATHER	YEAR	COUNTY	NAME OF MOTHER	YEAR	COUNTY
1	Fred Ebisch	Dead	Non-Citizen	Christianna Ebisch	Dead	Non-Citizen
2	Sam Paul	"	Chickasaw Roll	Francis Willis	1897	Pickens
3	No. 1			No. 2		
4	No. 1			No. 2		
5	No. 1			No. 2		
6	No. 1			No. 2		
7	No. 1			No. 2		

(NOTES)

Name of No. 1 C.F. Ebisch or Fred Ebisch. See his letter filed May 3, 1901.
No. 1 on Chickasaw Roll as Fred Ebbish *(No. 1 Dawes' Roll No. 118)*
No. 2 " " " " Mattie "
No. 4 " " " " C.A.F. "
No. 4 Proof of birth received and filed Oct. 27, 1902.
No. 6 Enrolled April 15, 1901.
No. 7 Born June 28, 1902; Enrolled July 25, 1902.

P.O. Province, I.T. Sept. 22/98.

RESIDENCE: Pickens **COUNTY** **CARD NO.**
POST OFFICE: Ardmore, Ind. Ter. **FIELD NO.**

	Name	Relationship to Person First Named	Age	Sex	Blood	Tribal Enrollment Year	County	Page
1	Webb, George H.		41	M	I.W.	1897	Pickens	83
2	" Stella Laflon	wife	35	F	1/16	1897	Pickens	17
3	" Guy Laflore	Son	13	M	1/32	1897	"	17
4	" Daisy Maude	Dau	4	F	1/32	1897	"	17

TRIBAL ENROLLMENT OF PARENTS

	Name of Father	Year	County	Name of Mother	Year	County
1	Geo W. Webb	Dead	Non-Citizen	Susan S. Webb		Non-Citizen
2	Charles Laflore		Choctaw roll	Mary A. Flore	Dead	Chickasaw Roll
3	Geo. H. Webb	1897	Pickens	No. 2		
4	" " "	"	"	No. 2		

(NOTES)

No. 1 enrolled Nov. 22/98. *(No. 1 Dawes' Roll No. 23)*
No. 2 on Chickasaw roll as Stella L. Webb
No. 3 " " " " Guy L. "
No. 4 " " " " Daisy N. " Sept. 22/98.

RESIDENCE: Pickens **COUNTY** **CARD NO.**
POST OFFICE: Marietta, Ind. Ter. **FIELD NO.**

	Name	Relationship to Person First Named	Age	Sex	Blood	Tribal Enrollment Year	County	Page
1	Love, Thomas B.		36	M	3/4	1897	Pickens	26
2	" Mary M.	wife	27	F	I.W.	1897	"	79
3	" Lena Belle	Dau	7	"	3/8	1897	"	26

4	" Robert Howard	Son	6	M	3/8	1897	"	26
5	" Clara Maude	Dau	5	F	3/8	1897	"	26
6	" Mary Hazel	"	3	F	3/8	1897	"	26

TRIBAL ENROLLMENT OF PARENTS

	NAME OF FATHER	YEAR	COUNTY	NAME OF MOTHER	YEAR	COUNTY
1	Robt. H. Love	Dead	Chickasaw Roll	Sallie Love	Dead	Chickasaw Roll
2	L.M. Huddleston		Non-Citizen	M.E. Huddleston		Non-Citizen
3	No. 1			No. 2		
4	No. 1			No. 2		
5	No. 1			No. 2		
6	No. 1			No. 2		

(NOTES)

No. 3 on Chickasaw Roll as Lena B. Love *(No. 2 Dawes' Roll No. 116)*
No. 4 " " " " Robert H. "
No. 5 " " " " Clara M. "
No. 6 " " " " Mary H. "

Sept. 22/98.

RESIDENCE: Pontotoc	**COUNTY**	**CARD NO.**	
POST OFFICE: Purcell, Ind. Ter.		**FIELD NO.**	

	NAME	RELATIONSHIP TO PERSON FIRST NAMED	AGE	SEX	BLOOD	TRIBAL ENROLLMENT YEAR	COUNTY	PAGE
1	Kimberlin, Izaah J.		23	M	1/16	1897	Pickens	26
2	" Lizzie	Wife	22	F	I.W.			

TRIBAL ENROLLMENT OF PARENTS

	NAME OF FATHER	YEAR	COUNTY	NAME OF MOTHER	YEAR	COUNTY
1	W.G. Kimberlin		white man	Elizabeth Kimberlin	Dead	Chickasaw roll
2		Dead	Non-Citizen		Dead	Non-Citizen

(NOTES)

No. 1 on Chickasaw roll as Zudie Kimberlin

Sept. 22/98.

RESIDENCE:	**COUNTY**	**CARD NO.**	
POST OFFICE:		**FIELD NO.**	

	NAME	RELATIONSHIP TO PERSON FIRST NAMED	AGE	SEX	BLOOD	TRIBAL ENROLLMENT YEAR	COUNTY	PAGE
1	Burney, W.B.		49	M	3/16	1897	Pickens	21
2	" Julian	Son	16	M	1/4	1897	"	21
3	" Una	Dau	13	F	3/32	1897	"	21

4	" Valey	"	11	"	3/32	1897	"	21
5	" Blanch	"	9	"	3/32	1897	"	21
6	" Vessie	"	6	"	3/32	1897	"	21
7	" Clay P.	Son	4	M	3/32	1897	"	21
8	" Minnie	Dau	6 mo	F	3/32			
9	" Douglas Johnson	Son	6 mo	M	3/32			
10	" Clefford	Wife	40	F	I.W.			

TRIBAL ENROLLMENT OF PARENTS

	NAME OF FATHER	YEAR	COUNTY	NAME OF MOTHER	YEAR	COUNTY
1	David Burney	Dead	Chickasaw Roll	Emily Burney	Dead	Chickasaw Roll
2	No. 1			Eliza Burney	"	" "
3	No. 1			Clifford C. Burney		
4	No. 1			"		
5	No. 1			"		
6	No. 1			"		
7	No. 1			"		
8	No. 1			"		
9	No. 1			Clefford C. Burney		
10	James Conder	Dead	Non-Citizen	Victoria Conder		Non-Citizen

(NOTES)

No. 1 husband of Clifford C. Burney Chickasaw Card No. D.60
No. 8 affidavit of attending physician to be supplied. Received Oct. 4/98
No. 8 Died March 4, 1899; Proof of death filed Nov. 1, 1902
No. 9 Enrolled June 6, 1900.
No. 10 transferred from Chickasaw Card D.60 *(No. 10 Dawes' Roll No. 184)*
See decision of May 5, 1902. Sept. 22/98.

RESIDENCE: Tishomingo ***COUNTY*** ***CARD NO.***
POST OFFICE: Baum, Ind. Ter. ***FIELD NO.***

	NAME	RELATIONSHIP TO PERSON FIRST NAMED	AGE	SEX	BLOOD	TRIBAL ENROLLMENT YEAR	COUNTY	PAGE
1	McGlasson, Emma		36	F	1/2	1897	Tishomingo	30
2	Fitch, Mary Ellen	Dau	17	"	1/4	1897	"	28
3	" Joe	"	13	"	1/4	1897	"	30
4	" Maude	"	11	"	1/4	1897	"	30
5	" Eliza Easter	"	8	"	1/4	1897	"	30
6	McGlasson, Jesse	Son	6	M	1/4	1897	"	28
7	" Lula	Dau	4Days	F	1/4		"	

TRIBAL ENROLLMENT OF PARENTS

	NAME OF FATHER	YEAR	COUNTY	NAME OF MOTHER	YEAR	COUNTY
1	Leonidus Colbert	Dead	Choctaw Roll	Easter Hillhouse	Dead	Chickasaw Roll
2	Daniel Fitch		Non-Citizen	No. 1.		
3	" "		" "	No. 1.		
4	" "		" "	No. 1.		
5	" "		" "	No. 1.		
6	James McGlasson		" "	No. 1.		
7	" "		" "	No. 1.		

(NOTES)

No. 1 on Chickasaw roll as Ema McGlossan
No. 2 " " " " Marvelton
No. 5 " " " " Eliza
No. 6 " " " " Kessoe
Nos. 2 to 5 inclusive are children of D.H. Fitch on Chickasaw card #D.335.
Nos. 6 & 7 enrolled Sept. 27/98.

Sept. 22/98.

RESIDENCE: Tishomingo COUNTY CARD NO.
POST OFFICE: Baum, Ind. Ter. FIELD NO.

	NAME	RELATION-SHIP TO PERSON FIRST NAMED	AGE	SEX	BLOOD	TRIBAL ENROLLMENT YEAR	COUNTY	PAGE
1	Brown, Joe		33	M	Full	1897	Tishomingo	32
2	" Mary	Dau	2	F	1/2	1897	"	32
3	" Joe	Son	7mo	M	1/2			
4	Sealy, Clarence	Nephew	13	"	Full	1897	Tishomingo	28
5	" Holmes	Nephew	11	"	"	1897	"	28
6	" Alice	Niece	9	F	"	1897	"	28
7	Brown, Guy	Son	2mo	M	1/2			
8	" Rolia	Wife	30	F	I.W.			

TRIBAL ENROLLMENT OF PARENTS

	NAME OF FATHER	YEAR	COUNTY	NAME OF MOTHER	YEAR	COUNTY
1	Aaron Brown	Dead	Chickasaw Roll	Millie Brown	Dead	Chickasaw Roll
2	No. 1			Rolia Brown		white woman
3	No. 1			" "		" "
4	Jewel Sealy	Dead	Chickasaw Roll	Lottie Sealy	Dead	Tishomingo
5	" "	"	" "	" "	"	"
6	" "	"	" "	" "	"	"
7	No. 1			Rolia Brown		

8	John F. Barnes	"	non citz	Vitura Barnes		non citz.

(NOTES)

Husband of Rolia Brown Chickasaw Card No. D.58.
Guy Brown, born Nov. 16/99, on card No. D.312.
No. 7 born November 16, 1899; transferred to this card February 1, 1902.
No. 8 transferred from Chickasaw Card No 58

Sept. 22/98.

RESIDENCE: Pickens COUNTY CARD NO.
POST OFFICE: Ardmore, I.T. FIELD NO.

	NAME	RELATIONSHIP TO PERSON FIRST NAMED	AGE	SEX	BLOOD	TRIBAL ENROLLMENT YEAR	COUNTY	PAGE
1	Bynum, B.M.		34	M	I.W.	1897	Pickens	77
2	" Effie	wife	24	F	1/32	1897	"	20
3	" Willis	Son	3 1/2	M	1/64	1897	"	20

TRIBAL ENROLLMENT OF PARENTS

	NAME OF FATHER	YEAR	COUNTY	NAME OF MOTHER	YEAR	COUNTY
1	E. Bynum	Dead	Non-Citizen	Mary F. Bynum		Non-Citizen
2	Wm Willis	"	Chickasaw Roll	Mincis Willis Hiser	1897	Pickens
3	No. 1			No. 2		

(NOTES)

Nos. 1, 2 and 3 admitted by Dawes Com. Case No. 22, and no appeal taken. *(No. 1 Dawes' Roll No. 316)*
Married first in Texas Dec. 28/1893 under U.S. Law; remarried Oct. 3, 1894 under Chickasaw law.
Marriage license and certificate on file with Dawes Com. in office at Muskogee, I.T.
No. 2 on Chickasaw roll as Effy Bynum.

Sept. 22/98.

RESIDENCE: Pickens COUNTY CARD NO.
POST OFFICE: Healdton, Ind. Ter. FIELD NO.

	NAME	RELATIONSHIP TO PERSON FIRST NAMED	AGE	SEX	BLOOD	TRIBAL ENROLLMENT YEAR	COUNTY	PAGE
1	Chase, Grove		37	M	1/4	1897	Pickens	13
2	" Roxie	Wife	29	F	I.W.	1897	"	78
3	" Gussie	Dau	12	"	1/8	1897	"	13
4	" Emmet	Son	10	M	1/8	1897	"	13
5	" Abel D, Jr.	"	8	M	1/8	1897	"	13
6	" Lennie Mabel	Dau	3mo	F	1/8			

	Name of Father	Year	County	Name of Mother	Year	County
	Tribal Enrollment of Parents					
1	Abel Chase I.W.	1897	Pickens	Nancy Chase	1897	Pickens
2	Zeke Henry		Non-Citizen	Elizabeth Henry		Non-Citizen
3	No. 1			No. 2		
4	No. 1			No. 2		
5	No. 1			No. 2		
6	No. 1			No. 2		

(Notes)

No. 1 on Chickasaw roll as Grove
No. 2 " " " " Roxie *(No. 2 Dawes' Roll No. 316)*
No. 4 " " " " Emie
No. 5 " " " " Abel, Jr.
No. 6 Enrolled May 24, 1900.

Sept. 22/98.

Residence: Pickens **County** **Card No.**
Post Office: Eastman, Ind. Ter. **Field No.**

	Name	Relationship to Person First Named	Age	Sex	Blood	Tribal Enrollment Year	County	Page
1	Bass, Jerry		41	M	I.W.			
2	" Margaret	Wife	40	F	Full	1897	Pickens	20

	Name of Father	Year	County	Name of Mother	Year	County
	Tribal Enrollment of Parents					
1	Howell Bass	Dead	Non-Citizen	Rhoda N. Bass		Non-Citizen
2	I-ah-ne-ah	Dead	Chickasaw Roll	She-no-ka-cha	Dead	Chickasaw Roll

(Notes)

No. 1 License and certificate on file in office of Dawes Com. Muskogee, Ind. Ter.
December 2, 1899; License this day filed with card *(No. 2 Dawes' Roll No. 1722)*
Certified copy of divorce proceedings between Margaret Pollard and Jake Pollard filed April 8, 1900.

Sept. 22/98.

Residence: Pickens **County** **Card No.**
Post Office: Eastman, Ind. Ter. **Field No.**

	Name	Relationship to Person First Named	Age	Sex	Blood	Tribal Enrollment Year	County	Page
1	Carlton, Roberson		35	M	Full	1897	Pickens	20
2	" Sarah	Wife	32	F	I.W.	1897	"	77

3	" Frances	Dau	10	"	1/2	1897	"	20
4	" Josie	"	9	"	1/2	1897	"	20
5	" Guy	Son	4	M	1/2	1897	"	20
6	" Pearlie	Dau	2	F	1/2			
7	" George R.	Son	3m	M	1/2			

TRIBAL ENROLLMENT OF PARENTS

	NAME OF FATHER	YEAR	COUNTY	NAME OF MOTHER	YEAR	COUNTY
1	I-ah-ne-ah	Dead	Chickasaw Roll	She-no-ka-cha	Dead	Chickasaw Roll
2	Lige Kirkwood	"	Non-Citizen	Susan Kirkwood	"	Non-Citizen
3	No. 1			No. 2		
4	No. 1			No. 2		
5	No. 1			No. 2		
6	No. 1			No. 2		
7	No. 1			No. 2		

(NOTES)

No. 1 died Oct. 1899. Proof of death filed Nov. 3, 1902
No. 1[sic] died May 13, 1899
No. 2 marriage license and certificate to be supplied. *(No. 2 Dawes' Roll No. 314)*
No. 2 also on 1897 roll, Page 96 as Sarah Robertson
No. 3 " " 1897 " " 96 " Frank "
No. 4 " " 1897 " " 96 " Joseph "
See testimony of No. 2 taken Oct. 30, 1902.

Sept. 22/98.

RESIDENCE: Pickens	**COUNTY**				**CARD NO.**			
POST OFFICE: Cheek, Ind. Ter.					**FIELD NO.**			
	NAME	RELATION-SHIP TO PERSON FIRST NAMED	AGE	SEX	BLOOD	TRIBAL ENROLLMENT		
						YEAR	COUNTY	PAGE
1	Bonner, John A.		28	M	I.W.	1897	Pickens	77

TRIBAL ENROLLMENT OF PARENTS

	NAME OF FATHER	YEAR	COUNTY	NAME OF MOTHER	YEAR	COUNTY
1	Freeman Bonner	Dead	Non-Citizen	Susan Bonner		Non-Citizen

(NOTES)

On Chickasaw roll as John Bonner. *(No. 1 Dawes' Roll No. 23)*
Wife of No. 1 is Lucy E. Garland on 1893 Chickasaw roll. No. 2, page 90.

Sept. 22/98.

RESIDENCE: Pickens ***COUNTY*** ***CARD NO.***
POST OFFICE: Healdton, Ind. Ter. ***FIELD NO.***

	NAME	RELATION-SHIP TO PERSON FIRST NAMED	AGE	SEX	BLOOD	TRIBAL ENROLLMENT		
						YEAR	COUNTY	PAGE
1	Newton, William Calvin		40	M	I.W.	1897	Pickens	78
2	" Ruthie V.	wife	29	F	1/16	1897	"	13
3	" Ed	son	14	M	1/32	1897	"	13
4	" Willie Ida	Dau	13	F	1/32	1897	"	13
5	" Calvin	Son	5	M	1/32	1897	"	14

TRIBAL ENROLLMENT OF PARENTS

	NAME OF FATHER	YEAR	COUNTY	NAME OF MOTHER	YEAR	COUNTY
1	Marion Newton	Dead	Non-Citizen	Evaline Newton	Dead	Non-Citizen
2	A.D. Chase		" "	Nancy Chase	1897	Pickens
3	No. 1			No. 2		
4	No. 1			No. 2		
5	No. 1			No. 2		

(NOTES)

No. 1 on Chickasaw Roll as W.C. Newton *(No. 1 Dawes' Roll No. 22)*
No. 2 " " " " Seith "
No. 4 " " " " Willie "

Sept. 22/98.

RESIDENCE: Pickens ***COUNTY*** ***CARD NO.***
POST OFFICE: Berwyn, Ind. Ter. ***FIELD NO.***

	NAME	RELATION-SHIP TO PERSON FIRST NAMED	AGE	SEX	BLOOD	TRIBAL ENROLLMENT		
						YEAR	COUNTY	PAGE
1	Warren, William F.		34	M	I.W.	1897	Pickens	79
2	" Nannie C.	Wife	26	F	1/16	1897	"	21
3	" Reuben	Son	6	M	1/32	1897	"	21
4	" Ma *(illegible)*	Dau	3	F	1/32	1897	"	21
5	" Mary Catherine	"	6mos	"	1/32			
6	" Ruth Bixby	"	1mo	"	1/32			
7	" William Byrd	Son	1mo	M	1/32			

TRIBAL ENROLLMENT OF PARENTS

	NAME OF FATHER	YEAR	COUNTY	NAME OF MOTHER	YEAR	COUNTY
1	John Warren	Dead	Non-Citizen	Mary J. Warren	Dead	Non-Citizen
2	Thos. C.T. Boyd	"	Chickasaw Roll	Sarah Boyd	"	" "
3	No. 1			No. 2		

4	No. 1			No. 2		
5	No. 1			No. 2		
6	No. 1			No. 2		
7	No. 1			No. 2		

(NOTES)

No. 1 on Chickasaw roll as William Warren *(No. 1 Dawes' Roll No. 21)*
No. 2 " " " " Nannie "
No. 3 " " " " Reubin "
No. 6 Enrolled, June 23, 1900
No. 7 Born April 22, 1902; enrolled May 14, 1902

Sept. 22/98.

RESIDENCE: Pickens *COUNTY* *CARD NO.*
POST OFFICE: Newport, Ind. Ter. *FIELD NO.*

	NAME	RELATION-SHIP TO PERSON FIRST NAMED	AGE	SEX	BLOOD	TRIBAL ENROLLMENT		
						YEAR	COUNTY	PAGE
1	McCauley, Elmer		23	M	1/4	1897	Pickens	19

TRIBAL ENROLLMENT OF PARENTS

	NAME OF FATHER	YEAR	COUNTY	NAME OF MOTHER	YEAR	COUNTY
1	James McCauley	1897	Pickens	Susan McCauley	Dead	Chickasaw Roll

(NOTES)

Sept. 22/98.

RESIDENCE: Pickens *COUNTY* *CARD NO.*
POST OFFICE: Newport, Ind. Ter. *FIELD NO.*

	NAME	RELATION-SHIP TO PERSON FIRST NAMED	AGE	SEX	BLOOD	TRIBAL ENROLLMENT		
						YEAR	COUNTY	PAGE
1	McCauley, James		68	M	I.W.	1897		
2	Garland, Jake	G.Son	6	"	1/4	1897	Pickens	19

TRIBAL ENROLLMENT OF PARENTS

	NAME OF FATHER	YEAR	COUNTY	NAME OF MOTHER	YEAR	COUNTY
1	Bryan McCauley	Dead	Non-Citizen	Margaret McCauley	Dead	Non-Citizen
2	Mich Garland	"	Choctaw roll	Lucy Garland	"	Chickasaw Roll

(NOTES)

Widower. Married in 1859 to Susan Watkins half blood Chickasaw and lived with her until her death in 1875. Both parties well known to Judge Love and to Messrs Hampton and Fulsom.

No. 1 Died Jany. 26, 1901: proof of death filed Sept. 18, 1902.

Sept. 22/98.

RESIDENCE: Pickens ***COUNTY***		***CARD NO.***	
POST OFFICE: Ardmore, Ind. Ter.		***FIELD NO.***	

	NAME	RELATION-SHIP TO PERSON FIRST NAMED	AGE	SEX	BLOOD	TRIBAL ENROLLMENT YEAR	COUNTY	PAGE
1	Alexander, James Arthur		31	M	1/4	1893	Pickens	P.R.#2 Pg. 30
2	" Arch	Son	6	"	1/8	1893	"	P.R.#2 Pg. 30
3	" Bob	"	10mos	"	1/8			
4	" Whit Hyden	Dau	3	F	1/8	1897	Pickens	93
5	" Charles F.	Son	8	M	1/8	1893	"	PR#2 30
6	" Mattie E.	Dau	6wks	F	1/8			
7	" Della	wife	31	F	I.W.	1897	Pickens	93

TRIBAL ENROLLMENT OF PARENTS

	NAME OF FATHER	YEAR	COUNTY	NAME OF MOTHER	YEAR	COUNTY
1	W.V. Alexander I.W.	1897	Pickens	Jennie Alexander	Dead	Chickasaw Roll
2	No. 1			Della Alexander		white woman
3	No. 1			" "		" "
4	No. 1			" "		" "
5	No. 1			Cornelia Garret Alexander I.W.	Dead	Pickens
6	No. 1			Della Alexander		Non-Citizen
7	?raat Poke	Dead	Non-Citizen	Mary Poke	Dead	" "

(NOTES)

No. 1 on Chickasaw roll as J.A. Alexander
No. 1 on 1896 Chickasaw Roll, Pickens County, Page 93
No. 2 " " " " " " " "
No. 3 Doed Feb. 26, 1901: Proof of Death filed Nov. 3, 1902.
No. 4 on Chickasaw roll as Baby Alexander
No. 4 Died March 2, 1901: Proof of Death filed Nov. 3, 1902.
No. 6 Enrolled Sept. 26, 1900.
Wife Della Alexander, on Chickasaw Card No. D.64.
Nos. 1 and 2 on Chickasaw 1893 payroll No. 2, page 30.
No. 7 on Chickasaw roll as D.A. Alexander *(No. 7 Dawes' Roll No. 133)*
No. 7 transferred from Chickasaw Card #D.64.
Nos. 1, 2 and 3 enrolled Sept. 22/98.
Nos. 4 and 5 enrolled Oct. 1/98.

P.O. of No 5 Charles, I.T. Sept. 22/98.

RESIDENCE: Pickens COUNTY					CARD NO.		
POST OFFICE: Ardmore, Ind. Ter.					FIELD NO.		
NAME	RELATION-SHIP TO PERSON FIRST NAMED	AGE	SEX	BLOOD	TRIBAL ENROLLMENT		
					YEAR	COUNTY	PAGE
1 Mulkey, John C.		25	M	I.W.			
2 " Elsie	wife	19	F	1/4	1897	Pickens	20
3 " Charles S.	son	1mo	M	1/8			

TRIBAL ENROLLMENT OF PARENTS

	NAME OF FATHER	YEAR	COUNTY	NAME OF MOTHER	YEAR	COUNTY
1	H.S. Mulkey		Non-Citizen	Bettie Mulkey		Non-Citizen
2	C.W. Henderson I.W.	1897	Pickens	Louisa Henderson	1897	Pickens
3	No. 1			No. 2		

(NOTES)

No. 2 on Chickasaw roll as Elsie Henderson *(No. 1 Dawes' Roll No. 177)*
No. 3 enrolled Nov. 3/99.

P.O. Berwyn, I.T. Sept. 22/98.

RESIDENCE: Tishomingo COUNTY					CARD NO.		
POST OFFICE: Davis, Ind. Ter.					FIELD NO.		
NAME	RELATION-SHIP TO PERSON FIRST NAMED	AGE	SEX	BLOOD	TRIBAL ENROLLMENT		
					YEAR	COUNTY	PAGE
1 Price, W.N. DEAD		63	M	I.W.	1897	Tishomingo	79
2 " Bisey	Wife	30	F	Full	1897	"	30
3 " Benjamin Franklin	Son	8	M	1/2	1897	"	30
4 " Jennie Belle	Dau	5	F	1/2	1897	"	30
5 " Ellis	Son	17	M	1/2	1893	"	P.R.#1 129
6 " Beulah	Dau	2mo	F	1/2			

TRIBAL ENROLLMENT OF PARENTS

	NAME OF FATHER	YEAR	COUNTY	NAME OF MOTHER	YEAR	COUNTY
1	Benj. Price	Dead	Non-Citizen	Betsey Price	Dead	Non-Citizen
2	Alfred Humes	1897	Pontotoc	Jennie Humes	"	Tishomingo
3	No. 1			No. 2		
4	No. 1			No. 2		
5	No. 1			Liney Tillower	Dead	Tishomingo
6	No. 1			No. 2		

(NOTES)

No. 1 on Chickasaw roll as Nathan Price, page 79, Pickens County
No. 3 " " " " Ben "
No. 4 " " " " Jennie "
No. 5 " " " " Alice "
No. 5 Enrolled Sept. 28/98.
No. 6 Enrolled June 23, 1900
No. 1 Died March 13th 1901; Proof of death filed February *(the remainder is illegible)*

Sept. 22/98.

RESIDENCE: Pickens COUNTY					CARD NO.		
POST OFFICE: Cheek, Ind Ter.					FIELD NO.		
NAME	RELATION-SHIP TO PERSON FIRST NAMED	AGE	SEX	BLOOD	TRIBAL ENROLLMENT		
					YEAR	COUNTY	PAGE
1 Collins, James P.		52	M	I.W.	1897	Pickens	77
2 Collins, Hettie	Wife	38	F	1/4	1897	Pickens	19
3 " James P.	Son	18	M	1/8	1897	"	19
4 " George H.	"	16	M	1/8	1897	"	19
5 " Audry B.	Dau	14	F	1/8	1897	"	19
6 " John	Son	12	M	1/8	1897	"	19
7 " Theodore	"	10	"	1/8	1897	"	19

TRIBAL ENROLLMENT OF PARENTS

NAME OF FATHER	YEAR	COUNTY	NAME OF MOTHER	YEAR	COUNTY
1 John Collins		Non-Citizen	Louisa Collins		Non-Citizen
2 James McCauley I.W.	1897	Pickens	Susan McCauley	Dead	Chickasaw Roll
3 J.P. Collins (I.W.)	1897	"	No. 2		
4 " " " "	1897	"	No. 2		
5 " " " "	1897	"	No. 2		
6 " " " "	1897	"	No. 2		
7 " " " "	1897	"	No. 2		

(NOTES)

No. 1 enrolled Oct. 4/98. *(No. 1 Dawes' Roll No. I.W. 313)*
No. 1 on Chickasaw roll as J.R. Collins
No. 2 wife of J.P. Collins, Intermarried white man.
No. 3 on Chickasaw roll as James Collins
No. 4 " " " " George "
No. 5 " " " " Andy "

Sept. 22/98.

RESIDENCE: Pickens COUNTY					CARD NO.		
POST OFFICE: Woodford, Ind. Ter.					FIELD NO.		
	NAME	RELATIONSHIP TO PERSON FIRST NAMED	AGE	SEX	BLOOD	TRIBAL ENROLLMENT		
						YEAR	COUNTY	PAGE
1	Crow, P.C.		18	M	I.W.	1897	Pickens	87

TRIBAL ENROLLMENT OF PARENTS

	NAME OF FATHER	YEAR	COUNTY	NAME OF MOTHER	YEAR	COUNTY
1	A.J. Crow		Non-Citizen	Annie Crow		Non-Citizen

(NOTES)

Sept. 22/98.

RESIDENCE: Pickens COUNTY					CARD NO.		
POST OFFICE: Whitebead, Ind. Ter.					FIELD NO.		

	NAME	RELATIONSHIP TO PERSON FIRST NAMED	AGE	SEX	BLOOD	TRIBAL ENROLLMENT YEAR	COUNTY	PAGE
1	Love, Will E.		25	M	1/16	1897	Pickens	24
2	" Alvia	Son	2	"	1/32	1897	"	24
3	" Frank	"	9Days	"	1/32			
4	" Lottie Lillian	Dau	3wks	F	1/32			

TRIBAL ENROLLMENT OF PARENTS

	NAME OF FATHER	YEAR	COUNTY	NAME OF MOTHER	YEAR	COUNTY
1	George Love	1897	Pickens	Melvina Love (I.W.)	1897	Pickens
2	No. 1			Betty Love		Non-Citizen
3	No. 1			" "		" "
4	No. 1			" "		" "

(NOTES)

No. 1 on Chickasaw roll as W.E. Love
No. 4 Born Sept. 22, 1902, enrolled Oct. 13, 1902. *(No. 4 Dawes' Roll No. 4443)*

Sept. 22/98.

RESIDENCE: Pontotoc COUNTY					CARD NO.		
POST OFFICE: Johnson, Ind. Ter.					FIELD NO.		

	NAME	RELATIONSHIP TO PERSON FIRST NAMED	AGE	SEX	BLOOD	TRIBAL ENROLLMENT YEAR	COUNTY	PAGE
1	Byars, Nathan H.		50	M	I.W.	1897	Pickens	80
2	" Catherine	Wife	36	F	1/8	1897	"	61
3	" Thomas N.	Son	16	M	1/16	1897	"	61

4	"	William C.	"	15	"	1/16	1897	"	61
5	"	Charlie T.	"	13	"	1/16	1897	"	61
6	"	Samuel T.	"	12	"	1/16	1897	"	61
7	"	Katie May	Dau	10	F	1/16	1897	"	61
8	"	Nancy E.	"	8	"	1/16	1897	"	61
9	"	Roy N.	Son	6	M	1/16	1897	"	61
10	"	Alice Ophelia	Dau	4Days	F	1/16			
11	"	Jim Jones	Son	3wks	M	1/16			

TRIBAL ENROLLMENT OF PARENTS

	NAME OF FATHER	YEAR	COUNTY	NAME OF MOTHER	YEAR	COUNTY
1	H. Byars	Dead	Non-Citizen	Nancy Byars	Dead	Non-Citizen
2	Thos. Johnson	"	" "	Elizabeth Johnson	"	Chickasaw Roll
3	No. 1			No. 2		
4	No. 1			No. 2		
5	No. 1			No. 2		
6	No. 1			No. 2		
7	No. 1			No. 2		
8	No. 1			No. 2		
9	No. 1			No. 2		
10	No. 1			No. 2		
11	No. 1			No. 2		

(NOTES)

No. 1 on Chickasaw roll as N.H. Byars *(No. 1 Dawes' Roll No. 115)*
2 " " " " Katie "
3 " " " " T.N. "
4 " " " " W.C. "
5 " " " " C.P. "
6 " " " " S.F. "
7 " " " " Katie " Jr.
8 " " " " Lizzie E. " "

Parents of No. 11 Father No. 1
Mother No. 2

Affidavit of attending physician as to birth of No. 10 to be supplied. Received Oct. 5/98.
Affidavit of Judge G.W. Wilson as to procurement of license to be suppliec. Received Oct. 11/98.
No. 9 Died Nov. 19, 1897. Proof of death filed Oct. 27/02.
No. 11 Born Oct. 12, 1901 and enrolled November 1, 1901.

P.O. Byars, I.T. 1/24-04 Sept. 22/98.

RESIDENCE: Pontotoc COUNTY					CARD NO.		
POST OFFICE: Johnson, Ind. Ter.					FIELD NO.		
	NAME	RELATIONSHIP TO PERSON FIRST NAMED	AGE	SEX	BLOOD	TRIBAL ENROLLMENT		
						YEAR	COUNTY	PAGE
1	Smith, Mary A.		18	F	1/16	1897	Pickens	61
2	" Lillian Estelle	Dau	3mos	"	1/32			
3	" Alfred M.	Husband	24	M	I.W.			

TRIBAL ENROLLMENT OF PARENTS

	NAME OF FATHER	YEAR	COUNTY	NAME OF MOTHER	YEAR	COUNTY
1	Nathan Byars		Non-Citizen	Catherine Byars	1897	Pickens
2	A.M. Smith		" "	No. 1		
3	E.S. Smith		" "	R. A. Adams		Non-Citizen

(NOTES)

No. 3 enrolled March 20/99.

P.O. Byars, I.T. 2/20/01

Sept. 22/98.

RESIDENCE: Pontotoc COUNTY					CARD NO.		
POST OFFICE: Purcell, Ind. Ter.					FIELD NO.		
	NAME	RELATIONSHIP TO PERSON FIRST NAMED	AGE	SEX	BLOOD	TRIBAL ENROLLMENT		
						YEAR	COUNTY	PAGE
1	Turnbull, Ryan		30	M	1/8	1897	Pontotoc	62
2	" Lottie	Wife	19	F	I.W.	1897	"	80
3	" Roy	Son	3mo	M	1/16			
4	" Virgil Oster	Son	5mo	M	1/16			

TRIBAL ENROLLMENT OF PARENTS

	NAME OF FATHER	YEAR	COUNTY	NAME OF MOTHER	YEAR	COUNTY
1	John Turnbull	Dead	Choctaw roll	Lucy Turnbull	Dead	Panola
2	Harry Weston	"	Non-Citizen	Ida Weston		Non-Citizen
3	No. 1			No. 2		
4	No. 1			No. 2		

(NOTES)

No. 3 enrolled Nov. 3/99
No. 4 enrolled Aug. 2/01

(No. 2 Dawes' Roll No. 114)

P.O. Lindsay, I.T. 10/24/02

Sept. 22/98.

RESIDENCE: Pickens COUNTY					CARD NO.		
POST OFFICE: Velma, Ind. Ter.					FIELD NO.		
NAME	RELATION-SHIP TO PERSON FIRST NAMED	AGE	SEX	BLOOD	TRIBAL ENROLLMENT		
					YEAR	COUNTY	PAGE
1 Stone, William		39	M	I.W.	1897	Pickens	78
2 " Josephine	Wife	30	F	1/4	1897	"	17
3 " James B.	Son	8	M	1/8	"	"	17
4 " Mary	Dau	2 1/2	F	1/8	"	"	17
5 " Lacy	Son	5mos	M	1/8			
6 " William C.	Son	1mo	M	1/8			

TRIBAL ENROLLMENT OF PARENTS

NAME OF FATHER	YEAR	COUNTY	NAME OF MOTHER	YEAR	COUNTY
1 James B. Stone	Dead	Non-Citizen	Sophia Stone	Dead	Non-Citizen
2 J.A. Smith (I.W.)	1897	Panola	Nancy Smith	1897	Panola
3 No. 1			No. 2		
4 No. 1			No. 2		
5 No. 1			No. 2		
6 No. 1			No. 2		

(NOTES)

No. 1 on Chickasaw Roll as Bill Stone
No. 2 " " " " Josie "
No. 5 affidavit of attending physician to be supplied. Received Oct. 11/98.
No. 6 Enrolled Aug. 29, 1900
No. 1 Died July 1, 1901; Proof of death filed Oct. 28, 1902.

Sept. 22/98.

RESIDENCE: Pickens COUNTY					CARD NO.		
POST OFFICE: Healdton, Ind. Ter.					FIELD NO.		
NAME	RELATION-SHIP TO PERSON FIRST NAMED	AGE	SEX	BLOOD	TRIBAL ENROLLMENT		
					YEAR	COUNTY	PAGE
1 Heald, William		17	M	1/2	1897	Pickens	17
2 " Benjamin	Bro	14	"	1/2	1897	"	17
3 " Charles H.	Son	2mo	M	1/4			

TRIBAL ENROLLMENT OF PARENTS

NAME OF FATHER	YEAR	COUNTY	NAME OF MOTHER	YEAR	COUNTY
1 C.H. Heald		white man	Eliza Jane Guy Heald	Dead	Tishomingo
2 " " "		" "	" " " "	"	"
3 No. 1			Belle Heald		Non-Citizen

(NOTES)

No. 1 is now the husband of Belle Heald a Non-Citizen; Jany 27, 1902.
No. 1 on Chickasaw roll as Willie
No. 2 " " " " Bennie
No. 3 born Nov. 13, 1901; Enrolled Jany. 27, 1902.
Father, C.H. Heald, on Chickasaw Card No. D55.

Sept. 22/98

RESIDENCE: Pickens COUNTY					CARD NO.		
POST OFFICE: Pike, Ind. Ter.					FIELD NO.		
NAME	RELATIONSHIP TO PERSON FIRST NAMED	AGE	SEX	BLOOD	TRIBAL ENROLLMENT		
					YEAR	COUNTY	PAGE
1 McMillan. Mary		18	F	3/8	1897	Pickens	19
2 Duroderigo, Albert Franklin	Bro	14	M	3/8	1897	"	18
3 " Eliza	Sister	11	F	3/8	1897	"	19
4 McMillan, Lillie Myrtle	Dau	1mo	F	3/16			

TRIBAL ENROLLMENT OF PARENTS

	NAME OF FATHER	YEAR	COUNTY	NAME OF MOTHER	YEAR	COUNTY
1	Osavior Duroderigo	Dead	Mexican	Jane Duroderigo	Dead	Chickasaw roll
2	" "	"	"	" "	"	" "
3	" "	"	"	" "	"	" "
4	W.A. McMillan		non-citizen	No. 1		

(NOTES)

No. 1 on Chickasaw roll as Mary Drawnguess
No. 2 " " " " Albert "
No. 3 " " " " Eliza "
A full brother, Columbus, on Chickasaw Card No. 1345
All living with Clara Coyle, widow of Ake Coyle, their on mother's side
No. 1 is now the wife of W.A. McMillan, non-citizen. Evidence of marriage filed herein May 17, 1901.
No. 4 Enrolled May 17, 1901. *(No. 4 Dawes' Roll No. 1660)*

Sept. 22/98

RESIDENCE: Pickens COUNTY					CARD NO.		
POST OFFICE: Pike, Ind. Ter.					FIELD NO.		
NAME	RELATIONSHIP TO PERSON FIRST NAMED	AGE	SEX	BLOOD	TRIBAL ENROLLMENT		
					YEAR	COUNTY	PAGE
1 Williams, Clara J.		31	F	I.W.	1897	Pickens	77
2 Coyle, James Thomas	Son	12	M	3/8	1897	"	22
3 " Albert Pike	"	10	"	3/8	1897	"	22

4	" Benjamin Harrison	"	8	M	3/8	1897	"	22
5	" Earnest Earl	"	6	"	3/8	1897	"	22
6	" Mabel Pearl	Dau	4	F	3/8	1897	"	22
7	" Lillie Audry	"	11/2	"	3/8			
8	" Violet Teresa	"	3mos	"	3/8			

TRIBAL ENROLLMENT OF PARENTS

	NAME OF FATHER	YEAR	COUNTY	NAME OF MOTHER	YEAR	COUNTY
1	John McMahon		Non citizen	Frances McMahon		Non citizen
2	Pike Coyle	Dead	Pickens	No. 1		
3	" "	"	"	No. 1		
4	" "	"	"	No. 1		
5	" "	"	"	No. 1		
6	" "	"	"	No. 1		
7	" "	"	"	No. 1		
8	" "	"	"	No. 1		

(NOTES)

No. 1 Surname is now Williams, Sept. 22, 1902. Duroderigo child on Card No. 555 living with No. 1.
No. 2 on Chickasaw roll as Jim Coyle *(No. 1 Dawes' Roll No. 22)*
No. 3 " " " " Albert "
No. 4 " " " " Bee "
No. 5 " " " " Earl "
No. 6 " " " " Pearl "
No. 7 Proof of birth received and filed Sept. 22, 1902. *(No. 7 Dawes' Roll No. 4441)*
No. 8 Proof of birth received and filed Sept. 22, 1902. *(No. 8 Dawes' Roll No. 4442)*

Sept. 22/98.

RESIDENCE: Pontotoc ***COUNTY*** ***CARD NO.***
POST OFFICE: Purcell, Ind. Ter. ***FIELD NO.***

	NAME	RELATION-SHIP TO PERSON FIRST NAMED	AGE	SEX	BLOOD	TRIBAL ENROLLMENT		
						YEAR	COUNTY	PAGE
1	Gibbons, Amelia J.		36	F	1/4	1897	Pontotoc	63
2	" Murray	Son	2	M	1/8	1897	"	63
3	" Margaret C.	Dau	5	F	1/8	1897	"	63
4	" Migs E.	Son	4mo	M	1/8			
5	" James E.	Husb	45	M	I.W.			

TRIBAL ENROLLMENT OF PARENTS

	NAME OF FATHER	YEAR	COUNTY	NAME OF MOTHER	YEAR	COUNTY
1	H.T. Murray (I.W.)	1897	Panola	Margaret Murray	Dead	Panola
2	James E. Gibbons		white man	No. 1		

3	" " "		" "	No. 1		
4	" " "		" "	No. 1		
5	James Gibbons	Dead	non citizen	Elizabeth Gibbons	Dead	non citizen

(NOTES)

No. 1 on Chickasaw roll as Emely J. Gibbons, wife of James E. Gibbon, Chickasaw Card No. D.53.
No. 3 on Chickasaw roll as M.C. Gibbons
Nos. 1, 2 and 3 admitted by Dawes Commission as citizens by blood in Chickasaw case #200: No appeal.
No. 5 transferred from Chickasaw card #D.53. See decision of March 5, 1904. Mar. 23, 1904

Sept. 21/98.

RESIDENCE: Pickens COUNTY CARD NO.
POST OFFICE: Woodford, Ind. Ter. FIELD NO.

	NAME	RELATION-SHIP TO PERSON FIRST NAMED	AGE	SEX	BLOOD	TRIBAL ENROLLMENT YEAR	COUNTY	PAGE
1	Brown, Hattie		21	F	1/8	1893	Pickens	P.R.#2 P. #210
2	Stephenson, Victoria	Sister	17	"	1/8	1893	"	P.R.#2 P.210
3	" Wayne	Niece[sic]	4mo	M	1/16			
4	Brown, Henry	Son	2mo	M	1/16			
5	Stephenson, Ivry	Niece	3mo	F	1/16			
6	Brown, Otto	Som	8mo	M	1/8			

TRIBAL ENROLLMENT OF PARENTS

	NAME OF FATHER	YEAR	COUNTY	NAME OF MOTHER	YEAR	COUNTY
1	John Taylor		Chick. Freedman	Martha McGee	Dead	Chickasaw Roll
2	Ben Williams		" "	" "	"	" "
3	Philip Stephenson		" "	No. 2		
4	John Brown		Chick. roll	No. 1		
5	Philip Stephenson		Chick. freedman	No. 2		
6	John Brown		Chick. Roll	No. 1		

(NOTES)

No. 1 on 1896 Chickasaw roll, page 97, Pickens County
No. 1 " 1893 " pay roll No. 2 page 210 as Hattie Jackson *(illegible)*
No. 1 is now the wife of John Brown
No. 2 on 1896 Chickasaw roll, page 97, Pickens County
No. 2 " 1893 " payroll No. 2, page 210
No. 2 on Chickasaw roll as Tora Taylor.
No. 2 is now wife of Philip Stephenson 1/23/00.
Husband of No. 2 Philip Stephenson on Chickasaw freedman card #600
No. 3 Enrolled Feby. 24, 1900.

No. 4 Enrolled May 24, 1900.
No. 5 Born Oct. 7, 1901; Enrolled Jany. 16, 1902.
No. 6 Born March 14, 1902; enrolled Nov. 11, 1902. *(No. 6 Dawes' Roll No. 4410)*

No. 2 P.O. Springer, I.T. 10/14/02. Sept. 21/98.

RESIDENCE: Pickens COUNTY					CARD NO.			
POST OFFICE: Woodford, Ind. Ter.					FIELD NO.			
	NAME	RELATIONSHIP TO PERSON FIRST NAMED	AGE	SEX	BLOOD	TRIBAL ENROLLMENT		
						YEAR	COUNTY	PAGE
1	McGee, Jesse		33	M	1/4	1897	Pickens	16

TRIBAL ENROLLMENT OF PARENTS

	NAME OF FATHER	YEAR	COUNTY	NAME OF MOTHER	YEAR	COUNTY
1	Arch McGee	Dead	Chickasaw Roll	Nancy McGee	Dead	Non-citizen

(NOTES)

On Chickasaw roll as Jessie McGee.
No. 1 is husband of Dora McGee and father of children on Chickasaw freedman card #572.

Sept. 21/98.

RESIDENCE: Pickens COUNTY					CARD NO.			
POST OFFICE: Ardmore, Ind. Ter.					FIELD NO.			
	NAME	RELATIONSHIP TO PERSON FIRST NAMED	AGE	SEX	BLOOD	TRIBAL ENROLLMENT		
						YEAR	COUNTY	PAGE
1	McLish, Richard H.		38	M	1/4	1897	Pickens	17
2	" Rose	Wife	31	F	I.W.	1897	"	78
3	" Jerry J.	Son	13	M	1/8	1897	"	17
4	" Richard R.	"	11	"	1/8	1897	"	17
5	" Otwell	"	7	"	1/8	1897	"	17
6	" Rosa	Dau	4	F	1/8	1897	"	17

TRIBAL ENROLLMENT OF PARENTS

	NAME OF FATHER	YEAR	COUNTY	NAME OF MOTHER	YEAR	COUNTY
1	Richard McLish	Dead	Chickasaw Roll	Nancy Love McLish	1897	Panola
2	Russ Washington		Non-citizen	*(Illegible)* Washington		Non-citizen
3	No. 1			No. 2		
4	No. 1			No. 2		
5	No. 1			No. 2		
6	No. 1			No. 2		

(NOTES)

No. 1 on Chickasaw Roll as R.H. McLish *(No. 2 Dawes' Roll No. 113)*
No. 3 " " " " Jirry "
No. 4 " " " " Richard "
No. 6 Died April 8, 1901; Proof of death filed Nov. 11, 1902.

Sept. 21/98.

RESIDENCE: Pickens COUNTY	CARD NO.
POST OFFICE: Heelton, Ind. Ter.	FIELD NO.

	NAME	RELATION-SHIP TO PERSON FIRST NAMED	AGE	SEX	BLOOD	TRIBAL ENROLLMENT		
						YEAR	COUNTY	PAGE
1	Ingram, W.R.		38	M	I.W.	1897	Pickens	78
2	" Mollie	Wife	28	F	1/16	1897	"	17
3	" Lyda	Dau	8	F	1/32	1897	"	17
4	" Gertie	"	6	"	1/32	1897	"	17
5	" Hettie	"	5	"	1/32	1897	"	17
6	" Clytie	"	4	"	1/32	1897	"	17
7	" William Hobart	Son	16mo	M	1/32	~~1897~~	"	~~86~~
8	Carter, John E.	StepSon	10	"	1/32	1897	Pickens	17
9	Ingram, Ruby	Dau	2wks	F	1/32			

TRIBAL ENROLLMENT OF PARENTS

	NAME OF FATHER	YEAR	COUNTY	NAME OF MOTHER	YEAR	COUNTY
1	Tony Ingram	Dead	Non-citizen	Martha Ingram		non citz
2	C.H. Heel (I.W.)	1897	Pickens	Eliza Gile Ingram	Dead	Tishomingo
3	No. 1			No. 2		
4	No. 1			No. 2		
5	No. 1			No. 2		
6	No. 1			No. 2		
7	No. 1			No. 2		
8	John Carter	Dead	Cherokee Citz.	No. 2		
9	No. 1			No. 2		

(NOTES)

No. 3 on Chickasaw roll as Lydia *(No. 1 Dawes' Roll No. 20)*
No. 7 " " " " William St. Ingram.
No. 9 Born May 29,1902; enrolled June 13, 1902.

Sept. 21/98.

RESIDENCE: Pickens **COUNTY** **CARD NO.**

POST OFFICE: Lone Grove, Ind. Ter. **FIELD NO.**

	NAME	RELATION-SHIP TO PERSON FIRST NAMED	AGE	SEX	BLOOD	TRIBAL ENROLLMENT YEAR	COUNTY	PAGE
1	Price, C.C.		45	M	I.W.	1897	Pickens	78
2	" Mollie	Wife	29	F	1/8	1897	"	12
3	" Thomas Guy	Son	10	M	1/16	1897	"	12
4	" Erie	Dau	1 1/2	F	1/16	1897		85
5	" Therean Bogart	Son	3mos	M	1/16			

TRIBAL ENROLLMENT OF PARENTS

	NAME OF FATHER	YEAR	COUNTY	NAME OF MOTHER	YEAR	COUNTY
1	John Price		Non-citizen	Louisa Price	Dead	Non-citizen
2	Henry Colbert	Dead	Chickasaw Roll	Louisa Colbert	1897	Pickens
3	No. 1			No. 2		
4	No. 1			No. 2		
5	No. 1			No. 2		

(NOTES)

No. 1 See decision of June 13/04. *(No. 1 Dawes' Roll No. 387)*
No. 1 On Chickasaw roll as Sweet Price
No. 3 " " " " Guy "
No. 5 Enrolled July 7, 1900.
No. 4 Died Nov. *(illegible)* Proof of death filed *(illegible)*.

Sept. 21/98.

RESIDENCE: Pickens **COUNTY** **CARD NO.**

POST OFFICE: Ardmore, Ind. Ter. **FIELD NO.**

	NAME	RELATION-SHIP TO PERSON FIRST NAMED	AGE	SEX	BLOOD	TRIBAL ENROLLMENT YEAR	COUNTY	PAGE
1	Herndon, Myrtle Gale		21	F	1/16	1897	Pickens	13
2	" John Milton	Son	2	M	1/32	1897	"	"
3	" Otto A.	"	1mo	"	1/32			
4	" Clyde Elwood	Son	1mo	"	1/32			
5	" Ellwood	Hus	35	"	I.W.			

TRIBAL ENROLLMENT OF PARENTS

	NAME OF FATHER	YEAR	COUNTY	NAME OF MOTHER	YEAR	COUNTY
1	M.W. Coffey (I.W.)	1897	Pickens	M.P. Coffey	1897	Pickens
2	Elwood Herndon		White man	No. 1		
3	" "		" "	No. 1		

4	" "		" "	No. 1		
5	J.M. Herndon		non citz.	Lafavorite Herndon	Dead	non citz.

(NOTES)

No. 1 on Chickasaw roll as Mirtie Hernden - wife of Ellwood Herndon Chickasaw Card No. D.50.
No. 2 on Chickasaw roll as Melton.
No. 4 Born June 25, 1902; Enrolled July 16, 1902.
No. 3 May 12/98.
No. 5 Transferred from Chickasaw Card D.50 8/22/03.

Sept. 21/98.

RESIDENCE: Pickens **COUNTY** **CARD NO.**
POST OFFICE: Woodford, Ind. Terr. **FIELD NO.**

	Name	Relationship to Person First Named	Age	Sex	Blood	Tribal Enrollment Year	Tribal Enrollment County	Tribal Enrollment Page
1	Johnson, John		40	M	I.W.	1897	Pickens	77
2	" Emely	Wife	33	F	Full	1897	"	19
3	" Maybell	Dau	10	"	1/2	1897	"	19
4	" Willie M	"	7	"	1/2	1897	"	19
5	" Lola Maude	"	4	"	1/2	1897	"	19
6	" Wesley R.	Son	2	M	1/2	1897	"	19
7	" Zella Marigold	Dau	2mo	F	1/2			
8	" Elba	"	1mo	F	1/2			

TRIBAL ENROLLMENT OF PARENTS

	Name of Father	Year	County	Name of Mother	Year	County
1	Geo. W. Johnson	Dead	Non-citizen	Frances Johnson	Dead	Non-citizen
2	Pinkney Brown	"	Chickasaw Roll	Hepsey Brown	1897	Tishomingo
3	No. 1			No. 2		
4	No. 1			No. 2		
5	No. 1			No. 2		
6	No. 1			No. 2		
7	No. 1			No. 2		
8	No. 1			No. 2		

(NOTES)

No. 1 better known as Six Shooter Johnson
No. 2 on Chickasaw Roll as Emly "
No. 4 " " " " William M. "
No. 5 " " " " Lola M. "
No. 6 " " " " Wesley W. "
No. 7 enrolled Mar. 6/99.
No. 8 enrolled May 29/1901.

P.O. Milo, I.T. 10/29/02. Sept. 21/98.

RESIDENCE: Pickens **COUNTY** **CARD NO.**
POST OFFICE: Ardmore, Ind. Ter. **FIELD NO.**

	NAME	RELATIONSHIP TO PERSON FIRST NAMED	AGE	SEX	BLOOD	TRIBAL ENROLLMENT YEAR	COUNTY	PAGE
1	Campbell, Viona S.		34	F	I.W.	1897	Pickens	79
2	Harris, Serena	Dau	16	"	1/2	1897	"	32
3	" Daisy	"	12	"	1/2	1897	"	32
4	" Bennie	Son	3	M	1/2	1897	"	32

TRIBAL ENROLLMENT OF PARENTS

	NAME OF FATHER	YEAR	COUNTY	NAME OF MOTHER	YEAR	COUNTY
1	Alex Wilson	Dead	Non-citizen	Cicily A. Wilson		Non-citizen
2	Ben Harris	"	Pickens	No. 1		
3	" "	"	"	No. 1		
4	" "	"	"	No. 1		

(NOTES)

No. 1 on Chickasaw Roll as V.S. Harris.
T.F. *(Illegible)* of Ardmore testifies under oath that he was present at the solemnization of the marriage between Ben Harris and V.S. Harris in 1880. Marriage license, certificate and court records destroyed.
(Last entry illegible, too light)

Sept. 21/98.

RESIDENCE: Pickens **COUNTY** **CARD NO.**
POST OFFICE: Brock, Ind. Ter. **FIELD NO.**

	NAME	RELATIONSHIP TO PERSON FIRST NAMED	AGE	SEX	BLOOD	TRIBAL ENROLLMENT YEAR	COUNTY	PAGE
1	Coffey, Ivy		23	M	1/16	1897	Pickens	13

TRIBAL ENROLLMENT OF PARENTS

	NAME OF FATHER	YEAR	COUNTY	NAME OF MOTHER	YEAR	COUNTY
1	Mint Coffey I.W.	1897	Pickens	*(Illegible)* Coffey	1897	Pickens

(NOTES)

Sept. 21/98.

RESIDENCE: Pickens COUNTY					CARD NO.			
POST OFFICE: Lone Grove, Ind. Ter.					FIELD NO.			
	NAME	RELATION-SHIP TO PERSON FIRST NAMED	AGE	SEX	BLOOD	TRIBAL ENROLLMENT YEAR	COUNTY	PAGE
1	Norman, Daniel S.		53	M	I.W.	1897	Pickens	78
2	" Catherine	Wife	41	F	1/8	1897	"	14

	NAME OF FATHER	YEAR	COUNTY	NAME OF MOTHER	YEAR	COUNTY
1	Wm. W. Norman	Dead	Non-citizen	Belinda Norman	Dead	Non-citizen
2	Josiah Brown	1897	Tishomingo	Frances V. Brown	"	Tishomingo

(NOTES)

No. 1 on Chickasaw roll as Dan Norman
No. 2 " " " " Katie "

P.O. Connerville, I.T. Sept. 21/98.

RESIDENCE: Tishomingo COUNTY					CARD NO.			
POST OFFICE: Nebo, Ind. Ter.					FIELD NO.			
	NAME	RELATION-SHIP TO PERSON FIRST NAMED	AGE	SEX	BLOOD	TRIBAL ENROLLMENT YEAR	COUNTY	PAGE
1	Wolf, Bella		50	F	Full	1897	Pickens	30
2	Norton, Henry	Son	11	M	1/2	1897	"	31

TRIBAL ENROLLMENT OF PARENTS

	NAME OF FATHER	YEAR	COUNTY	NAME OF MOTHER	YEAR	COUNTY
1	Butch Cartubby	Dead	Chickasaw Roll	Sena	Dead	Chickasaw Roll
2	Bud Norton		Non-citizen	No. 1		

(NOTES)

P.O. Drake, I.T. 3/21/04. Sept. 21/98.

RESIDENCE: Pickens COUNTY					CARD NO.			
POST OFFICE: Nebo, Ind. Ter.					FIELD NO.			
	NAME	RELATION-SHIP TO PERSON FIRST NAMED	AGE	SEX	BLOOD	TRIBAL ENROLLMENT YEAR	COUNTY	PAGE
1	Brown, Lou		40	F	Full	1897	Tishomingo	30
2	Greenwood, Betsey	Dau	20	"	"	1897	"	30
3	" Pearl	Gr. "	2	F	"	1897	"	31
4	Owens, Laura Vaginia	" "	1	"	1/2			

	TRIBAL ENROLLMENT OF PARENTS					
	NAME OF FATHER	YEAR	COUNTY	NAME OF MOTHER	YEAR	COUNTY
1	Butch Cartubby	Dead	Chickasaw Roll	Sena	Dead	Chickasaw Roll
2	Cubby Cochantubby	"	" "	No. 1		
3	Cubby Greenwood	1897	Pickens	No. 2		
4	Jessie Owens			No. 2		

(NOTES)

No. 4 born June 17, 1902; Application received March 7, 1905, under Act of Congress approved *(illegible)*

(No. 4 Dawes' Roll No. 4964)

Sept. 21/98.

RESIDENCE: Pickens COUNTY						CARD NO.		
POST OFFICE: Cheek, Ind. Ter.						FIELD NO.		
	NAME	RELATIONSHIP TO PERSON FIRST NAMED	AGE	SEX	BLOOD	TRIBAL ENROLLMENT		
						YEAR	COUNTY	PAGE
1	Parker, Wilson		37	M	Full	1897	Pickens	15
2	" Mary C.	Wife	36	F	I.W.	1897	"	78
3	" John T.	Son	16	M	1/2	1897	"	15
4	" Victoria Sophronia	Dau	14	F	1/2	1897	"	15
5	" Charles Benjamin	Son	12	M	1/2	1897	"	15
6	" William Guy	"	8	"	1/2	1897	"	15
7	" Laura Belle	Dau	5	F	1/2	1897	"	15

	TRIBAL ENROLLMENT OF PARENTS					
	NAME OF FATHER	YEAR	COUNTY	NAME OF MOTHER	YEAR	COUNTY
1	Thos. Parker	Dead	Chickasaw Roll	She-no-ke-cha	Dead	Chickasaw Roll
2	W.D. Smith		Non-citizen	Sophrona Smith		Non-citizen
3	No. 1			No. 2		
4	No. 1			No. 2		
5	No. 1			No. 2		
6	No. 1			No. 2		
7	No. 1			No. 2		

(NOTES)

No. 4 on Chickasaw roll as Victoria Parker
No. 5 " " " " Charley "
No. 6 " " " " William "
No. 7 " " " " Laura "
No. 3 Also on 1897 roll, Page 96, as Thomas Parker.
No. 4 " " 1897 " " 96 " Sophie "
No. 5 " " 1897 " " 96 " Benny "
No. 6 " " 1897 " " 96 " Guy "

No. 7 " " 1897 " " 96 " Laura B. "
Certified copy of marriage license & certificate of No 1 and 2 filed April 4/1903.

P.O. Cornish, I.T. Sept. 21/98.

RESIDENCE: Pickens **COUNTY**					**CARD NO.**			
POST OFFICE: Marietta, Ind. Ter.					**FIELD NO.**			
	NAME	**RELATION-SHIP TO PERSON FIRST NAMED**	**AGE**	**SEX**	**BLOOD**	**TRIBAL ENROLLMENT**		
						YEAR	**COUNTY**	**PAGE**
1	Washington, William Edward		38	M	I.W.	1897	Pickens	78
2	" May Ellen	Wife	33	F	1/4	1897	"	12
3	" John Richard	Son	15	M	1/8	1897	"	12

TRIBAL ENROLLMENT OF PARENTS

	NAME OF FATHER	YEAR	COUNTY	NAME OF MOTHER	YEAR	COUNTY
1	J.R. Washington		Non-citizen	Sally Washington	Dead	Non-citizen
2	? A. Smith I.W.	1897	Panola	Nancy Smith	1897	Panola
3	No. 1			No. 2		

(NOTES)

No. 2 on Chickasaw roll as M.E. Washington, also called Mollie *(No. 1 Dawes' Roll No. 18)*
No. 3 " " " " John R. "
See testimony of No. 1, taken Oct. 17, 1902.

Sept. 21/98.

RESIDENCE: Pickens **COUNTY**					**CARD NO.**			
POST OFFICE: Ardmore, Ind. Ter.					**FIELD NO.**			
	NAME	**RELATION-SHIP TO PERSON FIRST NAMED**	**AGE**	**SEX**	**BLOOD**	**TRIBAL ENROLLMENT**		
						YEAR	**COUNTY**	**PAGE**
1	Coffey, Melton W.		52	M	I.W.	1897	Pickens	78
2	" Amanda Virginia	Wife	42	F	1/8	1897	"	13
3	" William Lee	Son	27	M	1/16	1897	"	13
4	" Taylor Overton	"	25	"	1/16	1897	"	13
5	" Merritt Price	"	19	"	1/16	1897	"	13
6	" Earnest	"	16	"	1/16	1897	"	13
7	" Mary Alvirta	Dau	12	F	1/16	1897	"	13
8	" Anderson Wolford	Son	11	M	1/16	1897	"	13
9	" Sale	"	9	M	1/16	1897	"	13
10	" Walter	"	5	"	1/16	1897	"	13

	TRIBAL ENROLLMENT OF PARENTS					
	NAME OF FATHER	YEAR	COUNTY	NAME OF MOTHER	YEAR	COUNTY
1	Sale Coffey	Dead	Non-citizen	Nancy Coffey	Dead	Non-citizen
2	Bill Lewis I.W.	"	Tishomingo	Eliza Love Lewis	"	Chickasaw Roll
3	No. 1			No. 2		
4	No. 1			No. 2		
5	No. 1			No. 2		
6	No. 1			No. 2		
7	No. 1			No. 2		
8	No. 1			No. 2		
9	No. 1			No. 2		
10	No. 1			No. 2		

(NOTES)

No. 1 On Chickasaw roll as M.W. Coffey. Married in 1869. Certified copy of marriage record to be supplied.
No. 2 " " " " Amanda
No. 3 " " " " W. Lee
No. 4 " " " " Overton
No. 5 " " " " Marriet
No. 7 " " " " Allie
No. 8 " " " " Wolford
Jany 4, 1900; Certified copy of record of marriage received, but as seal was lacking same was returned.
Filed Jany. 19, 1900.

10/29/02. P.O. Brook, I.T. Sept. 21/98.

RESIDENCE: Pickens COUNTY					CARD NO.		
POST OFFICE: Ardmore, Ind. Ter.					FIELD NO.		
NAME	RELATION-SHIP TO PERSON FIRST NAMED	AGE	SEX	BLOOD	TRIBAL ENROLLMENT		
					YEAR	COUNTY	PAGE
1 Watkins, W.R. Jr.		24	M	1/16	1897	Pickens	13

	TRIBAL ENROLLMENT OF PARENTS					
	NAME OF FATHER	YEAR	COUNTY	NAME OF MOTHER	YEAR	COUNTY
1	W.R. Watkins (I.W.)	Dead	Pickens	Elizabeth Watkins	Dead	Pickens

(NOTES)

Husband of Edna Watkins, Choctaw roll, card No. 254.
Under sentence in Ardmore jail pending an appeal.

Sept. 23/98.

RESIDENCE: Texas **COUNTY** **CARD NO.**
POST OFFICE: Gainesville, Texas **FIELD NO.**

	NAME	RELATIONSHIP TO PERSON FIRST NAMED	AGE	SEX	BLOOD	TRIBAL ENROLLMENT YEAR	COUNTY	PAGE
1	Reagan, Stella		12	F	1/16	1897	Pickens	26
2	Montray, Perry	Bro	11	M	1/16	1897	"	26

TRIBAL ENROLLMENT OF PARENTS

	NAME OF FATHER	YEAR	COUNTY	NAME OF MOTHER	YEAR	COUNTY
1	M.G. Montray		white man	Liza Montray	Dead	Pickens
2	" " "		" "	" "	"	"

(NOTES)

Father, M.G. Montray on Chickasaw Card No. D.48. *(No. 1 Dawes' Roll No. 4944)*
Sir name on Chickasaw roll Montray *(No. 2 Dawes' Roll No. 4945)*
Further evidence taken Nov. 25, *(illegible)*
No. 1 is now the wife of Walker Reagan, non citizen
evidence of marriage filed, May 6, 1903.

Sept. 21/98.

RESIDENCE: Pickens **COUNTY** **CARD NO.**
POST OFFICE: Eastman, Ind. Ter. **FIELD NO.**

	NAME	RELATIONSHIP TO PERSON FIRST NAMED	AGE	SEX	BLOOD	TRIBAL ENROLLMENT YEAR	COUNTY	PAGE
1	Jenkins, Jennie		23	F	Full	1897	Pickens	20
2	" Minnie	Dau	4	"	1/2	1897	"	20
3	" Boyd	Son	1	M	1/2	1897	"	86
4	" James	Son	2mo	M	1/2			
5	" Peter	Hus	45	M	I W			

TRIBAL ENROLLMENT OF PARENTS

	NAME OF FATHER	YEAR	COUNTY	NAME OF MOTHER	YEAR	COUNTY
1	Eastman Burris	Dead	Chickasaw Roll	Lena Burris	1897	Pickens
2	Peter Jenkins			No. 1		
3	" "			No. 1		
4	" "			No. 1		
5		Dead	Mexican			Mexican

(NOTES)

Jennie Jenkins is wife of Peter Jenkins, Chickasaw roll Card No. D.47.
No. 3 Proof of birth received and filed Oct. 22, 1902. *(No. 3 Dawes' Roll No. 4409)*
No. 4 Enrolled June 23, 1900.
No. 5 Transferred from Chickasaw card D.47.

10/17/02 P.O. Cornish, I.T. Sept. 21/98.

RESIDENCE: Pickens COUNTY					CARD NO.		
POST OFFICE: Ardmore, Ind. Ter.					FIELD NO.		
NAME	RELATION-SHIP TO PERSON FIRST NAMED	AGE	SEX	BLOOD	TRIBAL ENROLLMENT		
					YEAR	COUNTY	PAGE
1 Merchant, E.E.		28	M	I.W.	1897	Pickens	78
2 " Malvina	Wife	22	F	1/4	1897	"	15
3 " Victoria	Dau	2	"	1/8	1897	"	16
4 " Harry	Son	1/2	M	1/8			
5 " Irene	Dau	2mo	F	1/8			
6 " Ellen	Dau	3wks	F	1/8			

TRIBAL ENROLLMENT OF PARENTS

	NAME OF FATHER	YEAR	COUNTY	NAME OF MOTHER	YEAR	COUNTY
1	James S.W. Merchant		Non-citizen	Fannie Merchant	Dead	Non-citizen
2	Wm. Hull		" "	Sippey Hull		Pickens
3	No. 1			No. 2		
4	No. 1			No. 2		
5	No. 1			No. 2		
6	No. 1			No. 2		

(NOTES)

No. 1 Admitted by Dawes Com, Case No. 101 and no appeal taken.
No. 2 on Chickasaw roll as Nelvie Hull.
No. 4 Affidavit of attending physician to be supplied. Received Sept. 24/98.
Marriage certificate and license with the Dawes Com. at Muskogee, I.T.
No. 5 enrolled June 5/1900.
No. 6 Born Aug. 1, 1902; enrolled Aug. 21, 1902.
Given name of wife is Lavina 10/20/02.

10/20/02 P.O. Marlow, I.T. Sept. 21/98.

RESIDENCE: Pickens COUNTY					CARD NO.		
POST OFFICE: Burneyville, Ind. Ter.					FIELD NO.		
NAME	RELATION-SHIP TO PERSON FIRST NAMED	AGE	SEX	BLOOD	TRIBAL ENROLLMENT		
					YEAR	COUNTY	PAGE
1 Thornton, Carrie Murray		18	F	3/8	1897	Pickens	15
2 " Robert	Son	2mo	M	3/16			
3 " Anita	Dau	1mo	F	3/16			

4	" William D.	Hus	31	M	I.W.			

TRIBAL ENROLLMENT OF PARENTS

	NAME OF FATHER	YEAR	COUNTY	NAME OF MOTHER	YEAR	COUNTY
1	Eph Murray	Dead	Non citz.	Patsey Myers	1897	Pickens
2	W.D. Thornton		" "	No. 1		
3	" " "		" "	No. 1		
4	G.G. Thornton	Dead	" "	M.A. Thornton		Non-citizen

(NOTES)

On Chickasaw roll as Carrie Murray, wife of W.D. Thornton, Chickasaw card D.45.

No. 2 Enrolled Mar. 20/99.

No. 3 Enrolled July 7, 1900.

No. 4 Transferred from Chick. card D.45

11/5/02 P.O. Marietta I.T. of Wm. D. Thornton. Sept. 21/98.

RESIDENCE: Pontotoc *COUNTY* *CARD NO.*

POST OFFICE: Purcell, Ind. Ter. *FIELD NO.*

	NAME	RELATION-SHIP TO PERSON FIRST NAMED	AGE	SEX	BLOOD	TRIBAL ENROLLMENT		
						YEAR	COUNTY	PAGE
1	Wolf, T.J.		29	M	I.W.	1897	Pontotoc	84
2	" Susan	Wife	37	F	1/2	1897	"	64
3	" Frank	Son	6	M	1/4	1897	"	64
4	" Jessie	Dau	4	F	1/4	1897	"	97
5	" Carrie	"	2	"	1/4	1897	"	64
6	" Dewey	Son	5mo	M	1/4			
7	Foster, Henry C.	StepSon	14	"	1/4	1897	Pontotoc	64
8	" George	" "	13	"	1/4	1897	"	64
9	" William	" "	11	"	1/4	1897	"	64
10	" Lizzie	" Dau	9	F	1/4	1897	"	66
11	" Florence	" "	8	"	1/4	1897	"	66
12	Wolf, May	Dau	2	F	1/4			

TRIBAL ENROLLMENT OF PARENTS

	NAME OF FATHER	YEAR	COUNTY	NAME OF MOTHER	YEAR	COUNTY
1	A.H. Wolf		Non-citizen	Sarah Wolf		Non-citizen
2	John Billee	Dead	Choctaw roll	Julia Haynes	1897	Chick. residing in Choctaw N. 1st D.
3	No. 1			No. 2		
4	No. 1			No. 2		
5	No. 1			No. 2		

6	No. 1			No. 2		
7	Hewlett Foster	Dead	Non citizen	No. 2		
8	" "	"	" "	No. 2		
9	" "	"	" "	No. 2		
10	" "	"	" "	No. 2		
11	" "	"	" "	No. 2		
12	No. 1			No. 2		

(NOTES)

No. 2 on Chickasaw roll as Susan Wolfe.
Nos. 3 and 5 " " " " Wolfe " *(No. 4 Dawes' Roll No. 4408)*
No. 1 Died Aug. 1, 1901 - proof of death filed March 27, 1902.
No. 12 Born March 1, 1901; enrolled March 31, 1902.
No. 4 Proof of birth filed Oct. 13, 1902.
No. 5 Proof of birth filed Oct. 13, 1902; Died Feby 10, 1899; proof of death filed Oct. 13, 1902.
No. 6 Died in Jany 1899 - proof of death filed Oct. 13, 1902.

P.O. Norman I.T. Sept. 21/98.

RESIDENCE: Pickens ***COUNTY*** ***CARD NO.***
POST OFFICE: Velma, Ind. Ter. ***FIELD NO.***

	NAME	RELATION-SHIP TO PERSON FIRST NAMED	AGE	SEX	BLOOD	TRIBAL ENROLLMENT		
						YEAR	COUNTY	PAGE
1	Doak, Dudley Nail		25	M	I.W	1897	Pickens	78
2	" Lorre Lee	Wife	20	F	1/16	1897	"	13
3	" Henry Love	Son	3wks	M	1/32			
4	Fitzhugh, John M.	Father of No. 2	41	M	I.W.			

TRIBAL ENROLLMENT OF PARENTS

	NAME OF FATHER	YEAR	COUNTY	NAME OF MOTHER	YEAR	COUNTY
1	Dudley Doak	Dead	Non-citizen	Elizabeth Doak	Dead	Non-citizen
2	John Fitzhugh		" "	Ida Fitzhugh	"	Pickens
3	No. 1			No. 2		
4	Robt. Fitzhugh	Dead	Non-citizen	Katie Fitzhugh	Dead	Non-citizen

(NOTES)

No. 4 admitted by U.S. Ct. at Ardmore, I.T., Dec. 22/97 Court Case # *(illegible)*
Nos. 2 & 4 admitted by Com. in 96 Chick. Case #66
No. 2 on Chickasaw roll as Love Lee Doak.
No. 3 Enrolled January 7, 1901.
No. 2 admitted by U.S. Court, So. Dist. Court case #46, as Love Lee Fitzhugh.
No. 4 Transferred to this card from C-66 July 20/04. *(No. 4 Dawes' Roll No. I.W. 43)*

Sept. 21/98.

RESIDENCE: Tishomingo COUNTY					CARD NO.		
POST OFFICE: Berwyn, Ind. Ter.					FIELD NO.		
	NAME	RELATION-SHIP TO PERSON FIRST NAMED	AGE	SEX	BLOOD	TRIBAL ENROLLMENT		
						YEAR	COUNTY	PAGE
1	Young, Granville W.		43	M	I.W.	1897	Pickens	79
2	" Adaline	Wife	34	F	3/4	1897	"	28
3	" Lizzie Bell	Dau	17	"	3/8	1897	"	28
4	" Lucy Branferd	"	15	"	3/8	1897	"	28
5	" Carrie Lee	"	10	"	3/8	1897	"	28
6	" Mattie Lou	"	7	"	3/8	1897	"	28
7	" James Granville	Son	5	M	3/8	1897	"	28
8	" Nancy Colbert	Dau	2	F	3/8	1897	"	28
9	" Patsey	"	1wk	"	3/8	1897	"	28
10	" Bettie May	Dau	1mo	F	3/8	1897	"	28

TRIBAL ENROLLMENT OF PARENTS

	NAME OF FATHER	YEAR	COUNTY	NAME OF MOTHER	YEAR	COUNTY
1	James L. Young		Non-citizen	Judy Young	Dead	Non-citizen
2	George Johnson		Chick. residing in Choctaw N. 1st Dist.	Lucy Johnson	"	Tishomingo
3	No. 1			No. 2		
4	No. 1			No. 2		
5	No. 1			No. 2		
6	No. 1			No. 2		
7	No. 1			No. 2		
8	No. 1			No. 2		
9	No. 1			No. 2		
10	No. 1			No. 2		

(NOTES)

No. 1 on Chickasaw roll as Greenville Young *(No. 1 Dawes' Roll No. I.W. 47)*
No. 3 " " " " Lizzie "
No. 4 " " " " Lucy "
No. 5 " " " " Carrie "
No. 6 " " " " Mattie "
No. 7 " " " " Jos. "
No. 8 " " " " Nancy "
No. 10 Born Oct. 13, 1901; enrolled Nov. 14, 1901.
No. 9 enrolled Dec. 13/98.
Affidavit of Mrs. I.J. Poyner as to marriage of Nos 1 and 2 filed Oct. 31, 1901.
Affidavit of C.W. Henderson as to marriage between Nos. 1 and 2 filed Nov. 6, 1902.

Statement of clerk of Pickens Co. as to marriage records being destroyed filed Nov. 6, 1902.

Sept. 21/98.

RESIDENCE: Pickens COUNTY CARD NO.

POST OFFICE: Berwyn, Ind. Ter. FIELD NO.

	NAME	RELATIONSHIP TO PERSON FIRST NAMED	AGE	SEX	BLOOD	TRIBAL ENROLLMENT		
						YEAR	COUNTY	PAGE
1	Henderson, Louisa		42	F	3/4	1897	Pickens	20
2	" Charles Colbert	Son	17	M	3/8	1897	"	20
3	" Grover Cleveland	"	13	"	3/8	1897	"	20
4	" Luella	Dau	7	F	3/8	1897	"	20
5	" John Thomas	Son	4	M	3/8	1897	"	20
6	" Thelma	Dau	2	F	3/8	1897	"	20
7	" Addie Ruth	"	8mos	"	3/8			
8	Thomas, Amanda	Niece in law	4	"	1/2	1897	Pickens	20
9	Humes, Buck	Step son	23	M	3/8	1897	"	20
10	Henderson, C.W.	Husband	56	"	I.W.	1897	"	77

TRIBAL ENROLLMENT OF PARENTS

	NAME OF FATHER	YEAR	COUNTY	NAME OF MOTHER	YEAR	COUNTY
1	Vann Colbert	Dead	Pickens	Elsie Colbert	Dead	Pickens
2	C.W. Henderson (I.W.)		"	No. 1		
3	" " "		"	No. 1		
4	" " "		"	No. 1		
5	" " "		"	No. 1		
6	" " "		"	No. 1		
7	" " "		"	No. 1		
8	Isaac Thomas	Dead	Tishomingo	Eliza Thomas	Dead	Tishomingo
9	Buck Humes	Dead	Non-citizen	No. 1		
10						

(NOTES)

No. 1 wife of C.W. Henderson, Chickasaw Card D.44.
No. 2 on Chickasaw roll as Charley Henderson
No. 3 " " " " Grover "
No. 4 " " " " Ella "
No. 5 " " " " Johnnie "
No. 6 " " " " Thelma "
No. 7 Affidavit of attending physician to be supplied. Received Sept. 26/98.
No. 3 Died Oct. 30, 1900. See testimony of C.W. Henderson May 2, 1902.
No. 9 Died July 11, 1900. See " " " " May 2, 1902. Sept. 21/98.

Residence: Pickens	***County***				***Card No.***			
Post Office: Addington, Ind. Ter.					***Field No.***			

	Name	Relation-ship to Person First Named	Age	Sex	Blood	Tribal Enrollment		
						Year	County	Page
1	Ryle, Whitmill A.		30	M	I.W.	1897	Chick. residing in Choctaw N. 3rd Dist.	82
2	" Mattie	Wife	20	F	1/8	1897	" " " "	75
3	" Emma	Dau	4	"	1/16	1897	" " " "	75
4	" Nannie May	"	2	"	1/16	1897	" " " "	75
5	" Jessie Lee	"	10mos	"	1/16			
6	" W.H.	Son	2wks	M	1/16			

Tribal Enrollment of Parents

	Name of Father	Year	County	Name of Mother	Year	County
1	M.D. Ryle		Non-citizen	Nancy Ryle	Dead	Non-citizen
2	Joe Hardwick	Dead	Chickasaw Roll	*(Illegible Name)*	Dead	" "
3	No. 1			No. 2		
4	No. 1			No. 2		
5	No. 1			No. 2		
6	No. 1			No. 2		

(Notes)

No. 3 on Chickasaw roll as Ema *(No. 1 Dawes' Roll No. 46)*
No. 4 " " " " Minnie May
No. 5 Affidavit of midwife to be furnished. Filed Nov. 3/99,
W.H. Ryle born Dec. 31, 1899 on Card No. D.313.
No. 6 born Dec. 31, 1899; transferred to this card February 7, 1902.

Sept. 20/98.

Residence: Pickens	***County***				***Card No.***			
Post Office: Brownsville, Ind. Ter.					***Field No.***			

	Name	Relation-ship to Person First Named	Age	Sex	Blood	Tribal Enrollment		
						Year	County	Page
1	Kaney, Margaret		36	F	Full	1897	Pickens	25
2	" Lottie	Dau	18	"	"	1897	"	25
3	" Billie	Son	15	M	"	1897	"	25
4	" Eastman	"	13	"	"	1897	"	25
5	" Lucy	Dau	11	F	"	1897	"	25
6	" Alice	"	8	"	"	1897	"	25

7	" Joanna	"	5	"	"	1897	"	25

TRIBAL ENROLLMENT OF PARENTS

	NAME OF FATHER	YEAR	COUNTY	NAME OF MOTHER	YEAR	COUNTY
1	Overton Keel	Dead	Pickens	Jane Keel	Dead	Pickens
2	Amos Kaney	"	"	No. 1		
3	" "	"	"	No. 1		
4	" "	"	"	No. 1		
5	" "	"	"	No. 1		
6	" "	"	"	No. 1		
7	" "	"	"	No. 1		

(NOTES)

No. 7 on Chickasaw roll as Guyamy Kaney *(No. 2 Dawes' Roll No. 4402) (No. 3 Dawes' Roll No. 4403)*
Affidavits of Janey Archeerson and J. Hamp. Willis as to the degree of Chickasaw blood possessed by father Nos. 2 to 7 inclusive filed Sept. 22, 1902. *(No. 4 Dawes' Roll No.4404) (No. 5 Dawes' Roll No. 4405) (No. 6 Dawes' Roll No. 4406) (No. 7 Dawes' Roll No. 4407)*

Oct. 3/98.

RESIDENCE: Pickens ***COUNTY*** ***CARD NO.***
POST OFFICE: Ardmore, Ind. Ter. ***FIELD NO.***

	NAME	RELATION-SHIP TO PERSON FIRST NAMED	AGE	SEX	BLOOD	TRIBAL ENROLLMENT		
						YEAR	COUNTY	PAGE
1	Greenwood, Samuel A.		25	M	I.W.			
2	" Myrtle	Wife	21	F	1/4	1897	Pickens	12

TRIBAL ENROLLMENT OF PARENTS

	NAME OF FATHER	YEAR	COUNTY	NAME OF MOTHER	YEAR	COUNTY
1	Benj. Greenwood	Dead	Non-citizen	Betty Greenwood		Non-citizen
2	Wyatt Wyndom	"	" "	Lizzie Wyndom	Dead	Pickens

(NOTES)

No. 2 on Chickasaw Roll as Myrtle Wyndom.

Sept. 20/98.

RESIDENCE: Pickens ***COUNTY*** ***CARD NO.***
POST OFFICE: Ardmore, Ind. Ter. ***FIELD NO.***

	NAME	RELATION-SHIP TO PERSON FIRST NAMED	AGE	SEX	BLOOD	TRIBAL ENROLLMENT		
						YEAR	COUNTY	PAGE
1	Brown, Roberson		35	M	Full	1897	Pickens	12
2	" Adaline	Wife	36	F	I.W.	1897	"	77
3	" Hattie	Dau	9	"	1/2	1897	"	12
4	" Leonard	Son	8	M	1/2	1897	"	12

5	" Jesse	"	4	M	1/2	1897	"	12
6	" Myrtle	Dau	1	F	1/2			

TRIBAL ENROLLMENT OF PARENTS

	NAME OF FATHER	YEAR	COUNTY	NAME OF MOTHER	YEAR	COUNTY
1	Houston Brown	Dead	Chickasaw Roll	Jennie Brown	Dead	Chickasaw Roll
2	Hewitt Cox	"	Non-citizen	Sarah Cox	"	Non-citizen
3	No. 1			No. 2		
4	No. 1			No. 2		
5	No. 1			No. 2		
6	No. 1			No. 2		

(NOTES)

No. 5 on Chickasaw Roll as Jessie

No. 6 affidavit of attending physician to be supplied. Received Sept. 21/98.

Affidavit of Lula Keel as to the marriage between Nos. 1 and 2 and destruction of same by fire in 1898; filed Nov. 8, 1902.

Sept. 20/98.

RESIDENCE: Pickens *COUNTY*	*CARD NO.*
POST OFFICE: Holder, Ind. Ter.	*FIELD NO.*

	NAME	RELATION-SHIP TO PERSON FIRST NAMED	AGE	SEX	BLOOD	TRIBAL ENROLLMENT		
						YEAR	COUNTY	PAGE
1	Harlin, George		21	M	1/2	1897	Pickens	15
2	" Belton	Son	1	"	1/4			
3	" Ruth G.	Dau	1mo	F	1/4			

TRIBAL ENROLLMENT OF PARENTS

	NAME OF FATHER	YEAR	COUNTY	NAME OF MOTHER	YEAR	COUNTY
1	George Harlin	Dead	Cherokee Citz.	Mary Harlin	Dead	Chickasaw Roll
2	No. 1			Pearl Harlin		Court citizen
3	No. 1			" "		" "

(NOTES)

Pearl Harlin, mother of No. 2 claims to be Chickasaw by blood.

No. 1 is the husband of Pearl harlin on Chickasaw card #C.169.

No. 2 affidavit of physician to be supplied. - Received Oct. 31/98.

No. 3 born Dec. 21, 1901. Enrolled Jany 14, 1902.

P.O. Ravia, I.T.

Sept. 20/98.

RESIDENCE: Pickens COUNTY					CARD NO.		
POST OFFICE: Fleetwood, Ind. Ter.					FIELD NO.		
NAME	RELATIONSHIP TO PERSON FIRST NAMED	AGE	SEX	BLOOD	TRIBAL ENROLLMENT		
					YEAR	COUNTY	PAGE
1 Hawkins, Joseph Walter		26	M	I.W.			
2 " Minnie	Wife	34	F	5/8	1897	Pickens	21

TRIBAL ENROLLMENT OF PARENTS

	NAME OF FATHER	YEAR	COUNTY	NAME OF MOTHER	YEAR	COUNTY
1	J.C. Hawkins		Non-citizen	Mandy Hawkins		Non-citizen
2	Charley Sealy	Dead	Chickasaw Roll	Emily Fleetwood	1897	Pickens

(NOTES)

No. 2 on Chickasaw roll as Minnie Coffee.

P.O. Terral, I.T. Oct. 16, 1902.

Sept. 20/98.

RESIDENCE: Pickens COUNTY					CARD NO.		
POST OFFICE: Fleetwood, Ind. Ter.					FIELD NO.		
NAME	RELATIONSHIP TO PERSON FIRST NAMED	AGE	SEX	BLOOD	TRIBAL ENROLLMENT		
					YEAR	COUNTY	PAGE
1 Gordon, Emily		57	F	1/4	1897	Pickens	21
2 Coffey, Charley	G.Son	8	M	1/16	1897	"	21
3 Gordon, Richard J.D.	Husband	40	"	I.W.			

TRIBAL ENROLLMENT OF PARENTS

	NAME OF FATHER	YEAR	COUNTY	NAME OF MOTHER	YEAR	COUNTY
1	Joseph Colbert	Dead	Chickasaw Roll	Elzira Oxberry Colbert	Dead	Chickasaw Roll
2	Hillary Coffey	"	Non-citizen	Ella Coffey	"	Pickens
3	Richard Gordon		" "	Nancy Gordon		Non-citizen

(NOTES)

No. 2 on Chickasaw roll as Charley Coffee
No. 1 " " " " Emly Fleetwood
No. 1 is now the wife of Richard J.D. Gordon on Chickasaw card #D.341. Feby. 13, 1901.
No. 3 originally listed for enrollment on Chickasaw card #D.341, Feb. 13, 1901
transferred to this card July 13, 1905.

Sept. 20/98.

RESIDENCE: Pickens COUNTY					CARD NO.		
POST OFFICE: Eastman, Ind. Ter.					FIELD NO.		
NAME	RELATIONSHIP TO PERSON FIRST NAMED	AGE	SEX	BLOOD	TRIBAL ENROLLMENT		
					YEAR	COUNTY	PAGE
1 Joel, Ella		21	F	1/2			
2 " Alice	Dau	2	"				
3 " Lee	"	1mo	"				
4 Shipman, Buck	Son	5mo	M	1/4			
5 " Willie Augustus	Son	8da	M	1/4			
6 " Kieth[sic]	Son	2wks	M	1/4			

TRIBAL ENROLLMENT OF PARENTS

NAME OF FATHER	YEAR	COUNTY	NAME OF MOTHER	YEAR	COUNTY
1 Willie Wachubby		Choctaw roll	Rhoda Watubby		Chickasaw Indian
2 Solomon Joel		" "	No. 1		
3 " "		" "	No. 1		
4 D.C. Shipman		" "	No. 1		
5 " " "		" "	No. 1		
6 " " "		" "	No. 1		

(NOTES)

No. 1 on Choctaw Census Roll No. 2, Page 308, *(the remainder illegible)*
No. 1 on Choctaw Roll 1896, Jack Fork County, No. 7352
See attached decree of divorce from Solomon Joel of No. 1 and marriage license to D.C. Shipman.
D.C. Shipman, father of No. 4 on Chickasaw card D.71.
No. 4 Enrolled May 24, 1900.
No. 5 Enrolled August 30, 1901.
No. 6 Born Aug. 25, 1902; enrolled Sept. 4, 1902.

Sept. 20/98.

RESIDENCE: Pickens COUNTY					CARD NO.		
POST OFFICE: Ardmore, Ind. Ter.					FIELD NO.		
NAME	RELATIONSHIP TO PERSON FIRST NAMED	AGE	SEX	BLOOD	TRIBAL ENROLLMENT		
					YEAR	COUNTY	PAGE
1 Nichols, Alexander		72	M	I.W.	1897	Pickens	78
2 " Susan M.	Wife	60	F	1/4	1897	"	14
3 " Robert H.	Son	24	M	1/8	1897	"	14
4 " Walter	"	22	"	1/8	1897	"	14
5 " Daisy	Dau	19	F	1/8	1897	"	14
6 " Clyde Cleveland	Son	13	M	1/8	1897	"	14

TRIBAL ENROLLMENT OF PARENTS						
	NAME OF FATHER	YEAR	COUNTY	NAME OF MOTHER	YEAR	COUNTY
1	George Nichols	Dead	Non-citizen	Elizabeth Nichols	Dead	Non-citizen
2	James Boyd I.W.	"	Chickasaw Roll	Nancy Love Boyd	"	Chickasaw Roll
3	No. 1			No. 2		
4	No. 1			No. 2		
5	No. 1			No. 2		

(NOTES)

No. 1 on Chickasaw Roll as A.M. Nichols. *(No. 1 Dawes' Roll No. 112)*
No. 2 " " " " Susan "
No. 3 " " " " Bob "
No. 6 " " " " Clyde "
Affidavit of R.L. Boyd as to marriage between No. 1 and No. 2 filed March 5, 1902.

Sept. 20/98.

RESIDENCE: Pickens COUNTY					CARD NO.			
POST OFFICE: Ardmore, Ind. Ter.					FIELD NO.			
	NAME	RELATION-SHIP TO PERSON FIRST NAMED	AGE	SEX	BLOOD	TRIBAL ENROLLMENT		
						YEAR	COUNTY	PAGE
1	Carter, C.D.		30	M	1/8	1897	Pickens	17
2	" Stella Laflore	Dau	6	F	1/16	1897	"	17
3	" Italy Cecil	"	4	"	1/16	1897	"	17
4	" Julia Josephine	"	2	"	1/16	~~1897~~	"	~~86~~
5	" Benjamin W.	Son	1mo	M	1/16			

TRIBAL ENROLLMENT OF PARENTS						
	NAME OF FATHER	YEAR	COUNTY	NAME OF MOTHER	YEAR	COUNTY
1	B.W. Carter	Dead	Cherokee Citz.	Serena Carter	1897	Pickens
2	No. 1			Ada Gertrude Carter		white woman
3	No. 1			" " "		" "
4	No. 1			" " "		" "
5	No. 1			" " "		" "

(NOTES)

No. 2 on Chickasaw roll as Stella F. Carter.
No. 4 " " " " Julia " *(No. 4 Dawes' Roll No. 4101)*
Correct name of No. 3 is Italy Cecil.
Wife of No. 1 and mother of children on this card is Ada Gertrude Carter on Chickasaw card #D.112.
No. 4 Proof of birth received and filed Nov. 1, 1901.

Sept. 20/98.

RESIDENCE: Tishomingo COUNTY					CARD NO.			
POST OFFICE: Dougherty, Ind. Ter.					FIELD NO.			
	NAME	RELATIONSHIP TO PERSON FIRST NAMED	AGE	SEX	BLOOD	TRIBAL ENROLLMENT		
						YEAR	COUNTY	PAGE
1	Schoeppe, Fred L.		66	M	I.W.	1897	Tishomingo	79
2	" Elizabeth	Wife	63	F	1/4	1897	"	30

TRIBAL ENROLLMENT OF PARENTS

	NAME OF FATHER	YEAR	COUNTY	NAME OF MOTHER	YEAR	COUNTY
1	John Schoeppe	Dead	Non-citizen	Christine Schoeppe	Dead	Non-citizen
2	Robt Aldridge	"	" "	*(Name illegible)*	"	Chickasaw Roll

(NOTES)

No. 2 on Chickasaw roll as Elizabeth Sheppa.
No. 1 " " " " Fred Shoeppe.
No. 1 was married to Lavina Davis, a Chickasaw in 1870, lived with her until her death in 1873; in 1877 married Martha Strickland, lived with her until her death in 1883. Married No. 2 Aug. 24, 1889.

No. 2 enrolled Sept. 20/98.
No. 1 enrolled " 21/98.

RESIDENCE: Pickens COUNTY					CARD NO.			
POST OFFICE: Ardmore, Ind. Ter.					FIELD NO.			
	NAME	RELATIONSHIP TO PERSON FIRST NAMED	AGE	SEX	BLOOD	TRIBAL ENROLLMENT		
						YEAR	COUNTY	PAGE
1	Carter, Serena		55	F	1/4	1897	Pickens	17
2	Fry, Sammie J.	Ward	18	M	1/4	1897	"	17
3	" Sophia	"	11	F	1/4	1897	"	17

TRIBAL ENROLLMENT OF PARENTS

	NAME OF FATHER	YEAR	COUNTY	NAME OF MOTHER	YEAR	COUNTY
1	William Guy	Dead	Non-citizen	Jane Guy	Dead	Chickasaw Roll
2	Jeff Fry I.W.	"	Pickens	Sophie Fry	"	" "
3	" "	"	"	" "	"	" "

(NOTES)

Sept. 20/98.

RESIDENCE: Pickens ***COUNTY*** ***CARD NO.***
POST OFFICE: Elk, Ind. Ter. ***FIELD NO.***

	NAME	RELATION-SHIP TO PERSON FIRST NAMED	AGE	SEX	BLOOD	TRIBAL ENROLLMENT		
						YEAR	COUNTY	PAGE
1	Hall, John W.		41	M	I.W.	1897	Pickens	78
2	" Henrietta	Wife	38	F	1/4	1897	"	14
3	" George J.	Son	13	M	1/8	1897	"	14
4	Collins, George	Step Son	18	"	1/8	1897	"	14

TRIBAL ENROLLMENT OF PARENTS

	NAME OF FATHER	YEAR	COUNTY	NAME OF MOTHER	YEAR	COUNTY
1	*(Name illegible)*	Dead	Non-citizen	Mary E. Hall	Dead	Non-citizen
2	Henry McKinney	"	Cherokee Citz.	Sally Harris McKinney	"	Chickasaw Roll
3	No. 1			No. 2		
4	John Collins	Dead	Non-citizen	No. 2		

(NOTES)

No. 1 on Chickasaw roll as John *(No. 1 Dawes' Roll No. 167)*
No. 3 " " " George

10/20/02. P.O. of No. 1 is Whitebead
" " " " 2 " Elk
Nos 1 & 2 separated in Jan. *(illegible)*

Sept. 20/98.

RESIDENCE: Pickens ***COUNTY*** ***CARD NO.***
POST OFFICE: Ardmore, Ind. Ter. ***FIELD NO.***

	NAME	RELATION-SHIP TO PERSON FIRST NAMED	AGE	SEX	BLOOD	TRIBAL ENROLLMENT		
						YEAR	COUNTY	PAGE
1	Hardy, Walter		28	M	I.W.	1897	Pickens	78
2	" Jennetta	Wife	22	F	1/8	1897	"	17
3	" Vinnie	Dau	3	"	1/16	1897	"	17
4	~~" Dewey~~	~~Son~~	~~9mos~~	~~M~~	~~1/16~~			
5	" Charles R.	Son	2wks	M	1/16			

TRIBAL ENROLLMENT OF PARENTS

	NAME OF FATHER	YEAR	COUNTY	NAME OF MOTHER	YEAR	COUNTY
1	Reuben Hardy		Non-citizen	Amanda Hardy		Non-citizen
2	Hobart Heel I.W.	1897	Pickens	Jane Heel	Dead	Tishomingo
3	No. 1			No. 2		
4	No. 1			No. 2		

5	No. 1			No. 2		

(NOTES)

No. 3 on Chickasaw roll as Venita
Sir name on Chickasaw roll as Hardie
No. 5 Enrolled November 27, 1900.
No. 4 Died May 23, 1899; Proof of death filed Dec. 24, 1902.

Sept. 20/98.

RESIDENCE: Pickens **COUNTY** **CARD NO.**
POST OFFICE: Woodford, Ind. Ter. **FIELD NO.**

	NAME	RELATION-SHIP TO PERSON FIRST NAMED	AGE	SEX	BLOOD	TRIBAL ENROLLMENT		
						YEAR	COUNTY	PAGE
1	Williford, Richard		9	M	1/4	1897	Pickens	19
2	McLane, Willie B.		15	M	1/2	1897	"	18

TRIBAL ENROLLMENT OF PARENTS

	NAME OF FATHER	YEAR	COUNTY	NAME OF MOTHER	YEAR	COUNTY
1	Joe Williford		white man	Margaret Williford	Dead	Pickens
2	Harrison McLane	Dead	Pickens	Mary Jane Callahan McLane	"	I.W/Chickasaw Roll

(NOTES)

No. 1 Father, Joe Williford, on Chickasaw roll, Card No. D.41.
No. 2 Stepson of Nannie Williford Chickasaw " " " 41.
No. 2 on Chickasaw roll as Willie McLane.

Sept. 20/98.

RESIDENCE: Pickens **COUNTY** **CARD NO.**
POST OFFICE: Eastman, Ind. Ter. **FIELD NO.**

	NAME	RELATION-SHIP TO PERSON FIRST NAMED	AGE	SEX	BLOOD	TRIBAL ENROLLMENT		
						YEAR	COUNTY	PAGE
1	Souse, Lina		45	M[sic]	Full	1897	Pickens	20
2	" Georgia	Dau	12	F	1/2	1897	"	20
3	" Lula	"	10	"	1/2	1897	"	20
4	" Hix	Son	7	"[sic]	1/2	1897	"	20
5	" Dory	Gr.Dau	4mo	F	1/2			
6	" John	Husband	43	M	I.W.			

TRIBAL ENROLLMENT OF PARENTS

	NAME OF FATHER	YEAR	COUNTY	NAME OF MOTHER	YEAR	COUNTY
1	Tish-e-of-ta	Dead	Chickasaw Roll	Lo-ah-te	Dead	Chickasaw Roll
2	John Souse		Non-citizen	No. 1		

3	" "		" "	No. 1		
4	" "		" "	No. 1		
5	Boss O. Saner			No. 2		
6	Hosea Souse	D'd	Mexican	Georgia Hosea	Dead	Mexican

(NOTES)

No. 1 on Chickasaw roll as Lind Souse.
No. 1 Died Jany. 15, 1902; proof of death filed Oct. 22, 1902.
No. 5 Born April 5, 1902; enrolled Aug. 29, 1902.
No. 5 is illegitimate
No. 6 transferred from Chickasaw Card *(the remainder illegible)*

P.O. Cornish, I.T. 10/14/02

Sept. 20/98.

RESIDENCE: Pickens ***COUNTY*** ***CARD NO.***
POST OFFICE: Burneyville, Ind. Ter. ***FIELD NO.***

	NAME	RELATION-SHIP TO PERSON FIRST NAMED	AGE	SEX	BLOOD	TRIBAL ENROLLMENT		
						YEAR	COUNTY	PAGE
1	Myers, Patsey		38	F	3/4	1897	Pickens	15
2	" Malinda	Dau	10	"	3/8	1897	"	15
3	" George	Son	5	M	3/8	1897	"	15
4	" Maude	Dau	3	F	3/8	1897	"	15
5	" Thomas David	Son	3mos	M	3/8			
6	Murray, Laura	Dau	15	F	3/8	1897	Pickens	15
7	Henderson, John	Son	13	M	3/8	1897	"	15

TRIBAL ENROLLMENT OF PARENTS

	NAME OF FATHER	YEAR	COUNTY	NAME OF MOTHER	YEAR	COUNTY
1	Governor Parker	Dead	Chickasaw roll	La-ditcha	Dead	Chickasaw Roll
2	John Myers		Non-citizen	No. 1		
3	" "		" "	No. 1		
4	" "		" "	No. 1		
5	" "		" "	No. 1		
6	Eph. Murray	Dead	" "	No. 1		
7	John Henderson		" "	No. 1		

(NOTES)

No. 2 on Chickasaw Roll as Malinda
No. 2 also on Page 22 as Lena Shipman

Sept. 20/98.

RESIDENCE: Tishomingo COUNTY					CARD NO.		
POST OFFICE: Nebo, Ind. Ter.					FIELD NO.		
NAME	RELATION-SHIP TO PERSON FIRST NAMED	AGE	SEX	BLOOD	TRIBAL ENROLLMENT		
					YEAR	COUNTY	PAGE
1 Krebbs, Robt. C.		30	M	1/4	1897	Tishomingo	30

	NAME OF FATHER	YEAR	COUNTY	NAME OF MOTHER	YEAR	COUNTY
1	Nathaniel Krebbs	Dead	Choctaw Roll	Elizabeth Krebbs	1897	Tishomingo

(NOTES)

On Chickasaw Roll as Robert Krebbs.

Sept. 20/98.

RESIDENCE: Pickens COUNTY						CARD NO.		
POST OFFICE: Eastman, Ind. Ter.						FIELD NO.		
	NAME	RELATION-SHIP TO PERSON FIRST NAMED	AGE	SEX	BLOOD	TRIBAL ENROLLMENT		
						YEAR	COUNTY	PAGE
1	Burris, Melton		23	M	Full	1897	Pickens	20
2	" Lillie	Dau	1 3/4	F	1/2	1897	"	86
3	" Bessie	"	4mo	"	1/2			
4	" Dewit	Son	2mo	M	1/2			
5	" Robert Lee	Son	3mo	M	1/2			

TRIBAL ENROLLMENT OF PARENTS

	NAME OF FATHER	YEAR	COUNTY	NAME OF MOTHER	YEAR	COUNTY
1	Eastman Burris	Dead	Chickasaw roll	Liney Burris	1897	Pickens
2	No. 1			Letha Burris		Non-citizen
3	No. 1			" "		" "
4	No. 1			" "		" "
5	No. 1			" "		" "

RESIDENCE: Pickens COUNTY	CARD NO.
POST OFFICE: Burneyville, Ind. Ter.	FIELD NO.

	NAME	RELATION-SHIP TO PERSON FIRST NAMED	AGE	SEX	BLOOD	TRIBAL ENROLLMENT		
						YEAR	COUNTY	PAGE
1	Kernel, Charley		27	M	1/2	1897	Pickens	15

TRIBAL ENROLLMENT OF PARENTS

	NAME OF FATHER	YEAR	COUNTY	NAME OF MOTHER	YEAR	COUNTY
1	Joseph Kernel	Dead	Creek citz.	Amy Parker Kernel	Dead	Pickens

(NOTES)

Also on Page 83.

Sept. 20/98.

RESIDENCE: Pickens COUNTY	CARD NO.
POST OFFICE: Thackerville, Ind. Ter.	FIELD NO.

	NAME	RELATION-SHIP TO PERSON FIRST NAMED	AGE	SEX	BLOOD	TRIBAL ENROLLMENT		
						YEAR	COUNTY	PAGE
1	Story, Sam		32	M	1/8	1897	Pickens	8

TRIBAL ENROLLMENT OF PARENTS

	NAME OF FATHER	YEAR	COUNTY	NAME OF MOTHER	YEAR	COUNTY
1	Elijah Story	Dead	Non-citizen	*(Illegible)* Story	Dead	Chickasaw roll

(NOTES)

Sept. 20/98.

RESIDENCE: Pickens COUNTY	CARD NO.
POST OFFICE: Burneyville, Ind. Ter.	FIELD NO.

	NAME	RELATION-SHIP TO PERSON FIRST NAMED	AGE	SEX	BLOOD	TRIBAL ENROLLMENT		
						YEAR	COUNTY	PAGE
1	Black, Kissie		22	F	3/8	1897	Pickens	15
2	" Mamie Wilbert	Dau	5	"	3/16	1897	"	15
3	Kernel, George	Bro	22	M	3/8	1893	"	P.R.#2 130

TRIBAL ENROLLMENT OF PARENTS

	NAME OF FATHER	YEAR	COUNTY	NAME OF MOTHER	YEAR	COUNTY
1	Joe Kernel	Dead	Creek Citz.	Amy Parker Kernel	Dead	Chickasaw Roll
2	Charley Black		Non-citizen	No. 1		
3	Joe Kernel	Dead	Creek Citizen	Amy Parker Kernel	Dead	Chickasaw Roll

(NOTES)

No. 1 on Chickasaw roll as Kizzi Block

No. 2 " " " " Mamie "
No. 3 also on 1897 Chickasaw roll as George Kernal

P.O. Hewitt, I.T. Sept. 20/98.

RESIDENCE: Pickens ***COUNTY***					***CARD NO.***			
POST OFFICE: Brownsville, Ind. Ter.					***FIELD NO.***			

	NAME	RELATION-SHIP TO PERSON FIRST NAMED	AGE	SEX	BLOOD	TRIBAL ENROLLMENT		
						YEAR	COUNTY	PAGE
1	Harney, Sison		55	F	Full	1897	Pickens	25
2	Iotontubby, Ginsy	Niece	15	F	"	1897	"	25
3	Kaney, Mary	Niece	15	"	"	1897	"	19
4	Vaughn, Jesse	Grand nephew	8	M	1/2	1897	"	22
5	Kaney, Robert Harmon	Son of No. 3	4mo	M	Full			

TRIBAL ENROLLMENT OF PARENTS

	NAME OF FATHER	YEAR	COUNTY	NAME OF MOTHER	YEAR	COUNTY
1	I-a-pa-hubby	1897	Pickens	Ah-co-na-he	Dead	Pickens
2	Iotontubby	Dead	"	Sulphie	"	"
3	Marshall Long	"	"	Jane Long	"	"
4	Vaughn		Non-citizen	Lowiney	"	"
5	Harmon Kaney on Chickasa	w Car	d #1027	No. 3		

(NOTES)

No. 2 Died Sept. 1900; Proof of death filed Nov. 6, 1902.
No. 2 on Chickasaw roll asGinsey Idonubby.
No. 4 " " " " Jessie Vaughn.
Father of No. 4 *(remainder illegible)*
No. 3 Now the wife of Harmon Kaney on Chickasaw Card #1027; Evidence of marriage requested July 22, 1901.
No. 5 Born March 25, 1902. Enrolled July 22, 1902.
Evidence of marriage between No. 3 and Harmon Kany filed Nov. 4, 1902.

P.O. of No. 3 Isom Springs, I.T. = is Woodville Oct. 3/98.

RESIDENCE: Pickens COUNTY					CARD NO.		
POST OFFICE: Berwyn, Ind. Ter.					FIELD NO.		
NAME	RELATION-SHIP TO PERSON FIRST NAMED	AGE	SEX	BLOOD	TRIBAL ENROLLMENT		
					YEAR	COUNTY	PAGE
1 King, Callie Boyd		21	D	1/8	1897	Pickens	21
2 " Marie Boyd	Dau	9mos	"	1/16			
3 " Clemmie Lelia	Dau	4mo	"	1/16			

TRIBAL ENROLLMENT OF PARENTS

	NAME OF FATHER	YEAR	COUNTY	NAME OF MOTHER	YEAR	COUNTY
1	*(Illegible)* Boyd	Dead	Chickasaw Roll	Sallie Boyd	Dead	Non-citizen
2	F.J. King		white man	No. 1		
3	" " "		" "	No. 1		

(NOTES)

No. 1 on roll as Callie Boyd; wife of F.J. King, Chickasaw Card No. D.37.
No. 2 Affidavit of attending physician to be supplied. Received Sept. 26/98.
No. 3 Enrolled May 24, 1900.
Evidence of marriage of F.J. King <u>and</u> Callie Boyd King attached to Chickasaw card D.37. Jan. 31, 1900.

P.O. Ardmore, I.T. Sept. 20/98.

RESIDENCE: Pickens COUNTY					CARD NO.		
POST OFFICE: McMillan, Ind. Ter.					FIELD NO.		
NAME	RELATION-SHIP TO PERSON FIRST NAMED	AGE	SEX	BLOOD	TRIBAL ENROLLMENT		
					YEAR	COUNTY	PAGE
1 McMillan, George W.		42	M	I.W.	1897	Pickens	77
2 " Nancy	Wife	35	F	Full	1897	"	9
3 " Millie	Dau	12	"	1/2	1897	"	11
4 " Rosie Rena	"	10	"	1/2	1897	"	11
5 " Joseph T.	Son	7	M	1/2	1897	"	11
6 " Bertha Frances	Dau	4	F	1/2	1897	"	11
7 " Alva Linzie	Son	3	M	1/2	1897	"	11
8 " Lillian Ethel	Dau	9mos	F	1/2			
9 Leader, Billie	StepSon	17	M	Full	1897	Pickens	11
10 Wolf, Monroe	Ward	11	M	"	1897	"	28

TRIBAL ENROLLMENT OF PARENTS

	NAME OF FATHER	YEAR	COUNTY	NAME OF MOTHER	YEAR	COUNTY
1	Edward McMillan	Dead	Non-citizen	Sarah McMillan	Dead	Non-citizen
2	Aaron Brown	"	Chickasaw Roll	Elsie Brown	"	Chickasaw Roll

3	No. 1			No. 2		
4	No. 1			No. 2		
5	No. 1			No. 2		
6	No. 1			No. 2		
7	No. 1			No. 2		
8	No. 1			No. 2		
9	Jim Leader	Dead	Chickasaw Roll	No. 2		
10	Murphy Wolf	"	" "	*(Illegible Name)*	Dead	Chickasaw Roll

(NOTES)

No. 10 in penitentiary at Leavenworth
No. 1 on Chickasaw Roll as George McMillan. Affidavits of Guy Keel, Henry Bourland.
No. 4 " " " " Rosie " J.S. Cate and Calvin Brown, relative to authority.
No. 6 " " " " Bertha " J.C. Lynn to solemnize marriages in 1889.
No. 7 " " " " Alva " filed May 22, 1903.
No. 8 affidavit of attending physician to be supplied. Received Sept. 23/98.
No. 8 Died Oct. 10, 1902; Proof of death filed Nov. 7, 1902.

Sept. 20/98.

RESIDENCE: Pickens **COUNTY** **CARD NO.**
POST OFFICE: Thackerville, Ind. Ter. **FIELD NO.**

	NAME	RELATION-SHIP TO PERSON FIRST NAMED	AGE	SEX	BLOOD	TRIBAL ENROLLMENT		
						YEAR	COUNTY	PAGE
1	Stewart, Ben M.		48	M	I.W.	1897	Pickens	79
2	" Mary Frances	Wife	49	F	1/2	1897	"	26
3	" Eugene	Son	13	M	1/4	1897	"	26
4	" Gertrude M.	Dau	10	F	1/4	1897	"	26

TRIBAL ENROLLMENT OF PARENTS

	NAME OF FATHER	YEAR	COUNTY	NAME OF MOTHER	YEAR	COUNTY
1	Ben Stewart	Dead	Non-citizen	Sarah Stewart	Dead	Non-citizen
2	Calvin S. Love	"	Chickasaw Roll	Sarah Love	"	Chickasaw Roll
3	No. 1			No. 2		
4	No. 1			No. 2		

(NOTES)

No. 1 married in 1868 *(No. 1 Dawes' Roll No. 312)*
No. 1 on Chickasaw roll as B.M.
No. 2 " " " " Mary F.
No. 4 " " " " G.M.
Evidence of marriage between No. 1 and No. 2 filed Feby. 21, 1902.

Sept. 20/98.

RESIDENCE: Pickens **COUNTY** **CARD NO.**
POST OFFICE: Ardmore, Ind. Ter. **FIELD NO.**

	NAME	RELATIONSHIP TO PERSON FIRST NAMED	AGE	SEX	BLOOD	TRIBAL ENROLLMENT YEAR	TRIBAL ENROLLMENT COUNTY	TRIBAL ENROLLMENT PAGE
1	Williams, Eva		26	F	3/4	1897	Pickens	15
2	Lester, Moran S.	Son	3	M	3/6	1897	"	15
3	" Wesley	"	1	"	3/8			
4	Williams, Orin	Son	4mo	M	3/8			

TRIBAL ENROLLMENT OF PARENTS

	NAME OF FATHER	YEAR	COUNTY	NAME OF MOTHER	YEAR	COUNTY
1	Wm Moore	Dead	Tishomingo	Jennie Moore	Dead	Tishomingo
2	Dave Booker		Non-citizen	No. 1		
3	" "		" "	No. 1		
4	G.M. Williams		" "	No. 1		

(NOTES)

No. 1 is now the wife of G.M. Williams, a non-citizen.
No. 2 on Chickasaw roll as S. Moran
No. 3 Affidavit of attending physician to be supplied.
No. 4 Enrolled, November 28, 1900.

Sept. 20/98.

RESIDENCE: Pickens **COUNTY** **CARD NO.**
POST OFFICE: Ryan, Ind. Ter. **FIELD NO.**

	NAME	RELATIONSHIP TO PERSON FIRST NAMED	AGE	SEX	BLOOD	TRIBAL ENROLLMENT YEAR	TRIBAL ENROLLMENT COUNTY	TRIBAL ENROLLMENT PAGE
1	Wray, William		29	M	I.W.			
2	" Daisy	Wife	20	F	1/4	1897	Pickens	20

TRIBAL ENROLLMENT OF PARENTS

	NAME OF FATHER	YEAR	COUNTY	NAME OF MOTHER	YEAR	COUNTY
1	David Wray	Dead	Non-citizen	*(Illegible)* Wray	Dead	Non-citizen
2	*(Illegible Name)*		Pickens	*(Illegible Name)*	"	Pickens

(NOTES)

10/29/98 See Choctaw Card No. 438 for family of No. 2
(No. 1 Dawes' Roll No. I.W. 273) *(No. 2 Dawes' Roll No. 1468)*

Sept. 20/98.

Residence: Choctaw Nation ***County*** ***Card No.***
Post Office: Antlers, Ind. Ter. ***Field No.***

	Name	Relationship to Person First Named	Age	Sex	Blood	Tribal Enrollment		
						Year	County	Page
1	Wasson, Nannie E.		36	F	3/8	1893	Pontotoc	P.R.#2 P.45
2	" Victor B.	Son	3	M	3/16	~~1896~~		~~89~~
3	" Clark B.	Husband	28	"	I.W.			
4	" Emma Janette Chloe	Dau	5w	F	3/16			
5	" Joseph J.	Son	1mo	M	3/16			

Tribal Enrollment of Parents

	Name of Father	Year	County	Name of Mother	Year	County
1	B.F. Byrd	1897	Pontotoc	Nannie Watson Byrd	Dead	Chickasaw Roll
2	Clark B. Wasson		Non-citizen	No. 1		
3	Joseph Wasson	1896	" "	Abbie Wasson	Dead	non citiz.
4	No. 3			No. 1		
5	No. 3			No. 1		

(Notes)

(Notations illegible)

Sept. 20/98.

Residence: Pontotoc ***County*** ***Card No.***
Post Office: Frank, Ind. Ter. ***Field No.***

	Name	Relationship to Person First Named	Age	Sex	Blood	Tribal Enrollment		
						Year	County	Page
1	Byrd, B.F.		49	M	1/4	1897	Pontotoc	58
2	" Mamie	Wife	32	F	1/32	1897	"	58
3	" Lonnie E	Son	7	M	9/64	1897	"	58
4	" Roy Neal	"	6	"	9/64	1897	"	58
5	" Lula May	Dau	4	F	9/64	1897	"	58
6	" Hattie Zelma	"	3	"	9/64	1897	"	58
7	" George Franklin	Son	20	M	3/8	1897	"	58
8	" William F. Jr.	"	18	"	3/8	1897	"	58
9	Guy, Douglas D.	StepSon	10	"	1/16	1897	"	58
10	Byrd, Benjamin Franklin	Son	3wks	"	9/64			

Tribal Enrollment of Parents

	Name of Father	Year	County	Name of Mother	Year	County
1	John Byrd	Dead	Non-citizen	Mary Moore Byrd	Dead	Pontotoc

2	P.R. Goldsby	"	" "	Nancy Ann Goldsby	"	Chickasaw Roll
3	No. 1			No. 2		
4	No. 1			No. 2		
5	No. 1			No. 2		
6	No. 1			No. 2		
7	No. 1			??olsie Colbert Byrd	Dead	Pontotoc
8	No. 1			" " "	"	"
9	Douglas Guy	Dead	Chickasaw Roll	No. 2		
10	No. 1			No. 2		

(NOTES)

No. 2 on Chickasaw Roll as Mrs. B.F. Byrd; Approved by Commission Mar. 29/99 and transferred from Chickasaw Card D.182.
No. 4 " " " " "Burd"
No. 5 " " " " Lula M
No. 6 " " " " Hattie H; No. 6 Died in April 1899; Proof of death filed Nov. 12, 1902.
No. 7 " " " " Geo. F.
No. 10 Enrolled Aug. 22, 1900.

Sept. 20/98.

RESIDENCE: Pontotoc	COUNTY	CARD NO.	
POST OFFICE: Norman, Okla. Ter.		FIELD NO.	

	NAME	RELATIONSHIP TO PERSON FIRST NAMED	AGE	SEX	BLOOD	TRIBAL ENROLLMENT		
						YEAR	COUNTY	PAGE
1	Adams, John C.		42	M	I.W.			
2	" Lucinda Brittain	Wife	37	F	3/4	1897	Pontotoc	93

TRIBAL ENROLLMENT OF PARENTS

	NAME OF FATHER	YEAR	COUNTY	NAME OF MOTHER	YEAR	COUNTY
1	John Adams	Dead	Non-citizen	Alice Adams	Dead	Non-citizen
2	Adam Gray	"	Chickasaw Roll	Elsie Gray	"	Chickasaw Roll

(NOTES)

No. 2 On Chickasaw Roll as Lucinda Brittain
On 1893 " Pay Roll No. 2 as Lucenda Briton
No. 2 is mother of children on Chickasaw Card #424
These parties live in Chickasaw Nation just across Canadian River from Oklahoma but get their mail at Norman, O.T. All questions as to residence eliminated Dec. 7, 1900.
See additional testimony of No. 1 taken Oct. 17, 1902
Certified copy of divorce of No. 2 from M.B. Brittain filed Feby. 10, *(illegible)*.

Sept. 19, 1898.

RESIDENCE: Pontotoc **COUNTY**					**CARD NO.**		
POST OFFICE: Purcell, Ind. Ter.					**FIELD NO.**		

	NAME	RELATION-SHIP TO PERSON FIRST NAMED	AGE	SEX	BLOOD	TRIBAL ENROLLMENT YEAR	COUNTY	PAGE
1	Turnbull, Dick		26	M	1/8	1897	Pontotoc	62
2	" Claude	Son	14mo	"	1/16	1897	"	90
3	" Fannie	Dau	3mo	F	1/16			
4	" Adel	"	1mo	"	1/16			
5	" Maude	Wife	28	F	I.W.			

TRIBAL ENROLLMENT OF PARENTS

	NAME OF FATHER	YEAR	COUNTY	NAME OF MOTHER	YEAR	COUNTY
1	John Turnbull	Dead	Choctaw Roll	Lucy Turnbull	Dead	Chickasaw Roll
2	No. 1			Maude "		Non-citizen
3	No. 1			" "		" "
4	No. 1			" "		" "
5	Lige Goode		Non-citizen	Fannie Goode		" "

(NOTES)

No. 1 Admitted by Dawes Commission in 1896 as a Chickasaw by blood; Chickasaw Case #90; No appeal.
No. 1 Husband of Maude Turnbull, Chickasaw Doubtful Card No. D.36.
No. 2 Registered under Act of Legislation, July 31st 1897, (Chick Roll Page 90)
No. 2 Proof of birth received and filed Sept. 30, 1902.
No. 3 Enrolled Nov. 3d 1899.
No. 4 Born Dec. 20, 1901; Enrolled Jany 23d 1902.
No. 5 transferred from Chickasaw card #D.36. See decision of March 5, 190? *(remainder illegible)*
No. 5 admitted by Domm in 1896; no appeal; case # *(illegible)*

Sept. 19/98.

RESIDENCE: Pickens **COUNTY**					**CARD NO.**		
POST OFFICE: Thackerville, Ind. Ter.					**FIELD NO.**		

	NAME	RELATION-SHIP TO PERSON FIRST NAMED	AGE	SEX	BLOOD	TRIBAL ENROLLMENT YEAR	COUNTY	PAGE
1	Nichols, R.L.		28	M	I.W.			
2	" Sarah Lottie	Wife	23	F	1/4	1897	Pickens	26
3	" Winnie Elsie	Dau	4	"	1/8	1897	"	26
4	" Joe B.	Son	2	M	1/8	~~1897~~	"	~~86~~
5	" Lee	"	3wks	"	1/8			

	Tribal Enrollment of Parents					
	Name of Father	Year	County	Name of Mother	Year	County
1	Robt. J. Nichols		Non-citizen	Mildred Nichols	Dead	Non-citizen
2	B.M. Stewart		Pickens	Frances Stewart		Pickens
3	No. 1			No. 2		
4	No. 1			No. 2		
5	No. 1			No. 2		

(Notes)

No. 2 On Chickasaw Roll as Lottie Nichols
No. 3 " " " " Winnie "
No. 4 " " " " Joe "
No. 4 Proof of birth received and filed Sept. 24. 1902.
No. 5 Enrolled Nov. 21/98.

P.O. Elmore, 9/30/02.

Sept. 19/98.

Residence: Pickens *County*					*Card No.*		
Post Office: Ishmael, Ind. Ter.					*Field No.*		
Name		Relationship to Person First Named	Age	Sex	Blood	Tribal Enrollment		

	Name	Relationship to Person First Named	Age	Sex	Blood	Tribal Enrollment Year	County	Page
1	Allison, Nancy		22	F	Full	1897	Pickens	20
2	" Josie	Dau	3	"	1/2	1897	"	20
3	" Wade	Son	3mos	M	1/2			
4	" Janey	Dau	1mo	F	1/2			

	Name of Father	Year	County	Name of Mother	Year	County
1	Eastman Burris	Dead	Chickasaw Roll	Liney Burris *(Illegible Name)*		Pickens
2	Will Allison		Non-citizen	No. 1		
3	" "		" "	No. 1		
4	?.W. Allison		" "	No. 1		

(Notes)

No. 4 Born June 18, 1902; Enrolled July 23, 1902.

P.O. Sugdew, I.T. 1/31/03.

Sept. 19/98.

RESIDENCE: Pickens *COUNTY*					*CARD NO.*		
POST OFFICE: Ardmore, Ind. Ter.					*FIELD NO.*		
	NAME	RELATION-SHIP TO PERSON FIRST NAMED	AGE	SEX	BLOOD	TRIBAL ENROLLMENT		
						YEAR	COUNTY	PAGE
1	Watkins, James		22	M	1/32	1897	Pickens	13
2	" Nora	Wife	18	F	I.W.	1897	"	78
3	" Henry Patton	Son	2	M	1/64	~~1897~~	"	~~85~~
4	" James Artie	"	3mo	"	1/64			
5	" William Eugene	"	2mo	"	1/64			

TRIBAL ENROLLMENT OF PARENTS

	NAME OF FATHER	YEAR	COUNTY	NAME OF MOTHER	YEAR	COUNTY
1	Bill Watkins	Dead	Non-citizen	Betty Watkins	Dead	Chickasaw Roll
2	Lee Su??att		" "	Sarah Su??att		Non-citizen
3	No. 1			No. 2		
4	No. 1			No. 2		
5	No. 1			No. 2		

(NOTES)

No. 3 Proof of birth received and filed Sept. 12, 1902. *(No. 2 Dawes' Roll No. I.W. 374)*
No. 4 Enrolled *(Illegible Month and date)*/99. *(No. 3 Dawes' Roll No. 1098)*
No. 5 Enrolled *(Illegible Month and date)*, 1902.
See affidavits of J.M. Campbell, J.J. Lee, R.W. Warren and
J.M. Colson relative to authority of Joseph Moseley to solemnize marriage.

Sept. 19/98

RESIDENCE: Pickens *COUNTY*					*CARD NO.*		
POST OFFICE: Marietta, Ind. Ter.					*FIELD NO.*		
	NAME	RELATION-SHIP TO PERSON FIRST NAMED	AGE	SEX	BLOOD	TRIBAL ENROLLMENT		
						YEAR	COUNTY	PAGE
1	Wolfenbarger, Rella		29	F	1/8	1897	Pickens	16
2	" Joseph	Son	12	M	1/16	1897	"	16
3	" Lula	Dau	10	F	1/16	1897	"	16
4	" Birdie	"	8	"	1/16	1897	"	16
5	" James Hanson	Son	6	M	1/16	1897	"	16
6	" Launa	Dau	4	F	1/16	1897	"	16
7	" Garnett	Son	2	M	1/16			
8	Johnson, Lucretia	Dau	20mo	F	1/16			

	TRIBAL ENROLLMENT OF PARENTS					
	NAME OF FATHER	**YEAR**	**COUNTY**	**NAME OF MOTHER**	**YEAR**	**COUNTY**
1	Sam Arnold	Dead	Non-citizen	Cyndie Arnold	Dead	Chickasaw Roll
2	Bert Wolfenbarger	"	" "	No. 1		
3	" "	"	" "	No. 1		
4	" "	"	" "	No. 1		
5	" "	"	" "	No. 1		
6	" "	"	" "	No. 1		
7	" "	"	" "	No. 1		
8	Henry Z. Johnson		" "	No. 1		

(NOTES)

No. 1 is now wife of Henry Z. Johnson, Non-citizen, Nov. 8, 1902.
No. 1 On Chickasaw Roll as Reila Woofenbarger
No. 3 " " " " Zula "
No. 5 " " " " James "
No. 6 " " " " Lorena "
No. 7 Affidavit of midwife to be supplied. Received Sept. 26/98.
No. 8 Born Feb. 6, 1901. Enrolled Nov. 8, 1902.

Sept. 19, 1898

RESIDENCE: Pickens ***COUNTY*** ***CARD NO.***
POST OFFICE: Ardmore, Ind. Ter. ***FIELD NO.***

	NAME	**RELATIONSHIP TO PERSON FIRST NAMED**	**AGE**	**SEX**	**BLOOD**	**TRIBAL ENROLLMENT**		
						YEAR	**COUNTY**	**PAGE**
1	Mayer, George		53	M	I.W.	1897	Pickens	78
2	" Betsie	Wife	49	F	3/4	1897	"	14

	TRIBAL ENROLLMENT OF PARENTS					
	NAME OF FATHER	**YEAR**	**COUNTY**	**NAME OF MOTHER**	**YEAR**	**COUNTY**
1	Henry Mayer	Dead	Non-citizen	Mary Mayer	Dead	Non-citizen
2	Daniel Davis	"	Chickasaw Roll	Nicey Davis	"	Chickasaw Roll

(NOTES)

Sir name of both persons on Chickasaw Roll as Myers
See testimony of No. 1 taken Oct. 28, 1902
No. 1 formerly husband of Amanda Mayer (nee Greenwood) a recognized Chickasaw by blood

Sept. 19/98.

RESIDENCE: Pickens **COUNTY** **CARD NO.**
POST OFFICE: Thackerville, Ind. Ter. **FIELD NO.**

	NAME	RELATION-SHIP TO PERSON FIRST NAMED	AGE	SEX	BLOOD	TRIBAL ENROLLMENT		
						YEAR	COUNTY	PAGE
1	Decherd, N.G.		54	M	I.W.	1897	Pickens	78
2	" Eugenia	Wife	48	F	3/4	1897	"	14

TRIBAL ENROLLMENT OF PARENTS

	NAME OF FATHER	YEAR	COUNTY	NAME OF MOTHER	YEAR	COUNTY
1	P.S. Decherd	Dead	Non-citizen	Frances Decherd	Dead	non citizen
2	Robert H. Love	"	Chickasaw Roll	Sally Love	"	Chickasaw Roll

(NOTES)

Sir name on Chickasaw Roll Dechard
No. 2 on Chickasaw Roll as Eugine

Sept. 19/1898.

RESIDENCE: Pickens **COUNTY** **CARD NO.**
POST OFFICE: Berwyn, Ind. Ter. **FIELD NO.**

	NAME	RELATION-SHIP TO PERSON FIRST NAMED	AGE	SEX	BLOOD	TRIBAL ENROLLMENT		
						YEAR	COUNTY	PAGE
1	Wheatley, Louisa		21	F	Full	1897	Tishomingo	29
2	Sealy, Acey	Son	7mo	M				

TRIBAL ENROLLMENT OF PARENTS

	NAME OF FATHER	YEAR	COUNTY	NAME OF MOTHER	YEAR	COUNTY
1	Manwell	Dead	Panola	Louisa Manwell	Dead	Tishomingo
2	Charlie Sealy		Tishomingo	No. 1		

(NOTES)

No. 1 was married May 29, 1898 to Thomas Crosby after his death
She was married to B.J. Holder, March 26, 1899, who promised a divorce from her June 25, 1900 and
She was married to G.W. Wheatley July 16, 1901, and her name is now Wheatley; May 5, 1902.
Evidence of marriage and of divorce as stated abve[sic] filed May 21, 1902
No. 2 Died Nov. 20, 1899. Proof of death filed Nov. 1, 1902.

Sept. 19/98.

RESIDENCE: Pickens **COUNTY** **CARD NO.**
POST OFFICE: Berwyn, Ind. Ter. **FIELD NO.**

	NAME	RELATION-SHIP TO PERSON FIRST NAMED	AGE	SEX	BLOOD	TRIBAL ENROLLMENT		
						YEAR	COUNTY	PAGE
1	Manwell, Wisdom		26	M	Full	1897	Tishomingo	27
2	" Malinda	Wife	19	F	"	1897	"	27

3	" Sampson	Son	4mo	M	"			
4	" Aaron	"	1mo	"	"			
5	" Birtha	Dau	2mo	F	"			

TRIBAL ENROLLMENT OF PARENTS

	NAME OF FATHER	YEAR	COUNTY	NAME OF MOTHER	YEAR	COUNTY
1	Manwell	Dead	Panola	Louisa Manwell	Dead	Tishomingo
2	Sampson Newbury	"	Tishomingo	Emily Newbury	"	"
3	No. 1			No. 2		
4	No. 1			No. 2		
5	No. 1			No. 2		

(NOTES)

No. 3 Enrolled 6/16/01
No. 3 Died Dec. 23rd 1900; Proof of Death filed Nov. 1st 1902.
No. 4 Enrolled July ?, 1900.
No. 4 Died April 19th 1901; Proof of Death filed Nov. 12, 1902.
No. 5 Born Dec. 19, 1901; Enrolled Feb. 20th 1902.

Sept. 11/98.

RESIDENCE: Pickens *COUNTY* *CARD NO.*
POST OFFICE: Willis, Ind. Ter. *FIELD NO.*

	NAME	RELATIONSHIP TO PERSON FIRST NAMED	AGE	SEX	BLOOD	TRIBAL ENROLLMENT		
						YEAR	COUNTY	PAGE
1	Bourland, Henry		40	M	1/32	1897	Pickens	9
2	" Frances Emma	Wife	35	F	I.W.	1897	"	77
3	" Clemmie	Dau	13	"	1/64	1897	"	9
4	" Ben	Son	8	M	1/64	1897	"	9
5	" Bessie	Dau	6	F	1/64	1897	"	9
6	" William	Son	2	M	1/64	1897	"	9
7	" Charles Howard	"	2wks	M	1/64			

TRIBAL ENROLLMENT OF PARENTS

	NAME OF FATHER	YEAR	COUNTY	NAME OF MOTHER	YEAR	COUNTY
1	Ben Bourland		Non-citizen	Mandy Bourland	Dead	Chickasaw Roll
2	Henry Dutton		" "	Harriet Dutton	"	Non-citizen
3	No. 1			No. 2		
4	No. 1			No. 2		
5	No. 1			No. 2		
6	No. 1			No. 2		
7	No. 1			No. 2		

(NOTES)

No. 2 On Chickasaw Roll as Francis Bourland
No. 7 Enrolled Sept 10, 1901
No. 3 is 18 years old. She was married to Bob Nolen, Feby 9, 1903.
See testimony of Nos. 1 and 3 of May 20, 1903.

No. 6 Enrolled Oct. 3/98.
All others " Sept. 19/98.

RESIDENCE: Pickens **COUNTY** **CARD NO.**
POST OFFICE: Ardmore, Ind. Ter. **FIELD NO.**

	NAME	RELATION-SHIP TO PERSON FIRST NAMED	AGE	SEX	BLOOD	TRIBAL ENROLLMENT		
						YEAR	COUNTY	PAGE
1	Bailey, O.S.		37	M	I.W.	1897	Pickens	78
2	" Annie L.	Wife	20	F	1/2	1897	"	16
3	" Richard Furman	Son	1 1/2	M	1/4	1897	"	86
4	" Pontotoc P.	"	1mo	"	1/4			
5	" Jewel	"	4mo	"	1/4			

TRIBAL ENROLLMENT OF PARENTS

	NAME OF FATHER	YEAR	COUNTY	NAME OF MOTHER	YEAR	COUNTY
1	P. Bailey		Non-citizen	Sarah E. Bailey		Non-citizen
2	Jack Paris	Dead	Cherokee Citizen	Rachael Owens Paris		Pickens
3	No. 1			No. 2		
4	No. 1			No. 2		
5	No. 1			No. 2		

(NOTES)

Nos. 1 & 2 Admitted by Dawes Com. Case No. 12 and No appeal taken.
Evidence of marriage of O.W.[sic] Bailey and Anna I.[sic] *(the remainder is illegible).*
No. 1 On Chickasaw Roll as E.S. Bailey
No. 2 " " " " Annie "
No. 3 Registered under Act of Legislative, July 31, 1897 (Chickasaw Roll Page 86).
No. 3 On Chickasaw Roll as Furman Bailey.
No. 3 Proof of Birth received and filed Sept. 23, 1902.
Son of Nos. 1 & 2 on Card D.295; Dec. 13/99.
No. 4 Born Nov. 6th 1899. Transferred to this card Feby 12, 1903.
No. 5 Born April 5th 1902. Enrolled Aug. 5, 1902.

Sept. 19/98.

RESIDENCE: Pickens **COUNTY**					**CARD NO.**			
POST OFFICE: Burneyville, Ind. Ter.					**FIELD NO.**			

	NAME	RELATION-SHIP TO PERSON FIRST NAMED	AGE	SEX	BLOOD	TRIBAL ENROLLMENT		
						YEAR	COUNTY	PAGE
1	Hays, John S.		36	M	I.W.	1897	Pickens	77
2	" Emma E.	Wife	25	F	1/4	1893	"	P.R.#2 P. 100
3	" Thomas Wesley	Son	6	M	1/8	1893	"	P.R.#2 100

TRIBAL ENROLLMENT OF PARENTS

	NAME OF FATHER	YEAR	COUNTY	NAME OF MOTHER	YEAR	COUNTY
1	J.W. Hayes		Non-citizen	Lizie E. Hays	Dead	Non-citizen
2	Thos. W. Bon	Dead	" "	Rhoda E. Bon	"	Tishomingo
3	No. 1			No. 2		

(NOTES)

No. 1 On Chickasaw Roll as J.S. Hays.
No. 1 & 2 are divorced. Evidence of Divorce filed Oct. 31, 1902.
No. 2 is now the wife of A.J. Brown, non-citizen; Evidence of marriage filed Oct. 31, 1902.
No. 2 On 1896 Chickasaw Roll Pickens County Page 94; On Chickasaw Roll as Emma E. Hoze.
No. 3 " " " " " " " " " " " " Thomas W. "
Nos. 2 & 3 on 1893 Chickasaw *(the remainder illegible).*

RESIDENCE: Pickens **COUNTY**					**CARD NO.**			
POST OFFICE: Ardmore, Ind. Ter.					**FIELD NO.**			

	NAME	RELATION-SHIP TO PERSON FIRST NAMED	AGE	SEX	BLOOD	TRIBAL ENROLLMENT		
						YEAR	COUNTY	PAGE
1	Gallatin, Perry		32	M	I.W.	1897	Pickens	77
2	" Minnie	Wife	28	F	1/16	1897	"	20
3	Watkins, Eugean	StepSon	12	M	1/32	1897	"	20

TRIBAL ENROLLMENT OF PARENTS

	NAME OF FATHER	YEAR	COUNTY	NAME OF MOTHER	YEAR	COUNTY
1	A.G. Gallatin	Dead	Non-citizen	Elizabeth Gallatin	Dead	Non-citizen
2	Calvin C. Colbert	"	Chickasaw Roll	Emma F. Colbert	"	Chickasaw Roll
3	R.L. Watkins	"	Non-citizen	No. 2		

(NOTES)

No. 1 Died Nov. 1st 1899. Proof of Death filed Nov. 3, 19<u>02</u>
No. 1 On Chickasaw Roll as Perry Gallaton.
No. 3 " " " " Eugine Watkins.

Sept. 19/98.

RESIDENCE: Pickens **COUNTY**					**CARD NO.**			
POST OFFICE: Paul Valley, Ind. Ter.					**FIELD NO.**			
	NAME	**RELATIONSHIP TO PERSON FIRST NAMED**	**AGE**	**SEX**	**BLOOD**	**TRIBAL ENROLLMENT**		
						YEAR	**COUNTY**	**PAGE**
1	Kimberlin, William H.		20	M	1/16	1897	Pickens	26
2	" Ira Earnest	Bro	16	M	1/16	1897	"	26
3	" William G.	Father	60	M	I.W.			

TRIBAL ENROLLMENT OF PARENTS

	NAME OF FATHER	YEAR	COUNTY	NAME OF MOTHER	YEAR	COUNTY
1	W.G. Kimberlin		Non-citizen	Lizzie Kimberlin	Dead	Pickens
2	" " "		" "	" "	"	"
3	R.S. "		" "	Eliza "	"	

(NOTES)

Nos. 1 & 2 are children of W.G. Kimberlin on Chickasaw Card #D.62.

No. 2 on Chickasaw Roll as Earnest.

No. 3 first married an Indian woman in 1870 and after her death took out a Chickasaw license and married a white woman.

No. 3 father of children on Chickasaw Card R#19

No. 3 transferred from Chickasaw *(remainder illegible).*

Sept. 16, 1898.

RESIDENCE: Pontotoc **COUNTY**					**CARD NO.**			
POST OFFICE: Waldon, Ind. Ter.					**FIELD NO.**			
	NAME	**RELATIONSHIP TO PERSON FIRST NAMED**	**AGE**	**SEX**	**BLOOD**	**TRIBAL ENROLLMENT**		
						YEAR	**COUNTY**	**PAGE**
1	Brown, William		32	M	3/4	1897	Pontotoc	65
2	" Annie	Wife	29	F	1/2	1897	"	65
3	" Nancy	Dau	12	"	5/8	1897	"	65
4	" Lucy	"	11	"	5/8	1897	"	65
5	" Frances	"	8	"	5/8	1893	"	P.R.#2 47

TRIBAL ENROLLMENT OF PARENTS

	NAME OF FATHER	YEAR	COUNTY	NAME OF MOTHER	YEAR	COUNTY
1	A-cu-id-ley Brown	Dead	Pontotoc	Minerva Brown	Dead	Pontotoc
2	Jackson Frazier	"	Choctaw Roll	Sarah Frazier	"	Chickasaw Roll
3	No. 1			No. 2		
4	No. 1			No. 2		
5	No. 1			No. 2		

(NOTES)

No. 5 On Chickasaw Roll as Francis Brown.

P.O. Newcastle *(date illegible).* Sept. 16/98.

RESIDENCE: Pickens COUNTY						CARD NO.		
POST OFFICE: Rush Springs, Ind. Ter.						FIELD NO.		
	NAME	RELATION-SHIP TO PERSON FIRST NAMED	AGE	SEX	BLOOD	TRIBAL ENROLLMENT		
						YEAR	COUNTY	PAGE
1	Sealy, Albert		28	M	Full	1897	Pontotoc	41
2	" Daily	Wife	16	F	I.W.			

TRIBAL ENROLLMENT OF PARENTS

	NAME OF FATHER	YEAR	COUNTY	NAME OF MOTHER	YEAR	COUNTY
1	Stephen Sealy	Dead	Tishomingo	Pey oh kia	Dead	Pontotoc
2	Geo. W. Tye	"	Non-citizen	Elizabeth Tye	"	Non-citizen

(NOTES)

No. 1 Died march 28th 1901; Proof of Death filed June 14, 1901.
No. 2 Enrolled March 20th 1899. *(No. 2 Dawes' Roll No. I.W. 271)*

P.O. *(Illegible),* I.T. 10/23/1902. Sept. 18/98.

RESIDENCE: Tishomingo COUNTY						CARD NO.		
POST OFFICE: Davis, Ind. Ter.						FIELD NO.		
	NAME	RELATION-SHIP TO PERSON FIRST NAMED	AGE	SEX	BLOOD	TRIBAL ENROLLMENT		
						YEAR	COUNTY	PAGE
1	Walker, Thomas		32	M	I.W.			
2	" Delia	Wife	22	F	1/8	1897	Tishomingo	30
3	" Thomas H.	Son	11mo	M	1/16	1897	"	88

TRIBAL ENROLLMENT OF PARENTS

	NAME OF FATHER	YEAR	COUNTY	NAME OF MOTHER	YEAR	COUNTY
1	Thos. Walker		Non-citizen	Mary Walker	Dead	Non-citizen
2	T.P. Howell		Choctaw Roll	Lizzie Howell	"	Pickens
3	No. 1			No. 2		

(NOTES)

See affidavit of W.D. Matthews and *(the remainder illegible).* *(No. 1 Dawes' Roll No. 811)*

P.O. Wynnewood, *(Date illegible).* Sept. 16/98.

RESIDENCE: Pickens **COUNTY** **CARD NO.**
POST OFFICE: Mansville, Ind. Ter. **FIELD NO.**

	NAME	RELATIONSHIP TO PERSON FIRST NAMED	AGE	SEX	BLOOD	TRIBAL ENROLLMENT YEAR	COUNTY	PAGE
1	Reel, Pearl		24	F	I.W.	1897	Pickens	78
2	" Ida	Dau	7	"	1/2	1897	"	17
3	" Dan	Son	5	M	1/2			

TRIBAL ENROLLMENT OF PARENTS

	NAME OF FATHER	YEAR	COUNTY	NAME OF MOTHER	YEAR	COUNTY
1	Jasper Canifan		Non-citizen	Mattie Canifan		non citizen
2	Daniel Reel	Dead	Pickens	No. 1		
3	" "	"	"	No. 1		

(NOTES)

(All notations illegible)

Feb. 3/98.

RESIDENCE: Pickens **COUNTY** **CARD NO.**
POST OFFICE: Pauls Valley, Ind. Ter. **FIELD NO.**

	NAME	RELATIONSHIP TO PERSON FIRST NAMED	AGE	SEX	BLOOD	TRIBAL ENROLLMENT YEAR	COUNTY	PAGE
1	Hill, John T.		47	M	I.W	1897	Pontotoc	80
2	" Susie E.	Wife	38	F	1/16	1897	"	48
3	" John Edgar	Son	12	M	1/32	1897	"	48
4	" Wm Riley	"	10	M	1/32	1897	"	48
5	" U de	Dau	7	F	1/32	1897	"	48
6	" Harry Vernon	Son	4	M	1/32	1897	"	48
7	" Susie	Dau	2	F	1/32			
8	" Thomas J.	Son	1mo	M	1/32			

TRIBAL ENROLLMENT OF PARENTS

	NAME OF FATHER	YEAR	COUNTY	NAME OF MOTHER	YEAR	COUNTY
1	Jas. A. Hill		Non-citizen	Mary A. Hill		Non-citizen
2	Wm. Walner	Dead	" "	Susan Carter Walner	Dead	Panola
3	No. 1			No. 2		
4	No. 1			No. 2		
5	No. 1			No. 2		
6	No. 1			No. 2		
7	No. 1			No. 2		
8	No. 1			No. 2		

(NOTES)

No. 2 Died September 10th 1901; Proof of Death filed Oct. 20th 1902.
No. 2 On Chickasaw Roll as S.C.
No. 3 " " " " J.E.
No. 4 " " " " W.R.
No. 5 " " " " Will
No. 7 Affidavit of attending physician to be supplied. Received Sept. 16/9?.
No. 8 Enrolled Sept. 24th 1900.

Sept. 10/98.

RESIDENCE: Pickens COUNTY					CARD NO.		
POST OFFICE: Davis, Ind. Ter.					FIELD NO.		
NAME	RELATION-SHIP TO PERSON FIRST NAMED	AGE	SEX	BLOOD	TRIBAL ENROLLMENT		
					YEAR	COUNTY	PAGE
1 Talley, Fannie		16	F	1/2	1897	Pickens	19
2 Talley, Willis N.	Bro	13	M	1/2	1897	"	19
3 " Thomas P.	"	13	"	1/2	1897	"	19
4 " Sudie B.	Sister	11	F	1/2	1897	"	19
5 " William	Father	47	M	I.W.	1893	"	210

TRIBAL ENROLLMENT OF PARENTS

NAME OF FATHER	YEAR	COUNTY	NAME OF MOTHER	YEAR	COUNTY
1 Wm Talley		white man	Agnes Talley	Dead	Pickens
2 " "		" "	" "	"	"
3 " "		" "	" "	"	"
4 " "		" "	" "	"	"
5 Allen D. Talley	Dead	Non citz.	Elizabeth Talley	Dead	Non Citz.

(NOTES)

Sir name of all, Falley on Chickasaw Roll.
Nos. 1 to 4 are children of William Talley on Chickasaw Card #D.52.
No. 1 married to Jesse Hoffman and *(the remainder illegible).*
No. 3 on Chickasaw roll as Tamsey P.
No. 5 transferred from Chickasaw Card #D.52. See decision of August 17, 1904.

P.O. Wynnewood, I.T. Sept. 12/98.

RESIDENCE: Pontotoc COUNTY					CARD NO.		
POST OFFICE: Purcell, Ind. Ter.					FIELD NO.		
NAME	RELATIONSHIP TO PERSON FIRST NAMED	AGE	SEX	BLOOD	TRIBAL ENROLLMENT		
					YEAR	COUNTY	PAGE
1 Casey, Newt F.		24	M	I.W.	1897	Pontotoc	81
2 " Lula	Wife	18	F	3/8	1897	"	63
3 " Charles Calvin	Son	14mo	M	3/16	1897	Pontotoc	85
4 " Effie May	Dau	6mo	F	3/16			

TRIBAL ENROLLMENT OF PARENTS

	NAME OF FATHER	YEAR	COUNTY	NAME OF MOTHER	YEAR	COUNTY
1	Andrew J. Casey		Non-citizen	*(Illegible)* Casey	Dead	Non-citizen
2	Ruder Goins		" "	Susan Goins	1897	Pontotoc
3	No. 1			No. 2		
4	No. 1			No. 2		

(NOTES)

(All notations illegible) Sept. ?/98.

RESIDENCE: Pickens COUNTY					CARD NO.		
POST OFFICE: Pauls Valley, Ind. Ter.					FIELD NO.		
NAME	RELATIONSHIP TO PERSON FIRST NAMED	AGE	SEX	BLOOD	TRIBAL ENROLLMENT		
					YEAR	COUNTY	PAGE
1 Kerr, Perry N.		27	M	I.W.	1897	Panola	83
2 " Irene	Wife	25	F	1/4	1897	Pickens	12
3 " Lockhart B.	Son	2 1/2	M	1/8	1897	"	12
4 " Rita	Fsu	1/2	F	1/8			
5 " Waite Tecumseh	Son	7mo	M	1/8			

TRIBAL ENROLLMENT OF PARENTS

	NAME OF FATHER	YEAR	COUNTY	NAME OF MOTHER	YEAR	COUNTY
1	W.F. Kerr		Non-citizen	Phoebe Kerr		Non-citizen
2	Thos F. Waite I.W.	Dead	Pickens	Catherine Waite	Dead	Pickens
3	No. 1			No. 2		
4	No. 1			No. 2		
5	No. 1			No. 2		

(NOTES)

Nos. 1 & 3 Admitted by Dawes Com. Case No. 65 and No appeal taken.
No. 1 On Chickasaw roll as P. N. Curr (Panola is Doubtful Dist).
No. 2 " " " " Isena Reer,
No. 3 " " " " Jackshort Reer.

No. 4 Affidavit of attending physician to be supplied. Received Sept. 16/98.
No. 5 Enrolled April 3, 1901.
See additional testimony by No. 1 date - Oct, 30th 1902.

Sept. 16/98.

RESIDENCE: Pontotoc **COUNTY** **CARD NO.**
POST OFFICE: Walker, Ind. Ter. **FIELD NO.**

	NAME	RELATIONSHIP TO PERSON FIRST NAMED	AGE	SEX	BLOOD	TRIBAL ENROLLMENT		
						YEAR	COUNTY	PAGE
1	Sealy, Eli		20	M	1/2	1897	Pickens	18
2	" Esau	Bro	17	"	1/2	1897	"	18
3	" Maggie	Sister	15	F	1/2	1897	"	19

TRIBAL ENROLLMENT OF PARENTS

	NAME OF FATHER	YEAR	COUNTY	NAME OF MOTHER	YEAR	COUNTY
1	Dave Sealy	Dead	Chickasaw Roll	Lottie Sealy	Dead	Pontotoc
2	" "	"	" "	" "	"	"
3	" "	"	" "	" "	"	"

(NOTES)

No. 2 On Chickasaw Roll as Esau
No. 3 is now the wife of R.D. Stanton - non-citizen, *(the remainder illegible).*

Sept. 16/98.

RESIDENCE: Pontotoc **COUNTY** **CARD NO.**
POST OFFICE: Purcell, Ind. Ter. **FIELD NO.**

	NAME	RELATIONSHIP TO PERSON FIRST NAMED	AGE	SEX	BLOOD	TRIBAL ENROLLMENT		
						YEAR	COUNTY	PAGE
1	Moore, J.B.		53	M	1/8	1897	Chickasaw residing in Choctaw N. 1st Dist.	71
2	" James E.	Son	19	"	1/8			
3	" Nancy E.	Dau	17	F	1/8			
4	" Mary Jennie	GrDau	1mo	"	1/16			

TRIBAL ENROLLMENT OF PARENTS

	NAME OF FATHER	YEAR	COUNTY	NAME OF MOTHER	YEAR	COUNTY
1	Christopher Moore	Dead	Non-citizen	Catherine Moore	Dead	Chickasaw Roll
2	No. 1			Jennie Moore	"	" "
3	No. 1			" "	"	" "
4	No. 2			Elizabeth Moore		non citizen

(NOTES)

No. 2 is now the Husband of Elizabeth Moore, non-citizen. Evidence of marriage filed Aug. 12th 1902.
No. 2 On Choctaw Roll 1896; at *(Illegible)* County; No. 8856.
No. 3 " " " 1896 " " " " 8857.
Nos. 2 & 3 found on Choctaw Census Record No. 2 Page 3576, transferred to *(remainder illegible)*.
No. 4 Born July 23, 1902; Enrolled Aug. 22, 1902.

Sept. 16/98.

RESIDENCE: Pontotoc COUNTY					CARD NO.		
POST OFFICE: Purcell, Ind. Ter.					FIELD NO.		
NAME	RELATION-SHIP TO PERSON FIRST NAMED	AGE	SEX	BLOOD	TRIBAL ENROLLMENT		
					YEAR	COUNTY	PAGE
1 Randolph, W.C.		57	M	I.W.	1897	Pontotoc	80
2 Hamm, Mattie L.	Dau	14	F	1/32	1897	"	62
3 Hamm, Charles Wesley	G.Son	1mo	M	1/64			

TRIBAL ENROLLMENT OF PARENTS

NAME OF FATHER	YEAR	COUNTY	NAME OF MOTHER	YEAR	COUNTY
1 James M. Randolph	Dead	Non-citizen	Tabitha Randolph		Non-citizen
2 No. 1			Sarah "	Dead	Pickens
3 Charles S. Hamm		Non-citizen	No. 2		

(NOTES)

No. 1 married 1863
No. 1 Admitted as an Intermarried Citizen and
No. 2 as a Citizen by blood by Dawes Commission in 1896 Chickasaw Case No. 121 No appeal.
No. 2 is now the wife of Charles S. Hamm, a non-citizen. Evidence of marriage filed Feb. 20th 1902.
No. 3 Born Jany 28, 1902; Enrolled Feb. 20, 1902.
See testimony of No. 1 taken Oct. 20, 1902.

Sept. 16/98.

RESIDENCE: Pickens COUNTY					CARD NO.		
POST OFFICE: Pauls Valley, Ind. Ter.					FIELD NO.		
NAME	RELATION-SHIP TO PERSON FIRST NAMED	AGE	SEX	BLOOD	TRIBAL ENROLLMENT		
					YEAR	COUNTY	PAGE
1 Stevenson, Malinda		30	F	3/4	1897	Pickens	16
2 " Mary	Dau	3	"	3/8	1897	"	16
3 " John H.	Hus	49	M	I.W.	1897	"	78

	TRIBAL ENROLLMENT OF PARENTS					
	NAME OF FATHER	YEAR	COUNTY	NAME OF MOTHER	YEAR	COUNTY
1	Tecumseh McClure	1897	Pickens	Mary McClure	Dead	Pickens
2	John Stevenson I.W.	1897	"	No. 1		
3	Lees Stevenson		Non-citizen	Lexas A. Gay		Non-citizen

(NOTES)

No. 1 is wife of John F. Stevenson on Chickasaw Card D.266.
No. 1 On Chickasaw Roll as Malinda Stephenson
No. 2 " " " " Mary "

No. 2 transferred from Chickasaw Card D.66 April 10, 1902.
See decision of March 25, 1902.

Sept. 26/98.

RESIDENCE: Pickens ***COUNTY*** ***CARD NO.***
POST OFFICE: Pauls Valley, Ind. Ter. ***FIELD NO.***

	NAME	RELATION-SHIP TO PERSON FIRST NAMED	AGE	SEX	BLOOD	TRIBAL ENROLLMENT		
						YEAR	COUNTY	PAGE
1	Martin, Tom F.		28	M	I.W.	1897	Pontotoc	78
2	" Ida R.	Wife	24	F	1/64	1897	"	17
3	" Tom G.	Son	4	M	1/128	1897	"	17
4	" Ida M.	Dau	3	F	1/128	1897	"	17
5	" Verbeth *(Illegible)*	"	4mo	"	1/128			

	TRIBAL ENROLLMENT OF PARENTS					
	NAME OF FATHER	YEAR	COUNTY	NAME OF MOTHER	YEAR	COUNTY
1	Saml. H. Martin		Non-citizen	Verlinda Martin	Dead	Non-citizen
2	W.G. Kimberlin		" "	Elizabeth Kimberlin	"	Pontotoc
3	No. 1			No. 2		
4	No. 1			No. 2		
5	No. 1			No. 2		

(NOTES)

No. 1 On Chickasaw Roll as Tom Martin. *(No. 1 Dawes' Roll No. 13)*
No. 2 " " " " Ida "
No. 3 " " " " Tom S. "

Sept. 16/98.

RESIDENCE: Pickens COUNTY					CARD NO.		
POST OFFICE: Davis, Ind. Ter.					FIELD NO.		
NAME	RELATION-SHIP TO PERSON FIRST NAMED	AGE	SEX	BLOOD	TRIBAL ENROLLMENT		
					YEAR	COUNTY	PA
1 Howell, Brunetta		11	F	1/4	1897	Tishomingo	2

TRIBAL ENROLLMENT OF PARENTS

	NAME OF FATHER	YEAR	COUNTY	NAME OF MOTHER	YEAR	COUNTY
1	John T. Howell		Choctaw residing in Chickasaw Dist.	Jane Colbert Howell	Dead	Tishomingo

(NOTES)

Father, John T. Howell, On Chickasaw Roll Card No. 175.

Sept. 16, 1898.

RESIDENCE: Pontotoc COUNTY						CARD NO.		
POST OFFICE: Purcell, Ind. Ter.						FIELD NO.		
	NAME	RELATION-SHIP TO PERSON FIRST NAMED	AGE	SEX	BLOOD	TRIBAL ENROLLMENT		
						YEAR	COUNTY	PAGE
1	Williams, Jennie L.		32	F	1/32	1897	Pontotoc	62
2	" Lelia	Dau	14	"	1/64	1897	"	62
3	" Wade	Son	12	M	1/64	1897	"	62
4	" Alonzo	"	10	"	1/64	1897	"	62
5	" Allie	Dau	8	F	1/64	1897	"	62
6	" Sam Jr.	Son	6	M	1/64	1897	"	62
7	" Susan Elizabeth	Dau	2	F	1/64	1897	"	62
8	" David S.	Son	4mo	M	1/64			
9	" Samuel L.	Husb	45	M	I.W.			

TRIBAL ENROLLMENT OF PARENTS

	NAME OF FATHER	YEAR	COUNTY	NAME OF MOTHER	YEAR	COUNTY
1	Phillip Wilson	Dead	Non-citizen	Susan Wilson Mays	1897	Pontotoc
2	Samuel L. Williams		White man	No. 1		
3	" " "		" "	No. 1		
4	" " "		" "	No. 1		
5	" " "		" "	No. 1		
6	" " "		" "	No. 1		
7	" " "		" "	No. 1		
8	" " "		" "	No. 1		
9	Sam Williams	Dead	Non-citizen	Kittie Williams	Dead	non citizen

(NOTES)

All except David S. admitted by Dawes Com. Case No. 100 and No appeal taken.
No. 1 Wife of Samuel L. Williams Chickasaw Doubtful Card No. 32.
No. 4 On Chickasaw Roll as Elonzo.
No. 7 On " " " Bessie.
No. 8 Affidavit of attending physician to be supplied. Received Sept. 24/98.
No. 9 transferred from Chickasaw card #D.32. See decision of March 5, 1904. Mar. 23, 1904.
No. 9 Admitted by Comin 1896 Case No. 100 no appeal. *(No. 9 Dawes' Roll No. I.W. 270)*

Sept. 16/98.

RESIDENCE: Pickens **COUNTY** **CARD NO.**

POST OFFICE: Hennapin, Ind. Ter. **FIELD NO.**

	NAME	RELATIONSHIP TO PERSON FIRST NAMED	AGE	SEX	BLOOD	TRIBAL ENROLLMENT		
						YEAR	COUNTY	PAGE
1	Brittenburg, Don A.		40	M	I.W.	1897	Pickens	77
2	" Maria	Wife	44	F	1/8	1897	"	19
3	" Alice M.	Dau	16	"	1/16	1897	"	19
4	" James B,	Son	15	M	1/16	1897	"	19
5	" Mary Ann	Dau	12	F	1/16	1897	"	19
6	" Norma S.	"	10	"	1/16	1897	"	19

TRIBAL ENROLLMENT OF PARENTS

	NAME OF FATHER	YEAR	COUNTY	NAME OF MOTHER	YEAR	COUNTY
1	Brittenburg	Dead	Non-citizen	Mary Ann Courtney		Non-citizen
2	James N. McLish	"	Chickasaw Roll	Polly Ann McLish	Dead	Chickasaw Roll
3	No. 1			No. 2		
4	No. 1			No. 2		
5	No. 1			No. 2		
6	No. 1			No. 2		

(NOTES)

No. 1 See decision of June 13/04. *(No. 1 Dawes' Roll No. 383)*
No. 2 Died December 9,1900; Evidence of Death filed Oct. 24, 1902. *(No. 2 Dawes' Roll No. 381)*
No. 3 Marriage to Winfield S. Myers and
No. 5 On Chickasaw Roll as Mary
No. 6 " " " " Norma.
Certified copy of divorce proceedings between No. 2 and her former husband filed Feby 28, 1902.

Sept. 16/98.

RESIDENCE: Pickens COUNTY CARD NO.
POST OFFICE: Doyle, Ind. Ter. FIELD NO.

	NAME	RELATION-SHIP TO PERSON FIRST NAMED	AGE	SEX	BLOOD	TRIBAL ENROLLMENT		
						YEAR	COUNTY	PAGE
1	Sadler, Joseph		40	M	I.W.	1897	Pickens	77
2	" Ginsey	Wife	38	F	Full	1897	"	22
3	" Lavina	Dau	13	"	1/2	1897	"	22

TRIBAL ENROLLMENT OF PARENTS

	NAME OF FATHER	YEAR	COUNTY	NAME OF MOTHER	YEAR	COUNTY
1	Wm Sadler	Dead	Non-citizen	Louvina Sadler		Non-citizen
2	Chilly Alexander	1809	Pontotoc	Caroline Alexander	Dead	Chickasaw Roll
3	No. 1			No. 2		

(NOTES)

No. 1 On Roll Saddler *(No. 1 Dawes' Roll No. 12)*
(Remainder of notations illegible)

Sept. 16/98.

RESIDENCE: Pontotoc COUNTY CARD NO.
POST OFFICE: Purcell, Ind. Ter. FIELD NO.

	NAME	RELATION-SHIP TO PERSON FIRST NAMED	AGE	SEX	BLOOD	TRIBAL ENROLLMENT		
						YEAR	COUNTY	PAGE
1	Staton, Elijah		29	M	I.W.	1897	Pontotoc	91
2	" Laura	Wife	20	F	1/16	1897	"	64
3	" Will	Son	2mo	M	1/32			
4	" Ludie David	"	2mo	"	1/32			
5	" Nita May	Dau	3mo	F	1/32			

TRIBAL ENROLLMENT OF PARENTS

	NAME OF FATHER	YEAR	COUNTY	NAME OF MOTHER	YEAR	COUNTY
1	Wm Staton	Dead	Non-citizen	Ruthie Staton	Dead	Non-citizen
2	L.L. Johnston	1897	Pontotoc	Georgia Johnston (I.W.)	1897	Pontotoc
3	No. 1			No. 2		
4	No. 1			No. 2		
5	No. 1			No. 2		

(NOTES)

No. 1 On Chickasaw Roll as Elijah Staten. *(No. 1 Dawes' Roll No. 108)*
No. 2 " " " " Laura Johnston.
No. 4 Enrolled Aug. 22nd 1900.
No. 5 Born March 16th 1902; Enrolled June 20th 1902.
See additional testimony of No 1 taken *(date illegible)*. Sept. 16/98.

RESIDENCE: Pickens COUNTY					CARD NO.			
POST OFFICE: Whitebead, Ind. Ter.					FIELD NO.			
	NAME	RELATIONSHIP TO PERSON FIRST NAMED	AGE	SEX	BLOOD	TRIBAL ENROLLMENT		
						YEAR	COUNTY	PAGE
1	Douglas, Nancy L.		28	F	1/8	1897	Pickens	86

TRIBAL ENROLLMENT OF PARENTS

	NAME OF FATHER	YEAR	COUNTY	NAME OF MOTHER	YEAR	COUNTY
1	Lafayette Love	Dead	Panola	Susan Stacey Baker		White woman

(NOTES)

No. 1 found on 1893 Pay Roll #2 Page 12 No. 379.
Registered under act of Legislature July 31 '97 *(remainder illegible)*
Mother Susan Stacey Baker *(remainder illegible)*

Sept. 15, 1898.

RESIDENCE: Pontotoc COUNTY					CARD NO.			
POST OFFICE: Wynnewood, Ind. Ter.					FIELD NO.			
	NAME	RELATIONSHIP TO PERSON FIRST NAMED	AGE	SEX	BLOOD	TRIBAL ENROLLMENT		
						YEAR	COUNTY	PAGE
1	Blevins, Lemuel		24	M	1/4	1897	Pontotoc	61
2	" Susie	Sister	22	F	1/4	1897	"	61
3	" Wirtie Clyde	Son	5mo	M	1/8			
4	" Robert Earl	"	4mo	"	1/8			
5	" Susie P.	Dau	3mo	F	1/8			

TRIBAL ENROLLMENT OF PARENTS

	NAME OF FATHER	YEAR	COUNTY	NAME OF MOTHER	YEAR	COUNTY
1	Toad Blevins	Dead	Non-citizen	Josephine Stewart	1897	Pontotoc
2	" "	"	" "	" "	"	"
3	No. 1			Willie Blevins		Non-citizen
4	No. 1			" "		" "
5	No. 1			" "		" "

(NOTES)

(All notations illegible)

Sept. 15/98.

RESIDENCE: Pickens COUNTY					CARD NO.			
POST OFFICE: Pauls Valley, Ind. Ter.					FIELD NO.			
	NAME	RELATIONSHIP TO PERSON FIRST NAMED	AGE	SEX	BLOOD	TRIBAL ENROLLMENT		
						YEAR	COUNTY	PAGE
1	Clayton, W.S.		35	M	I.W.	1897	Pickens	78

2	" Tamsey A.	Wife	29	F	1/4	1897	"	15
3	" Indianola D.	Dau	4	"	1/8	1897	"	15
4	" Lockie S.	"	2	"	1/8	1897	"	15
5	" William Herbert	Son	8mo	M	1/8			
6	" Paul Sharpe	"	2mo	"	1/8			

TRIBAL ENROLLMENT OF PARENTS

	NAME OF FATHER	YEAR	COUNTY	NAME OF MOTHER	YEAR	COUNTY
1	Benj. F. Clayton		Non-citizen	Rebecca Clayton		Non-citizen
2	James Arnold		" "	Sippie Hull	1897	Pickens
3	No. 1			No. 2		
4	No. 1			No. 2		
5	No. 1			No. 2		
6	No. 1			No. 2		

(NOTES)

No. 2 On Chickasaw Roll as Tamsey Clayton.
No. 3 " " " " Indola "
No. 6 Enrolled Dec. 16/99.
Nos. 1 & 2 Certificate of Marriage filed April *(illegible)*.

Sept. 15/98.

RESIDENCE: Pontotoc COUNTY CARD NO.
POST OFFICE: Waldon, Ind. Ter. FIELD NO.

	NAME	RELATIONSHIP TO PERSON FIRST NAMED	AGE	SEX	BLOOD	TRIBAL ENROLLMENT YEAR	COUNTY	PAGE
1	Waldon, Tom		52	M	I.W.	1897	Pontotoc	81
2	" Sophia	Wife	52	F	Full	1897	"	64
3	" Jimmie	Son	16	M	1/2	1897	"	64
4	" Lisa Maria	Dau	11	F	1/2	1897	"	64
5	" Bill Byrd	Son	9	M	1/2	1897	"	64
6	Brown, Benson	Nephew	18	M	1/2	1897	Pickens	18
7	James, George	Ward	11	"	Full	1897	Pontotoc	65
8	Brown, Minerva Lee	Dau of No. 6	6mo	F	1/4			

TRIBAL ENROLLMENT OF PARENTS

	NAME OF FATHER	YEAR	COUNTY	NAME OF MOTHER	YEAR	COUNTY
1	Joe Waldon	Dead	Non-citizen	Maria Waldon	Dead	Non-citizen
2	A-co-ead-le Brown	"	Chickasaw Roll	Liza Brown		Chickasaw Roll
3	No. 1			No. 2		
4	No. 1			No. 2		
5	No. 1			No. 2		

6	A-co-ead-le Brown	"	Chickasaw Roll	Minerva Brown	Dead	Non-citizen
7	Martin James	"	" "	Margaret McLane	1897	Pontotoc
8	No. 6			Cleo Brown		Non-citizen

(NOTES)

No. 1 On Chickasaw Roll as Thomas Waldon
No. 3 " " " " Jennie
No. 4 " " " " L.M.
No. 5 " " " " Byrd
No. 6 is now the husband of Cleo Brown, non-citizen. Evidence of marriage filed Sept. 11, 1902.
No. 7 Also on Chickasaw Roll Pickens County Page 18 as George James.
No. 8 Born May 3, 1902; Enrolled Sept. 11, 1902.
See testimony of No. 1 taken Oct. 15, 1902.

PO No. 6, Newcastle, I.T. 10/15/02. Sept. 15/98.

RESIDENCE: Pickens **COUNTY** **CARD NO.**
POST OFFICE: Pauls Valley, Ind. Ter. **FIELD NO.**

	NAME	RELATION-SHIP TO PERSON FIRST NAMED	AGE	SEX	BLOOD	TRIBAL ENROLLMENT		
						YEAR	COUNTY	PAGE
1	Love, G.W.		50	M	1/4	1897	Pickens	23
2	" Melvina	Wife	51	F	I.W.	1897	"	79
3	" Lauta Overton	Son	16	M	1/8	1897	"	24
4	" Annie	Dau	13	F	1/8	1897	"	24
5	" George	Son	9	M	1/8	1897	"	24

TRIBAL ENROLLMENT OF PARENTS

	NAME OF FATHER	YEAR	COUNTY	NAME OF MOTHER	YEAR	COUNTY
1	Wm Love	Dead	Panola	Cary Ann Love	Dead	Non-citizen
2	Lindsay	"	Non-citizen	*(Name Illegible)*	"	" "
3	No. 1			No. 2		
4	No. 1			No. 2		
5	No. 1			No. 2		

(NOTES)

Certified copy of marriage certificate to be supplied. Received Sept. 21/98.
No. 1 Died Jany 13, 1902. Proof of Death filed Oct. 23, 1902. *(No. 2 Dawes' Roll No. 289)*
No. 3 On Chickasaw Roll as Lawt.
No. 5 " " " " Georgia
See additional testimony of No. 2, taken Oct. 22, 1902.

P.O. Whitebead 10/22/02. Sept. 15, 1898.

RESIDENCE: Pickens COUNTY					CARD NO.		
POST OFFICE: Whitebead, Ind. Ter.					FIELD NO.		
NAME	RELATION-SHIP TO PERSON FIRST NAMED	AGE	SEX	BLOOD	TRIBAL ENROLLMENT		
					YEAR	COUNTY	PAGE
1 Love, Sam		23	M	1/16	1897	Pickens	24
2 " Clarence	Son	7mos	"	1/32			
3 " Ruby Jewel	Dau	1mo	F	1/32			
4 " Lizzie Melvina	"	1mo	"	1/32			

TRIBAL ENROLLMENT OF PARENTS

	NAME OF FATHER	YEAR	COUNTY	NAME OF MOTHER	YEAR	COUNTY
1	George Love	1897	Pickens	Melvina Love (I.W.)	1897	Pickens
2	No. 1			Nona Love		Non-citizen
3	No. 1			" "		" "
4	No. 1			" "		" "

(NOTES)

Wife of Sam Love - Nona Love a U.S. Citizen
No. 2 Affidavit of attending midwife to be furnished. Received Sept. 16, 1898.
No. 2 Died March 22, 1901; Proof of Death filed Oct. 24, 1902.
No. 3 Enrolled Oct. 16th 1900
No. 4 Born March 14th 1902; Enrolled May 3rd 1902.

P.O. Antioch, 10/20/02. Sept. 18/98.

RESIDENCE: Pontotoc COUNTY					CARD NO.		
POST OFFICE: Wynnewood, Ind. Ter.					FIELD NO.		
NAME	RELATION-SHIP TO PERSON FIRST NAMED	AGE	SEX	BLOOD	TRIBAL ENROLLMENT		
					YEAR	COUNTY	PAGE
1 Walner, Robert		19	M	1/16	1897	Pontotoc	60
2 " John	Bro	17	"	1/16	1897	"	60
3 " Jim	"	14	"	1/16	1897	"	60
4 " Ebb.	"	12	"	1/16	1897	"	60
5 " Frank	"	8	"	1/16	1897	"	60

TRIBAL ENROLLMENT OF PARENTS

	NAME OF FATHER	YEAR	COUNTY	NAME OF MOTHER	YEAR	COUNTY
1	Wm Walner	Dead	Pontotoc	Lena Walner	Dead	Non-citizen
2	" "	"	"	" "	"	" "
3	" "	"	"	" "	"	" "
4	" "	"	"	" "	"	" "

5	" "	"	"	" "		"	" "	

(NOTES)

No. 4 On Chickasaw Roll as Ed Walner.

Sept. 15, 1898.

RESIDENCE: Pickens *COUNTY* *CARD NO.*
POST OFFICE: Pauls Valley, Ind. Ter. *FIELD NO.*

	NAME	RELATION-SHIP TO PERSON FIRST NAMED	AGE	SEX	BLOOD	TRIBAL ENROLLMENT		
						YEAR	COUNTY	PAGE
1	Hewitt, Thomas		20	M	1/8	1897	Pickens	14
2	" Stella	Sister	17	F	1/8	1897	"	14
3	" Julius	Bro	16	M	1/8	1897	"	14
4	" Nora	Sister	13	F	1/8	1897	"	14
5	" Sam	Bro	11	M	1/8	1897	"	14

TRIBAL ENROLLMENT OF PARENTS

	NAME OF FATHER	YEAR	COUNTY	NAME OF MOTHER	YEAR	COUNTY
1	Saml. Hewitt	Dead	Non-citizen	Louvina Hewitt	Dead	Pickens
2	" "	"	" "	" "	"	"
3	" "	"	" "	" "	"	"
4	" "	"	" "	" "	"	"
5	" "	"	" "	" "	"	"

(NOTES)

No. 1 On Chickasaw Roll as Tom.
No. 2 is now the Wife of Geo B. Rennie on Chickasaw Card 456; Evidence of marriage filed Oct. 29th 1902.
No. 3 On Chickasaw Roll as Jude.
No. 4 " " " " Maude.
No. 4 Died March 10, 1900; Proof of Death filed Oct. 23rd 1902.

Sept. 15, 1898

RESIDENCE: Chickasaw Nation *COUNTY* *CARD NO.*
POST OFFICE: Pauls Valley, Ind. Ter. *FIELD NO.*

	NAME	RELATION-SHIP TO PERSON FIRST NAMED	AGE	SEX	BLOOD	TRIBAL ENROLLMENT		
						YEAR	COUNTY	PAGE
1	Elliott, John Cyrus		29	M	I.W.			
2	" Hannah	Wife	36	F	1/4	1897	Pickens	14
3	Burks, Royden	StepSon	16	M	1/8	1897	"	14
4	" William	" "	13	"	1/8	1897	"	14
5	" Vera	" Dau	11	F	1/8	1897	"	14

6	" Rowena	" "	9	"	1/8	1897	"	14
7	" Johnie Wenona	" "	7	"	1/8	1897	"	14
8	Elliott, Olivia	Dau	3mo	"	1/8			

TRIBAL ENROLLMENT OF PARENTS

	NAME OF FATHER	YEAR	COUNTY	NAME OF MOTHER	YEAR	COUNTY
1	J.C. Elliott		Non-citizen	Martha Elliott	Dead	Non-citizen
2	Thos. Waite	Dead	" "	Catherine Waite	"	Chickasaw Roll
3	John Burks	"	" "	No. 2		
4	" "	"	" "	No. 2		
5	" "	"	" "	No. 2		
6	" "	"	" "	No. 2		
7	" "	"	" "	No. 2		
8	No. 1			No. 2		

(NOTES)

No. 2 On Chickasaw Roll as Hanna Burks
No. 3 " " " " Roy "
No. 5 " " " " Verra "
No. 6 " " " " Roma "
No. 7 " " " " Johnnie "
No. 8 Enrolled June 25th 1900

(No. 1 Dawes' Roll No. 107)

No. 1 Enrolled March 20/99.
All others " Sept. 15, 1898.

RESIDENCE: Pickens ***COUNTY***					***CARD NO.***			
POST OFFICE: Pauls Valley, Ind. Ter.					***FIELD NO.***			
	NAME	RELATION-SHIP TO PERSON FIRST NAMED	AGE	SEX	BLOOD	TRIBAL ENROLLMENT		
						YEAR	COUNTY	PAGE
1	Rennie, Catherine Rooks		19	F	3/8	1897	Pickens	26
2	" George Burney	Bro	17	M	3/8	1897	"	26

TRIBAL ENROLLMENT OF PARENTS

	NAME OF FATHER	YEAR	COUNTY	NAME OF MOTHER	YEAR	COUNTY
1	James Rennie		Non-citizen	Georgia D. Spain	1897	Pickens
2	" "		" "	" " "	1897	"

(NOTES)

No. 1 On Chickasaw Roll as R.R.
No. 2 " " " " G.B.
James Rennie, father of Nos 1 & 2, on Chickasaw Card #1575.
No. 2 is now the husband of Stella He *(remainder illegible)* on Chickasaw Card 458. Oct. 29, 1902.

Sept. 15, 1898.

RESIDENCE: Pickens COUNTY					CARD NO.		
POST OFFICE: Pauls Valley, Ind. Ter.					FIELD NO.		
NAME	RELATIONSHIP TO PERSON FIRST NAMED	AGE	SEX	BLOOD	TRIBAL ENROLLMENT		
					YEAR	COUNTY	PAGE
1 Paul, Jennie		33	F	I.W.	1897	Pickens	78

TRIBAL ENROLLMENT OF PARENTS

NAME OF FATHER	YEAR	COUNTY	NAME OF MOTHER	YEAR	COUNTY
1 Danl. Tolbert		Non-citizen	Laura Tolbert		Non-citizen

(NOTES)

Certified copy of divorce proceedings *(remainder illegible)* *(No. 1 Dawes' Roll No. 162)*

Sept. 15, 1898.

RESIDENCE: Pontotoc COUNTY					CARD NO.		
POST OFFICE: Purcell, Ind. Ter.					FIELD NO.		
NAME	RELATIONSHIP TO PERSON FIRST NAMED	AGE	SEX	BLOOD	TRIBAL ENROLLMENT		
					YEAR	COUNTY	PAGE
1 Criner, Joe W.		27	M	1/16	1897	Pontotoc	63
2 " Lizzie	Wife	26	F	I.W.			

TRIBAL ENROLLMENT OF PARENTS

NAME OF FATHER	YEAR	COUNTY	NAME OF MOTHER	YEAR	COUNTY
1 George Criner	Dead	Non-citizen	Matilda Criner	Dead	Pickens
2 John Harmon		" "	Laura Harmon		Non-citizen

(NOTES)

See Chickasaw Card #D.270 *(No. 2 Dawes' Roll No. 11)*
No. 2 Transferred from Chickasaw card #D.270 March 29, 1903. See decision of March 13, 1903.

P.O. Ireton, I.T. Sept. 15, 1898.

RESIDENCE: Pickens COUNTY					CARD NO.		
POST OFFICE: Burt, Ind. Ter.					FIELD NO.		
NAME	RELATIONSHIP TO PERSON FIRST NAMED	AGE	SEX	BLOOD	TRIBAL ENROLLMENT		
					YEAR	COUNTY	PAGE
1 Hogue, Henry		19	M	1/4	1897	Pickens	23
2 " Beulah	Wife	19	F	I.W.			

TRIBAL ENROLLMENT OF PARENTS						
	NAME OF FATHER	YEAR	COUNTY	NAME OF MOTHER	YEAR	COUNTY
1	Henry Hogue	Dead	Non-citizen	Kitty Howard	1897	Pickens
2	Henry Buchanan		" "	Lonnie Daors		non citz.

(NOTES)

No. 1 is the Husband of Beulah Hogue on Chickasaw Card #D.379 Oct. 22, 1902.
No. 2 transferred from Chickasaw Card #D.379. *(No. 2 Dawes' Roll No. 182)*
See decision of *(date illegible)*

P.O. Bailey, I.T.
P.O. Kitts I.T. 3/7/03 Sept. 15, 1898.

RESIDENCE: Pickens COUNTY CARD NO.
POST OFFICE: Burt, Ind. Ter. FIELD NO.

	NAME	RELATION-SHIP TO PERSON FIRST NAMED	AGE	SEX	BLOOD	TRIBAL ENROLLMENT YEAR	COUNTY	PAGE
1	Howard, Kitty		49	F	1/2	1897	Pickens	23

TRIBAL ENROLLMENT OF PARENTS						
	NAME OF FATHER	YEAR	COUNTY	NAME OF MOTHER	YEAR	COUNTY
1	Samuel Allen (I.W.)	Dead	Chickasaw Roll	Nancy Allen	Dead	Chickasaw Roll

(NOTES)

No. 1 is wife of Frank Howard on Chickasaw Card #D.274.
On Chickasaw Roll as C.C. Jolly.

P.O. Bailey, I.T. Sept. 15, 1898.

RESIDENCE: Pontotoc COUNTY CARD NO.
POST OFFICE: Purcell, Ind. Ter. FIELD NO.

	NAME	RELATION-SHIP TO PERSON FIRST NAMED	AGE	SEX	BLOOD	TRIBAL ENROLLMENT YEAR	COUNTY	PAGE
1	Baker, Mary H.		48	F	1/2	1897	Tishomingo	32
2	" H.F.	Hus.	62	M	I.W.			

TRIBAL ENROLLMENT OF PARENTS						
	NAME OF FATHER	YEAR	COUNTY	NAME OF MOTHER	YEAR	COUNTY
1	Richard T. Cabb	Dead	Non-citizen	She-ma-ho-ga	Dead	Chickasaw Roll
2	Saml. D. Baker	"	" "	Angeline Baker	"	Non Citizen

(NOTES)

No. 2 See Decision of June 14/04 *(No. 2 Dawes' Roll No. 385)*
Wife of H.T. Baker, Chickasaw Doubtful No. D.28

No. 2 transferred from Chickasaw Card #D-38 July 2-'04. See Decisin of June 16 '04.

Sept. 15, 1898.

RESIDENCE: Pontotoc **COUNTY**						**CARD NO.**		
POST OFFICE: Chickasha, Ind. Ter.						**FIELD NO.**		
	NAME	**RELATIONSHIP TO PERSON FIRST NAMED**	**AGE**	**SEX**	**BLOOD**	**TRIBAL ENROLLMENT**		
						YEAR	**COUNTY**	**PAGE**
1	Lee, Kate		12	F	3/16	1893	Pontotoc	P.R.#2 P.141
2	" Sam	Bro	7	M	3/16	1893	"	PR#2 P141

TRIBAL ENROLLMENT OF PARENTS

	NAME OF FATHER	**YEAR**	**COUNTY**	**NAME OF MOTHER**	**YEAR**	**COUNTY**
1	Sam S. Lee		White man	Biddie Lee	Dead	Pontotoc
2	" " "		" "	" "	"	"

(NOTES)

No. 1 On 1896 Chickasaw Roll Page 95 Pontotoc County
No. 2 " " " " " " " "
Father, Sam S. Lee, On Chickasaw Card No. D.27.
Nos. 1 & 2 On 1893, Chickasaw Pay Roll No. *(illegible)*.

Sept. *(illegible)*

RESIDENCE: Pontotoc **COUNTY**						**CARD NO.**		
POST OFFICE: Purcell, Ind. Ter.						**FIELD NO.**		
	NAME	**RELATIONSHIP TO PERSON FIRST NAMED**	**AGE**	**SEX**	**BLOOD**	**TRIBAL ENROLLMENT**		
						YEAR	**COUNTY**	**PAGE**
1	Shannon, J.R.		33	M	I.W.	1897	Pontotoc	80
2	" Nora	Wife	30	F	1/16	1897	"	60

TRIBAL ENROLLMENT OF PARENTS

	NAME OF FATHER	**YEAR**	**COUNTY**	**NAME OF MOTHER**	**YEAR**	**COUNTY**
1	Jim Shannon	Dead	Non citizen	Sarah Shannon		Non citizen
2	George Criner	"	" "	Matilda Criner	Dead	Pickens

(NOTES)

James R. Shannon and Nora Shannon admitted by Dawes Com. Card No. 8 and No Appeal taken
No. 2 On Chickasaw Roll as Nora Shannon *(No. 1 Dawes' Roll No. 268)*

Sept. 15, 1898

RESIDENCE: Pontotoc **COUNTY**					**CARD NO.**			
POST OFFICE: Purcell, Ind. Ter.					**FIELD NO.**			

	NAME	RELATIONSHIP TO PERSON FIRST NAMED	AGE	SEX	BLOOD	TRIBAL ENROLLMENT YEAR	COUNTY	PAGE
1	Love, R.J.		46	M	I.W.	1897	Pontotoc	81
2	" Sallie G.	Wife	37	F	1/16	1897	"	63
3	" Buck	Son	17	M	1/32	1897	"	63
4	" Frank C.	"	15	"	1/32	1897	"	63
5	" Robert B.	"	13	"	1/32	1897	"	63
6	" Grace E.	Dau	11	F	1/32	1897	"	63
7	" Pearl G.	"	9	"	1/32	1897	"	63
8	" George C.	Son	7	M	1/32	1897	"	63
9	" Joe	"	4	"	1/32	1897	"	63
10	" Nona E.	Dau	2	F	1/32	1897	"	63
11	" R.F. Jr.	Son	2mo	M	1/32			
12	" Hattie Simpson	Wife of No. 3	17	F	I.W.			

TRIBAL ENROLLMENT OF PARENTS

	NAME OF FATHER	YEAR	COUNTY	NAME OF MOTHER	YEAR	COUNTY
1	William Love	Dead	Non citizen	Elizabeth Love	Dead	Non Citizen
2	George Criner	"	" "	Matilda Criner	"	Pickens
3	No. 1			No. 2		
4	No. 1			No. 2		
5	No. 1			No. 2		
6	No. 1			No. 2		
7	No. 1			No. 2		
8	No. 1			No. 2		
9	No. 1			No. 2		
10	No. 1			No. 2		
11	No. 1			No. 2		
12	Johnm W. Simpson			Nannie E. Simpson		

(NOTES)

No. 1 Died January 19, 1899. Proof of Death filed Oct. 25, 1902.
No. 10 Died April 11th 1899. Proof of Death filed Nov. 25, 1902.
No. 2 On Chickasaw Roll as F.G.
No. 4 " " " " Frank
No. 5 " " " " R.B.
No. 6 " " " " G.M.
No. 8 " " " " G.C.
No. 11 Affidavit of attending physician to be furnished. Rec'd. Sept 16/98.

Affidavit of John B. Criner, as to issuance of marriage license to be furnished. Received Sept. 21/98.
No. 12 transferred from Chickasaw Card #D.580 Nov. 22-1906. See decision of Nov. 6, 1906.

Sept. 16/98.

RESIDENCE: Pontotoc ***COUNTY*** ***CARD NO.***
POST OFFICE: McGee, Ind. Ter. ***FIELD NO.***

	NAME	RELATION-SHIP TO PERSON FIRST NAMED	AGE	SEX	BLOOD	TRIBAL ENROLLMENT		
						YEAR	COUNTY	PAGE
1	Cook, William V.		40	M	I.W.	1897	Pontotoc	80
2	" Mary	Wife	30	F	1/8	1897	"	47
3	" Charles	Son	12	M	1/16	1897	"	47
4	" Stella	Dau	10	F	1/16	1897	"	47
5	" Levera	"	7	"	1/16	1897	"	47
6	" Cabey Celess	"	4	"	1/16	1897	"	47
7	" William Nye	Son	2	M	1/16	1897	"	47
8	" Cleo	Dau	5mo	F	1/16			
9	~~Chisholm, Cora~~	~~Sister in Law~~	~~25~~	~~"~~	~~1/8~~	~~1897~~	~~Pontotoc~~	~~47~~

TRIBAL ENROLLMENT OF PARENTS

	NAME OF FATHER	YEAR	COUNTY	NAME OF MOTHER	YEAR	COUNTY
1	Ananias Cook	Dead	Non-Citizen	Mary Cook	Dead	Non citizen
2	Wm Chisholm	"	Creek "	Julia McLish	"	Chickasaw Roll
3	No. 1			No. 2		
4	No. 1			No. 2		
5	No. 1			No. 2		
6	No. 1			No. 2		
7	No. 1			No. 2		
8	No. 1			No. 2		
9	~~Wm Chisholm~~	~~Dead~~	~~Creek Citizen~~	~~Julia McLish~~	~~Dead~~	~~Chickasaw Roll~~

(NOTES)

No. 1 On Chickasaw Roll as W.V. Cook. *(No. 1 Dawes' Roll No. 106)*
No. 6 " " " " C.C. "
No. 6 Died Dec. 9/99; Proof of Death filed Oct. 25, 1902.

Sept. 15/98.

Residence: Pontotoc ***County*** ***Card No.***
Post Office: McGee, Ind. Ter. ***Field No.***

	Name	Relation-ship to Person First Named	Age	Sex	Blood	Tribal Enrollment		
						Year	County	Page
1	Asbury, Allen S.		31	M	I.W.	1897	Pontotoc	80
2	" Alice	Wife	28	F	1/8	1897	"	44
3	" Myrtle	Dau	7	"	1/16	1897	"	44
4	" Wm Douglas	Son	5	M	1/16	1897	"	44
5	" Nellie	Dau	3	F	1/16	1897	"	44
6	" Edgar Allen	Son	2	M	1/16			
7	" Eula	Dau	2wks	F	1/16			
8	" Rual O.	Son	1mo	M	1/16			

Tribal Enrollment of Parents

	Name of Father	Year	County	Name of Mother	Year	County
1	David F. Asbury	Dead	Non citizen	Mary Asbury	Dead	Non citizen
2	Wm Chisholm	"	Creek Citizen	Julia McLish		
3	No. 1			No. 2		
4	No. 1			No. 2		
5	No. 1			No. 2		
6	No. 1			No. 2		
7	No. 1			No. 2		
8	No. 1			No. 2		

(Notes)

No. 1 On Chickasaw Roll as A.S. Asberry
No. 4 " " " " Douglas "
No. 5 " " " " Sallie "
No. 8 Born April 20, 1902; Enrolled May 24, 1902.

Sept. 15, 1898.

Residence: Pickens ***County*** ***Card No.***
Post Office: Pauls Valley, Ind. Ter. ***Field No.***

	Name	Relation-ship to Person First Named	Age	Sex	Blood	Tribal Enrollment		
						Year	County	Page
1	Paul, Smith W.		23	M	1/4	1897	Pickens	16
2	" Wm H.	Bro	22	"	1/4	1897	"	16

Tribal Enrollment of Parents

	Name of Father	Year	County	Name of Mother	Year	County
1	Sam Paul	Dead	Pickens	Sarah J. Paul (I.W.)	1897	Pickens

2	" "	"	"	" " "	1897	"	

(NOTES)

No. 1 On Chickasaw Roll as S.W. Paul. *(No. 1 Dawes' Roll No. 4090)*
No. 1 is also called "Buck Paul".

RESIDENCE: Pickens **COUNTY** **CARD NO.**
POST OFFICE: Whitebead, Ind. Ter. **FIELD NO.**

	NAME	RELATION-SHIP TO PERSON FIRST NAMED	AGE	SEX	BLOOD	TRIBAL ENROLLMENT		
						YEAR	COUNTY	PAGE
1	Spain, Georgia D.		39	F	1/2	1897	Pickens	23
2	" Mary E.	Dau	12	"	1/4	1897	"	23
3	" Jessie	"	10	"	1/4	1897	"	23
4	" McKnightie	"	7	"	1/4	1897	"	23
5	" Georgia	"	5	"	1/4	1897	"	23
6	" Sallie P.	"	15mo	"	1/4	~~1897~~	~~"~~	~~86~~

TRIBAL ENROLLMENT OF PARENTS

	NAME OF FATHER	YEAR	COUNTY	NAME OF MOTHER	YEAR	COUNTY
1	Simon J. James		Chickasaw Roll	Elsie Gaines James	Dead	Chickasaw Roll
2	David M. Spain		Choctaw residing in Chickasaw Dist.	No. 1		
3	" " "		" "	No. 1		
4	" " "		" "	No. 1		
5	" " "		" "	No. 1		
6	" " "		" "	No. 1		

(NOTES)

No. 1 Died April 30, 1899; See testimony of David M. Spain.
No. 1 On Chickasaw Roll as Georgia D. Spaine; Wife of David M. Spain Choctaw Card #144.
No. 2 " " " " Mary "
No. 3 " " " " Jessie "
No. 4 " " " " McKnight "
No. 5 " " " " Georgia "
No. 6 registered under Act of Legislature July 31, 1897 Chickasaw Roll Page *(illegible)*.
No. 6 Proof of Birth received and filed Oct. 11, 1902. *(No. 6 Dawes' Roll No. 4094)*

Sept. 14, 1898.

RESIDENCE: Pickens COUNTY					CARD NO.			
POST OFFICE: Pauls Valley, Ind. Ter.					FIELD NO.			
	NAME	RELATION-SHIP TO PERSON FIRST NAMED	AGE	SEX	BLOOD	TRIBAL ENROLLMENT		
						YEAR	COUNTY	PAGE
1	Burks, William D.		72	M	I.W.	1897	Pickens	78
2	" Susan D.	Wife	62	F	1/2	1897	"	14

TRIBAL ENROLLMENT OF PARENTS

	NAME OF FATHER	YEAR	COUNTY	NAME OF MOTHER	YEAR	COUNTY
1	Benj. G. Burks	Dead	Non citizen	Susan Burks	Dead	Non citizen
2	David E. Burney	"	Chickasaw Roll	Lucy Burney	"	Chickasaw Roll

(NOTES)

No. 1 On Chickasaw Roll as Dr. Burks.
No. 2 " " " " Susan "
Died July 10th 1902; Proof of Death filed Oct. 24, 1902.

Sept. 14, 1898.

RESIDENCE: Pontotoc COUNTY					CARD NO.			
POST OFFICE: Purcell, Ind. Ter.					FIELD NO.			
	NAME	RELATION-SHIP TO PERSON FIRST NAMED	AGE	SEX	BLOOD	TRIBAL ENROLLMENT		
						YEAR	COUNTY	PAGE
1	Wilson, Joseph B.		39	M	1/32	1897	Pontotoc	63
2	" Emma B.	Wife	37	F	I.W.	1897	"	81
3	" Sue Ellen	Dau	14	"	1/64	1897	"	63
4	" Claude Allen	Son	11	M	1/64	1897	"	63

TRIBAL ENROLLMENT OF PARENTS

	NAME OF FATHER	YEAR	COUNTY	NAME OF MOTHER	YEAR	COUNTY
1	Philip Wilson	Dead	Non citizen	Susan E. Wilson Mrs. Mays	1897	Pontotoc
2	C.R. Worley	"	" "	Martha Worley		Non citizen
3	No. 1			No. 2		
4	No. 1			No. 2		

(NOTES)

Nos. 2, 3 & 4 Admitted by Dawes Com. on Nov. 11, 1896, Chickasaw Card No. 133.
No. 1 On Chickasaw Roll as J.B. Wilson. *(No. 2 Dawes' Roll No. 266)*
No. 3 " " " " S.E. " *(No. 3 Dawes' Roll No. 1092)*
No. 4 " " " " C.A. " *(No. 4 Dawes' Roll No. 1093)*
See additional testimony of No. 1 taken Oct. 20, 1902.

Sept. 14, 1898.

RESIDENCE: Pontotoc COUNTY					CARD NO.		
POST OFFICE: Purcell, Ind. Ter.					FIELD NO.		
NAME	RELATION-SHIP TO PERSON FIRST NAMED	AGE	SEX	BLOOD	TRIBAL ENROLLMENT		
					YEAR	COUNTY	PAGE
1 Brady, Mike N.		71	M	I.W.	1897	Pontotoc	81
2 " Caroline	Wife	64	F	1/16	1897	"	63

TRIBAL ENROLLMENT OF PARENTS

	NAME OF FATHER	YEAR	COUNTY	NAME OF MOTHER	YEAR	COUNTY
1	John Brady	Dead	Non citizen	Bridget Brady	Dead	Non citizen
2	Christopher Moore	"	" "	Catherine Moore	"	Chickasaw Roll

(NOTES)

No. 1 See decision of June 13 '04.
No. 1 On Chickasaw Roll as M.N. Brady.
See additional testimony of No. 1 taken Oct. 16, 1902.

Sept. 14/98.

RESIDENCE: Pontotoc COUNTY					CARD NO.		
POST OFFICE: Purcell, Ind. Ter.					FIELD NO.		
NAME	RELATION-SHIP TO PERSON FIRST NAMED	AGE	SEX	BLOOD	TRIBAL ENROLLMENT		
					YEAR	COUNTY	PAGE
1 Bell, J.E.		25	M	I.W.			
2 " Alta Pearl	Wife	17	F	1/32	1897	Pontotoc	63
3 " Joe Edgar	Son	1mo	M	1/64			
4 " Charles D.	"	2wk	"	1/64			
5 " James Smith	"	2mo	"	1/64			

TRIBAL ENROLLMENT OF PARENTS

	NAME OF FATHER	YEAR	COUNTY	NAME OF MOTHER	YEAR	COUNTY
1	J.S. Bell		Non citizen	Anna Bell		Non citizen
2	J.B. Wilson	1897	Pontotoc	Emma B. Wilson (I.W.)	1897	Pontotoc
3	No. 1			No. 2		
4	No. 1			No. 2		
5	No. 1			No. 2		

(NOTES)

No. 2 Admitted by Dawes Com. on Nov. 11, 1896 Page No. 133 Chickasaw
No. 2 On Chickasaw Roll as A.T. Wilson
No. 4 Enrolled Sept. 10th 1900
No. 4 Died Nov. 18, 1900. Proof of Death filed Oct. 12, 1902.
No. 5 Born March 13th 1902; Enrolled May 10th 1902.
No. 3 Enrolled April 9, 1899

See additional testimony of No. 1 taken *(date illegible)*.

P.O. Story, Ind. Ter. Sept. 14, 1898.

RESIDENCE: Pickens ***COUNTY***						***CARD NO.***			
POST OFFICE: Rush Springs, Ind. Ter.						***FIELD NO.***			
	NAME	**RELATION-SHIP TO PERSON FIRST NAMED**	**AGE**	**SEX**	**BLOOD**	**TRIBAL ENROLLMENT**		
						YEAR	**COUNTY**	**PAGE**
1	Fryrear, S. Burl		37	M	I.W.	1897	Pontotoc	81
2	" Roda	Wife	27	F	3/4	1897	"	64
3	" Ema	Dau	9	M[sic]	3/8	1897	"	64
4	" Annie May	"	6	F	3/8	1897	"	64
5	" Emet	Son	4	M	3/8	1897	"	64
6	" Frank	"	2	M	3/8			
7	Pettenridge, Charley	StepSon	12	"	3/8	1897	Pontotoc	64
8	Fryrear, Robert O.	Son	2mo	"	3/8			

TRIBAL ENROLLMENT OF PARENTS

	NAME OF FATHER	**YEAR**	**COUNTY**	**NAME OF MOTHER**	**YEAR**	**COUNTY**
1	Frank Fryrear	Dead	Non citizen	Elizabeth Fryrear	Dead	Non citizen
2	Quidley Brown	"	Chickasaw Roll	*(Illegible)* Brown	"	Chickasaw Roll
3	No. 1			No. 2		
4	No. 1			No. 2		
5	No. 1			No. 2		
6	No. 1			No. 2		
7	John Pettenridge	Dead	Pontotoc	No. 2		
8	No. 1			No. 2		

(NOTES)

No. 1 On Chickasaw Roll as S.B. Fryrear *(remainder illegible)*.
No. 2 " " " " Roda Fryrear.
No. 3 " " " " Ema "
No. 4 " " " " A.M. "
No. 5 " " " " Emet "
No. 6 Affidavit of midwife to be furnished. Received Sept 22/98.
No. 6 Died Nov. 1st 1900. Proof of Death filed Oct. 18th 1902.
No. 7 On Chickasaw Roll as C. Pettenridge.
No. 8 Enrolled Nov. 3, 1899.
Affidavits of W.M. Brown as to marriage of Nos. 1 and 2 filed Feby. 16, 1903.
10/15/02 Given name of No. 3 is "Emma"

Sept. 14th 1898.

RESIDENCE: Pontotoc **COUNTY** **CARD NO.**
POST OFFICE: Paola, Ind. Ter. **FIELD NO.**

	NAME	RELATIONSHIP TO PERSON FIRST NAMED	AGE	SEX	BLOOD	TRIBAL ENROLLMENT YEAR	COUNTY	PAGE
1	Dulin, Simpson		25	M	1/16	1897	Pontotoc	61
2	" Ola Lee	Dau	14mo	F	1/32			

TRIBAL ENROLLMENT OF PARENTS

	NAME OF FATHER	YEAR	COUNTY	NAME OF MOTHER	YEAR	COUNTY
1	Jim Dulin	Dead	Non citizen	Pocahontas Dulin	Dead	Pontotoc
2	No. 1			Janie May "		White woman

(NOTES)

No. 1 Husband of Janie May Dulin, Chickasaw Doubtful Card No. D.26.
No. 2 Affidavit of attending physician *(remainder illegible).*

Sept. 14, 1898.

RESIDENCE: Pickens **COUNTY** **CARD NO.**
POST OFFICE: Hennepin, Ind. Ter. **FIELD NO.**

	NAME	RELATIONSHIP TO PERSON FIRST NAMED	AGE	SEX	BLOOD	TRIBAL ENROLLMENT YEAR	COUNTY	PAGE
1	Lannom, Cordelia		14	F	1/2	1897	Pickens	14
2	" Annie Myrtle	Dau	2 1/2 mo	"	1/4			
3	" Bertha	"	5mo	"	1/4			
4	" William R.	Husband	29	M	I.W.			

TRIBAL ENROLLMENT OF PARENTS

	NAME OF FATHER	YEAR	COUNTY	NAME OF MOTHER	YEAR	COUNTY
1	George Poe		Non citizen	Sarah Dennis	1897	Pickens
2	William R. Lannom		" "	No. 1		
3	" " "		" "	No. 1		
4	R.T. Lannom		" "	Samantha J. Lannom	Dead	Non citizen

(NOTES)

No. 1 is the wife of William R. Lannom on Chickasaw Card D#265.
No. 2 Enrolled January 2nd 1901.
No. 3 Born March 7th 1902; Enrolled Aug. 5th 1902.
No. 4 transferred from Chickasaw Card #D.265; Oct. 1, 1904; *(remainding illegible).*

Sept. 14/98.

RESIDENCE: Pickens **COUNTY**					**CARD NO.**			
POST OFFICE: Foster, Ind. Ter.					**FIELD NO.**			
	NAME	**RELATIONSHIP TO PERSON FIRST NAMED**	**AGE**	**SEX**	**BLOOD**	**TRIBAL ENROLLMENT**		
						YEAR	**COUNTY**	**PAGE**
1	Bell, Eliza		25	F	1/2			
2	Lawrence, Azzie Anna	Dau	3	"	1/4			
3	Bell, Emma O.	"	4mo	"	1/4			
4	Gibson, Douglas	Bro	9	M	1/4			
5	Bell, Delila Lucinda	Dau	4mo	F	1/4			
6	" Grant	Son	1mo	M	1/4			

TRIBAL ENROLLMENT OF PARENTS

	NAME OF FATHER	**YEAR**	**COUNTY**	**NAME OF MOTHER**	**YEAR**	**COUNTY**
1	Calvin Gibson	Dead	Choctaw Roll	Nancy Gibson	Dead	Chickasaw Roll
2	Osborne Lawrence		" "	No. 1		
3	Grant Bell		Non citizen	No. 1		
4	Calvin Gibson	Dead	Choctaw Roll	Nancy Gibson	Dead	Chickasaw Roll
5	Grant Bell		Non citizen	No. 1		
6	A.G. Bell		" "	No. 1		

(NOTES)

Nos. 1 & 2 On Choctaw Census Card No. 2 Page 331, Tobucksy County, transferred by Dawes Com.
No. 4 " " " " " " " 200 " " " " " "
No. 1 " " " " as Eliza Lawrence.
No. 1 On Chickasaw Roll 1896, Tobucksy Co. No. 7885 as Eliza Lawrence
No. 2 " " " 1896 " " " 7886 as Anne "
No. 4 " " " 1896 " " " 4690
No. 3 Evidence of Birth received & filed Aug. 4th 1902.
No. 5 Enrolled Nov. 6th 1900.
No. 6 Born Feb. 2, 1902; Enrolled March 22, 1902.

No. 4 Enrolled Sept. 14/98.
All others " Sept. 30/98.

RESIDENCE: Choctaw Nation **COUNTY**					**CARD NO.**			
POST OFFICE: Tuskahoma, Ind. Ter.					**FIELD NO.**			
	NAME	**RELATIONSHIP TO PERSON FIRST NAMED**	**AGE**	**SEX**	**BLOOD**	**TRIBAL ENROLLMENT**		
						YEAR	**COUNTY**	**PAGE**
1	Gibson, Johnie		16	M	1/2			
2	" Louisa	Sister	13	F	1/2			

TRIBAL ENROLLMENT OF PARENTS						
	NAME OF FATHER	YEAR	COUNTY	NAME OF MOTHER	YEAR	COUNTY
1	Calvin Gibson	Dead	Choctaw Roll	Nancy Gibson	Dead	Choctaw Roll
2	" "	"	" "	" "	"	" "

(NOTES)

Both on Choctaw Census Record No. 2 Page 214 transferred to Chickasaw Roll by Dawes Com.
No. 1 On Choctaw Roll, 1896, Jacks Fork County, No. 5008 as Johnnie Gibson.
No. 2 " " " 1896 " " " " 5009.

Sept. 14, 1898.

RESIDENCE: Pickens COUNTY CARD NO.
POST OFFICE: Pauls Valley, Ind. Ter. FIELD NO.

	NAME	RELATIONSHIP TO PERSON FIRST NAMED	AGE	SEX	BLOOD	TRIBAL ENROLLMENT		
						YEAR	COUNTY	PAGE
1	Waite, Mary		28	F	1/4	1897	Pickens	17
2	" Katie	Niece	15	"	1/8	1897	"	17

TRIBAL ENROLLMENT OF PARENTS						
	NAME OF FATHER	YEAR	COUNTY	NAME OF MOTHER	YEAR	COUNTY
1	T.F. Waite	Dead	Non citizen	Catherine Waite	Dead	Pickens
2	Fred Waite	"	Pickens	Mary Waite Jones		Non citizen

(NOTES)

No. 1 On Chickasaw Roll as Mary Wait
No. 2 " " " " Katie "
Katie Waite is a *(remainder illegible)*.

Sept. 14, 1898.

RESIDENCE: Pontotoc COUNTY CARD NO.
POST OFFICE: Wayne, Ind. Ter. FIELD NO.

	NAME	RELATIONSHIP TO PERSON FIRST NAMED	AGE	SEX	BLOOD	TRIBAL ENROLLMENT		
						YEAR	COUNTY	PAGE
1	Seifried, Wm		21	M	1/4	1897	Pontotoc	62

TRIBAL ENROLLMENT OF PARENTS						
	NAME OF FATHER	YEAR	COUNTY	NAME OF MOTHER	YEAR	COUNTY
1	Wm F. Seifried	Dead	Non citizen	Julia Siefried	Dead	Chickasaw Roll

(NOTES)

On Chickasaw Roll as William Seifried.
Nov. 13/99 Should be placed upon Choctaw Card, mother, Julia Siefried, *(remainder illegible)*.
Nov. 13/99 Wife Mary L. Seifried has this day been enrolled on Choctaw Card No. D.519.
Nov. 18/99 Placed upon Choctaw Card No. 4933.

RESIDENCE: Pickens ***COUNTY***					***CARD NO.***			
POST OFFICE: Pauls Valley, Ind. Ter.					***FIELD NO.***			
	NAME	**RELATION-SHIP TO PERSON FIRST NAMED**	**AGE**	**SEX**	**BLOOD**	**TRIBAL ENROLLMENT**		
						YEAR	**COUNTY**	**PAGE**
1	Oliphant, Jennie		32	F	1/4	1897	Pickens	17
2	" Willie	Dau	4	"	1/8	1897	"	17
3	" Claude Waite	Sone	2	M	1/8	~~1897~~	"	~~86~~
4	" Lucile M	Dau	8mo	F	1/8			
5	" Oscar Paul	Son	2mo	M	1/8			
6	" Ruth O.	Dau	5wks	F	1/8			
7	" Sam R.	Hus	40	M	I.W.			

TRIBAL ENROLLMENT OF PARENTS

	NAME OF FATHER	**YEAR**	**COUNTY**	**NAME OF MOTHER**	**YEAR**	**COUNTY**
1	Thos. F. Waite	Dead	Non citizen	Catherine Waite	Dead	Pickens
2	Sam R. Oliphant		White man	No. 1		
3	" " "		" "	No. 1		
4	" " "		" "	No. 1		
5	" " "		" "	No. 1		
6	" " "		" "	No. 1		
7	W.D. Oliphant		Non citz.	Belle Oliphant	Dead	Non citz.

(NOTES)

No. 1 Wife of Sam R. Oliphant, Chickasaw Doubtful Card No. 24.
No. 3 Proof of Birth received and filed Sept. 15th 1902. *(No. 3 Dawes' Roll No. 4091)*
No. 4 Affidavit of attending physician to be furnished. Received March 27th 1899.
No. 5 Born Oct. 12th 1901. Enrolled Dec. 20th 1901.
No. 6 Born Dec. 4, 1899; On Card D.314 and transferred to this card Feb. 1st 1902.
No. 7 Transferred from Chickasaw Card D.24. 8/25/03.

Sept. 14/98.

RESIDENCE: Pontotoc ***COUNTY***					***CARD NO.***			
POST OFFICE: Wynnewood, Ind. Ter.					***FIELD NO.***			
	NAME	**RELATION-SHIP TO PERSON FIRST NAMED**	**AGE**	**SEX**	**BLOOD**	**TRIBAL ENROLLMENT**		
						YEAR	**COUNTY**	**PAGE**
1	Lasater, Sarah		29	F	1/4	1897	Pickens	17
2	" Corinne	Dau	3mo	"	1/8			
3	" Milas	Husb	31	M	I.W.			

	TRIBAL ENROLLMENT OF PARENTS					
	NAME OF FATHER	YEAR	COUNTY	NAME OF MOTHER	YEAR	COUNTY
1	Thos. F. Waite	Dead	Non citizen	Catherine Waite	Dead	Pickens
2	Milas Lasater		" "	No. 1		
3	Geo. M. Lasater		" "	Sophronia Lasater	Dead	non citz.

(NOTES)

No. 1 is wife of Milas Lasater on Chickasaw Card #D.23.
On Chickasaw Roll as Sarah Laster.
No. 2 Enrolled May 29th 1900.
No. 3 transferred from Chickasaw card #D23. See decision of March 5, 1904. Mar. 23, 1904.

Sept. 14, 1898.

RESIDENCE: Pontotoc **COUNTY** **CARD NO.**
POST OFFICE: Purcell, Ind. Ter. **FIELD NO.**

	NAME	RELATIONSHIP TO PERSON FIRST NAMED	AGE	SEX	BLOOD	TRIBAL ENROLLMENT		
						YEAR	COUNTY	PAGE
1	Waite, Emely		34	F	1/4	1897	Pontotoc	48

	TRIBAL ENROLLMENT OF PARENTS					
	NAME OF FATHER	YEAR	COUNTY	NAME OF MOTHER	YEAR	COUNTY
1	T.F. Waite	Dead	Non citizen	Catherine Waite	Dead	Pickens

(NOTES)

On Chickasaw Roll as Emely Wait.

Sept. 14/98.

RESIDENCE: Pontotoc **COUNTY** **CARD NO.**
POST OFFICE: Purcell, Ind. Ter. **FIELD NO.**

	NAME	RELATIONSHIP TO PERSON FIRST NAMED	AGE	SEX	BLOOD	TRIBAL ENROLLMENT		
						YEAR	COUNTY	PAGE
1	Waite, A.R.		40	M	1/4	1897	Pontotoc	63
2	" Mary E.	Wife	33	F	I.W.	1897	"	81
3	" Verdi V.	Son	9 1/2	M	1/8	1897	"	63
4	" Grace C.	Dau	8	F	1/8	1897	"	63
5	" Winifred	"	5	"	1/8	1897	"	63
6	" Leo E.	Son	3	M	1/8	1897	"	63

	TRIBAL ENROLLMENT OF PARENTS					
	NAME OF FATHER	YEAR	COUNTY	NAME OF MOTHER	YEAR	COUNTY
1	T.F. Waite	Dead	Non citizen	Catherine Waite	Dead	Pickens

2	E.R. Spear		" "	Mary Spear		Non citizen
3	No. 1			No. 2		
4	No. 1			No. 2		
5	No. 1			No. 2		
6	No. 1			No. 2		

(NOTES)

Surname on Chickasaw Roll as Wait
No. 3 On Chickasaw Roll as Verdie V.
No. 4 " " " " Gracie C.

11/15/02 Stonewall, I.T.

Sept. 14/98.

RESIDENCE: Pickens COUNTY	CARD NO.
POST OFFICE: Whitebead, Ind. Ter.	FIELD NO.

	NAME	RELATIONSHIP TO PERSON FIRST NAMED	AGE	SEX	BLOOD	TRIBAL ENROLLMENT		
						YEAR	COUNTY	PAGE
1	Hull, Jesse		19	M	1/4	1897	Pickens	15
2	" Belle Langdon	Wife	20	F	I.W.			
3	" Joseph K.	Son	7mo	M	1/8			
4	" William Jesse	"	5wks	M	1/8			

TRIBAL ENROLLMENT OF PARENTS

	NAME OF FATHER	YEAR	COUNTY	NAME OF MOTHER	YEAR	COUNTY
1	Wm Hull (I.W.)	1897	Pickens	Sippey Hull	1897	Pickens
2	Joe Langdon	Dead	Non citizen	Libbie Langdon		Non-citizen
3	No. 1			No. 2		
4	No. 1			No. 2		

(NOTES)

No. 3 Enrolled Nov. 3/99.
No. 4 Enrolled Feb. 28th 1901.

Sept. 14/98.

RESIDENCE: Pickens COUNTY	CARD NO.
POST OFFICE: Pauls Valley, Ind. Ter.	FIELD NO.

	NAME	RELATIONSHIP TO PERSON FIRST NAMED	AGE	SEX	BLOOD	TRIBAL ENROLLMENT		
						YEAR	COUNTY	PAGE
1	Gardner, Edna O.		18	F	I.W.	1897	Pickens	78
2	Paul, Samuel Jackson	Son	1	M	1/8			

	TRIBAL ENROLLMENT OF PARENTS					
	NAME OF FATHER	YEAR	COUNTY	NAME OF MOTHER	YEAR	COUNTY
1	F.A. Casey		non citizen	Folina Casey	Dead	Non citizen
2	Smith W. Paul	1897	Pickens	No. 1		

(NOTES)

No. 1 is married to Grant Gardner. See letter filed herein Sept. 27th 1902.
No. 1 On Chickasaw Roll as E.O. Paul *(No. 1 Dawes' Roll No. 161)*
No. 1 See copy of letter attached 1/11/00
No. 2 Proof of Birth received & filed Sept. 27th 1902. *(No. 2 Dawes' Roll No. 1095)*
See additional testimony of No. 1 taken Oct. 22nd 1902.

Sept. 14/98.

RESIDENCE: Pickens *COUNTY* *CARD NO.*
POST OFFICE: Whitebead, Ind. Ter. *FIELD NO.*

	NAME	RELATION-SHIP TO PERSON FIRST NAMED	AGE	SEX	BLOOD	TRIBAL ENROLLMENT		
						YEAR	COUNTY	PAGE
1	Hull, William		51	M	I.W.	1897	Pickens	97
2	" Sippia	Wife	45	F	1/2	1897	"	15
3	" Theodore	Son	11	M	1/4	1897	"	94
4	" Lucius Irvin	"	8	"	1/4	1897	"	15
5	" Flora	Dau	5	F	1/4	1897	"	15
6	" Bessue	"	9mo	"	1/4			

	TRIBAL ENROLLMENT OF PARENTS					
	NAME OF FATHER	YEAR	COUNTY	NAME OF MOTHER	YEAR	COUNTY
1	Wm Hull	Dead	Non citizen	Mary Hull	Dead	Non citizen
2	Smith Paul	"	" "	Ellen Paul	"	Chickasaw Roll
3	No. 1			No. 2		
4	No. 1			No. 2		
5	No. 1			No. 2		
6	No. 1			No. 2		

(NOTES)

No. 1 On Chickasaw Roll as W.M. Hull *(No. 1 Dawes' Roll No. 234)*
No. 3 On 1893 Chickasaw Pay Roll, No. 2 Page 100.
No. 4 On Chickasaw Roll as Lucian Hull.
No. 6 Affidavit of attending physician to be furnished. *(Remainder illegible).*
No. 6 Evidence of Birth *(remainder illegible).*

Sept. 14, 1898.

RESIDENCE: Pontotoc	COUNTY				CARD NO.		
POST OFFICE: Norman, Okl. Ter.					FIELD NO.		
NAME	RELATIONSHIP TO PERSON FIRST NAMED	AGE	SEX	BLOOD	TRIBAL ENROLLMENT YEAR	COUNTY	PAGE
1 Moore, Helen Foster		17	F	1/2	1897	Pontotoc	64
2 " Lillie	Dau	3	"	1/4	1897	"	64
3 " Willie	Son	11mos	M	1/4			
4 " Gracie	Dau	16mos	F	1/4			

TRIBAL ENROLLMENT OF PARENTS

	NAME OF FATHER	YEAR	COUNTY	NAME OF MOTHER	YEAR	COUNTY
1	Huler Foster	Dead	Non citizen	Susan Wolfe	1897	Pontotoc
2	E.L. Moore		" "	No. 1		
3	" " "		" "	No. 1		
4	" " "		" "	No. 1		

(NOTES)

(All notations illegible)

Sept. 14, 1898.

RESIDENCE: Pontotoc	COUNTY				CARD NO.		
POST OFFICE: Norman, Okl. Ter.					FIELD NO.		
NAME	RELATIONSHIP TO PERSON FIRST NAMED	AGE	SEX	BLOOD	TRIBAL ENROLLMENT YEAR	COUNTY	PAGE
1 Brittain, Frank		16	M	1/2	1897	Pontotoc	62
2 " Eveline	Sister	13	F	1/2	1897	"	62

TRIBAL ENROLLMENT OF PARENTS

	NAME OF FATHER	YEAR	COUNTY	NAME OF MOTHER	YEAR	COUNTY
1	M.L. Brittain		White man	Lucinda Adams	1897	Pontotoc
2	" " "		" "	" "	"	"

(NOTES)

Father, M.L. Brittain. on Chickasaw Doubtful Card No. D.21.
Mother, Lucinda Brittain Adams, on Chick. 498.

Sept. 14/98.

RESIDENCE: Pontotoc	COUNTY				CARD NO.		
POST OFFICE: Purcell, Ind. Ter.					FIELD NO.		
NAME	RELATIONSHIP TO PERSON FIRST NAMED	AGE	SEX	BLOOD	TRIBAL ENROLLMENT YEAR	COUNTY	PAGE
1 Shannon, William T.		36	M	I.Q.	1897	Pontotoc	80

2	" Laura G.	Wife	28	F	1/16	1897	"	62
3	" Thressa May	Dau	10	"	1/32	1897	"	62
4	" Joseph Scott	Son	8	M	1/32	1897	"	62
5	" Robert Lee	"	6	"	1/32	1897	"	62
6	" Charlie Foster	"	4	"	1/32	1897	"	62
7	" Annie Laura	Dau	2	F	1/32	1897	"	62
8	" Murphy Lena	"	3mos	"	1/32			
9	" Ida Estella	"	1mo	"	1/32			
10	" Willie Inez	"	1mo	"	1/32			

TRIBAL ENROLLMENT OF PARENTS

	NAME OF FATHER	YEAR	COUNTY	NAME OF MOTHER	YEAR	COUNTY
1	T.F. Shannon	Dead	Non-Citizen	S. E. Shannon		Non citizen
2	David Mays	1897	Pontotoc	Susan E. Mays	1897	Pontotoc
3	No. 1			No. 2		
4	No. 1			No. 2		
5	No. 1			No. 2		
6	No. 1			No. 2		
7	No. 1			No. 2		
8	No. 1			No. 2		
9	No. 1			No. 2		
10	No. 1			No. 2		

(NOTES)

No. 1 On Chickasaw Roll as William Shannon.
No. 3 " " " " Thressa "
No. 4 " " " " Scott "
No. 5 " " " " Lee "
No. 6 " " " " Charley "
No. 7 " " " " Annie "
No. 8 Affidavit of attending physicia to be furnished. Received Sept. 15/98.
No. 9 Enrolled June 15th 1900
No. 10 Born Aug. 25, 1902; Enrolled Sept. 30, 1902.

No. 1 Admmitted[sic] as an Intermarried Citizen and Nos. 2,3,4,5,6 and 7 as Citizens by blood by Dawes *(Illegible)* on 1896 Chickasaw Case #80. No Appeal.

Sept. 14/98

RESIDENCE: Pickens ***COUNTY*** ***CARD NO.***
POST OFFICE: Wynnewood, Ind. Ter. ***FIELD NO.***

	NAME	RELATION-SHIP TO PERSON FIRST NAMED	AGE	SEX	BLOOD	TRIBAL ENROLLMENT		
						YEAR	COUNTY	PAGE
1	Speed, James L.		M	38	I.W.	1897	Pickens	77

2	" Annie	Wife	F	29	1/16	1897	"	22
3	" Willie Grant	Son	M	9	1/32	1897	"	22
4	" Charles J.	"	"	3	1/32	1897	"	22
5	" Samuel J.	"	"	11mos	1/32			

Tribal Enrollment of Parents

	Name of Father	Year	County	Name of Mother	Year	County
1	Sam Speed	Dead	Non citizen	Mary Speed	Dead	Non citizen
2	Tom Grant	1897	Pickens	Jane Grant	"	Pickens
3	No. 1			No. 2		
4	No. 1			No. 2		
5	No. 1			No. 2		

(Notes)

No. 1 On Chickasaw Roll as J.L. Speed
No. 2 Died Nov. 17th 1900; Proof of Death filed Oct. 28th 1902
No. 3 On Chickasaw Roll as Willie G. Speed.
No. *(Remainder illegible).*

Sept. 14, 1898.

Residence: Pickens ***County*** ***Card No.***
Post Office: Pauls Valley, Ind. Ter. ***Field No.***

	Name	Relationship to Person First Named	Age	Sex	Blood	Tribal Enrollment Year	Tribal Enrollment County	Tribal Enrollment Page
1	Grant, C.J.		37	M	1/16	1897	Pickens	26
2	" Carrie L.	Wife	32	F	I.W.	1897	"	78
3	" *(Illegible)* F.	Son	10	M	1/32	1897	"	26
4	" Tom P.	"	8	"	1/32	1897	"	26
5	" Mattie C.	Dau	6	F	1/32	1897	"	26
6	" Nora J.	"	4	"	1/32	1897	"	26

Tribal Enrollment of Parents

	Name of Father	Year	County	Name of Mother	Year	County
1	Thos. Grant	1897	Pickens	*(Illegible)* Grant	Dead	Pickens
2	Charles F. Witten		non citizen	Matilda Witten		Non Citizen
3	No. 1			No. 2		
4	No. 1			No. 2		
5	No. 1			No. 2		
6	No. 1			No. 2		

(Notes)

No. 2 On Chickasaw Roll as C.F. Grant
No. 5 " " " " *(Illegible Name)*

Sept. 14, 1898.

RESIDENCE: Pickens COUNTY					CARD NO.		
POST OFFICE: Pauls Valley, Ind. Ter.					FIELD NO.		
NAME	RELATIONSHIP TO PERSON FIRST NAMED	AGE	SEX	BLOOD	TRIBAL ENROLLMENT		
					YEAR	COUNTY	PAGE
1 Branum, T.C.		42	M	I.W.	1897	Pickens	87
2 " Mattie	Wife	23	F	1/8	1897	Pontotoc	48

TRIBAL ENROLLMENT OF PARENTS

NAME OF FATHER	YEAR	COUNTY	NAME OF MOTHER	YEAR	COUNTY
1 Merritt Branum		Non citizen	Ellen Branum		Non-citizen
2 W.A. Wilson		" "	Alice Welch	Dead	Chickasaw Roll

(NOTES)

No. 1 On Chickasaw Roll as T.C. Branum *(the remainder illegible)*

No. 2 On Chickasaw Roll as Mattie Welch. Also on Page 23

Copy of marriage license file on file in office of Dawes Com. *(Remainder illegible)*

Sept. 14, 1898.

RESIDENCE: Choctaw Nation COUNTY					CARD NO.		
POST OFFICE: Kiowa, Ind. Ter.					FIELD NO.		
NAME	RELATIONSHIP TO PERSON FIRST NAMED	AGE	SEX	BLOOD	TRIBAL ENROLLMENT		
					YEAR	COUNTY	PAGE
1 Blackwood, A.C.		49	M	I.W.			
2 " Amelia C.	Wife	30	F	3/4	1897	Chick. residing in Choctaw N. 1st Dist.	70
3 " Georgia M.	Dau	12	"	3/8	1897	" " " " "	70
4 " Nobe? G.	Son	10	M	3/8	1897	" " " " "	70
5 " Nora I.	Dau	7	F	3/8	1897	" " " " "	70
6 " Jemima C.	"	5	"	3/8	1897	" " " " "	70
7 " Andrew C. Jr.	Son	6mo	M	3/8			

TRIBAL ENROLLMENT OF PARENTS

NAME OF FATHER	YEAR	COUNTY	NAME OF MOTHER	YEAR	COUNTY
1 John Blackwood	Dead	non citizen	Mary Blackwood	Dead	non citizen
2 James Collins	"	Chickasaw Roll	Mary Colbert	"	Chickasaw Roll
3 No. 1			No. 2		
4 No. 1			No. 2		
5 No. 1			No. 2		
6 No. 1			No. 2		
7 No. 1			No. 2		

(NOTES)

No. 1 Admitted by Dawes Commission On Intermarried Choctaw Case No. 928. No appeal.
All others " " " " " Choctaw by Blood " " 928. " "
Marriage license and certificate *(the remainder illegible)*
No. 1 On Choctaw Int. Roll, Tobucksy Co, Page 7 transferred to Chickasaw Roll by Dawes Com.
No. 1 On Choctaw Roll 1896, Tobucksy County, No. 14307 *(the remainder illegible).*
No. 2 " " " as Emily C.
No. 3 " " " " Georgia
No. 4 " " " " Robert J.
No. 5 " " " " Nora I.
No. 7 Enrolled Nov. 3rd 1899
No. 1 Died March, 1899; Proof of Death filed *(date illegible).*

Sept. 12, 1898.

RESIDENCE: Pontotoc **COUNTY** **CARD NO.**
POST OFFICE: Purcell, Ind. Ter. **FIELD NO.**

	NAME	RELATIONSHIP TO PERSON FIRST NAMED	AGE	SEX	BLOOD	TRIBAL ENROLLMENT YEAR	COUNTY	PAGE
1	Moore, E.M.		40	M	I.W.	1897	Pontotoc	80
2	" Jessie E.	Wife	27	F	1/16	1897	"	62
3	" Carrie Imogene	Dau	9mo	"	1/32			

	NAME OF FATHER	YEAR	COUNTY	NAME OF MOTHER	YEAR	COUNTY
1	Elisha Moore	Dead	Non citizen	*(Illegible)* Moore	Dead	Non citizen
2	W.C. Randolph			Sadie Randolph	"	Pickens
3	No. 1			No. 2		

(NOTES)

No. 1 Admitted as a Intermarried Citizen and
No. 2 as a Citizen by Blood by Dawes Commission, 1896. Chickasaw Case #113 - No appeal.
No. 3 Enrolled Aug 23rd 1901.

10/20/02. P.O. Pauls Valley, I.T.

Sept. ??, 1898.

RESIDENCE: Pickens **COUNTY** **CARD NO.**
POST OFFICE: Hennapin, Ind. Ter. **FIELD NO.**

	NAME	RELATIONSHIP TO PERSON FIRST NAMED	AGE	SEX	BLOOD	TRIBAL ENROLLMENT YEAR	COUNTY	PAGE
1	Morris, William Franklin		42	M	I.W.	1897	Pickens	78
2	" Selina	Wife	33	F	3/4	1897	"	15
3	" Caline	Dau	9	"	3/8	1897	"	15

4	" *(Illegible)*	"	7	"	3/8	1897	"	15
5	" *(Illegible)*	Son	6	M	3/8	1897	"	15
6	" Susie	Dau	4	F	3/8	1897	"	15
7	" *(Illegible)*	"	3mo	"	3/8			
8	" Salina	"	2mo	"	3/8			

TRIBAL ENROLLMENT OF PARENTS

	NAME OF FATHER	YEAR	COUNTY	NAME OF MOTHER	YEAR	COUNTY
1	Joe Morris	Dead	non citizen	Ellen Morris	Dead	Non Citizen
2	Tecumseh McClure	1897	Pickens	Mary McClure	"	Pickens
3	No. 1			No. 2		
4	No. 1			No. 2		
5	No. 1			No. 2		
6	No. 1			No. 2		
7	No. 1			No. 2		
8	No. 1			No. 2		

(NOTES)

No. 1 On Chickasaw Roll as Frank Morris.
No. 2 Died Sept. 20th 1900. Proof of death filed *(illegible)* 1902.
No. 6 Died Oct. 10th 1902; Proof of Death filed *(date illegible)*.
No. 8 Enrolled November 17th 1900.
No. 8 Died November 28th 1900. Proof of Death filed Oct. 24th 1902.

Sept. 14th 1898.

RESIDENCE: Pontotoc ***COUNTY*** ***CARD NO.***
POST OFFICE: Dibble, Ind. Ter. ***FIELD NO.***

	NAME	RELATION-SHIP TO PERSON FIRST NAMED	AGE	SEX	BLOOD	TRIBAL ENROLLMENT		
						YEAR	COUNTY	PAGE
1	Pybas, Boy		35	M	I.W.	?	Pontotoc	81
2	" Dora	Wife	27	F	1/2	?	"	66
3	" Fannie Belle	Dau	8	"	1/4	?	"	66
4	" Pat	Son	6	M	1/4	?	"	66
5	" Daisy	Dau	3	F	1/4	?	"	66
6	" Lee Winston	Son	1	M	1/4			
7	" Nellie H.	Dau	2mo	F	1/4			

TRIBAL ENROLLMENT OF PARENTS

	NAME OF FATHER	YEAR	COUNTY	NAME OF MOTHER	YEAR	COUNTY
1	K.M. Pybas		non-citizen	E.C. Pybas		non citizen
2	Jos Kennel	Dead	" "	Mamie Kennel	Dead	Chickasaw Roll
3	No. 1			No. 2		

4	No. 1			No. 2		
5	No. 1			No. 2		
6	No. 1			No. 2		
7	No. 1			No. 2		

(NOTES)

No. 1 was admitted as an Intermarried Citizen and *(No. 1 Dawes' Roll No. 261)*
Nos. 2, 3, 4 and 5 as Citizens by Blood by Dawes Commission in 1896; Case #119. No appeal.
No. 2 On Chickasaw Roll as Dora Pybes.
No. 3 " " " " F.B. "
No. 6 Affidavit of attending physician to be furnished. Received *(date illegible)*
No. 7 Nellie H. Pybas born Nov. 6/99 *(the remainder illegible)*.

P.O. Purcell, IT Oct. 23 *(Year illegible)*. Sept. 14/98.

RESIDENCE: Pontotoc ***COUNTY***					***CARD NO.***			
POST OFFICE: Purcell, Ind. Ter.					***FIELD NO.***			
	NAME	**RELATION-SHIP TO PERSON FIRST NAMED**	**AGE**	**SEX**	**BLOOD**	**TRIBAL ENROLLMENT**		
						YEAR	**COUNTY**	**PAGE**
1	Mays, David		61	M	I.W.	1897	Pontotoc	80
2	" Susan E.	Wife	58	F	1/16	1897	"	62
3	" Willie	Son	23	M	1/32	1897	"	62
4	" T.G.	"	21	"	1/32	1897	"	62
5	" Clarence	"	18	"	1/32	1897	"	62

TRIBAL ENROLLMENT OF PARENTS

	NAME OF FATHER	**YEAR**	**COUNTY**	**NAME OF MOTHER**	**YEAR**	**COUNTY**
1	Dave Mays	Dead	Non Citizen	Sally Mays	Dead	Non Citizen
2	Joe Mitchell	"	Chickasaw Roll	Jane Mitchell	"	*(illegible)*
3	No. 1			No. 2		
4	No. 1			No. 2		
5	No. 1			No. 2		

(NOTES)

No. 1 was admitted as an intermarried Citizen and *(No. 1 Dawes' Roll No. I.W. 266)*
Nos. 2, 3, 4, & 5 as citizens by blood by Dawes Commission 1896, Chickasaw Case #278. No Appeal.
No. 2 On Chickasaw Roll as Susan Mays.
No. 4 is now Husband of *(Name Illegible)* on Chickasaw Card #122. *(Remainder illegible)*.

P.O. Beef Creek Sept. 14/98.

RESIDENCE: Pickens **COUNTY**					**CARD NO.**			
POST OFFICE: Pauls Valley, Ind. Ter.					**FIELD NO.**			
	NAME	**RELATION-SHIP TO PERSON FIRST NAMED**	**AGE**	**SEX**	**BLOOD**	**TRIBAL ENROLLMENT**		
						YEAR	**COUNTY**	**PAGE**
1	Paul, Sarah J.		44	F	I.W.			

TRIBAL ENROLLMENT OF PARENTS

	NAME OF FATHER	YEAR	COUNTY	NAME OF MOTHER	YEAR	COUNTY
1	Hiram Lambert	Dead	Non-Citizen	Emily Lambert	Dead	Non-citizen

(NOTES)

Certified copy of divorce proceedings between Samuel and Lucy Paul filed *(date and remainder illegible.*

Sept. 14th 1898.

RESIDENCE: Pontotoc **COUNTY**					**CARD NO.**			
POST OFFICE: Purcell, Ind.					**FIELD NO.**			
	NAME	**RELATION-SHIP TO PERSON FIRST NAMED**	**AGE**	**SEX**	**BLOOD**	**TRIBAL ENROLLMENT**		
						YEAR	**COUNTY**	**PAGE**
1	Jones, Winfield Scott		37	M	I.W.	1897	Pontotoc	87
2	" Mary Ella	Wife	26	F	1/16	1897	"	62
3	" Eaman Mays	Son	3wks	M	1/32			
4	" Erin Marray	Dau	1mo	F	1/32			

TRIBAL ENROLLMENT OF PARENTS

	NAME OF FATHER	YEAR	COUNTY	NAME OF MOTHER	YEAR	COUNTY
1	N.B. Jones	Dead	Non-Citizen	Eliza Jones	Dead	Non-Citizen
2	David Mays (I.W.)	1897	Pontotoc	Susan E. Mays	1897	Pontotoc
3	Winfield Scott Jones	1897	"	No. 2		
4	" " "	1897	"	No. 2		

(NOTES)

No. 1 Transferred from white Card No. 2 in 1898.
No. 1 Registered under Act of Legislature, July 31st 1897.
No. 2 Also 1897 Roll, Page 97.
No. 3 Evidence of Birth received and filed June 5th 1902.
No. 4 Enrolled June 8, 1900.
See additional testimony of No. 1 taken Oct. 15th 1902.

P.O. Chickasha, I.T. 10/15/??

Sept. 13, 1898.

RESIDENCE: Pontotoc COUNTY					CARD NO.		
POST OFFICE: Bradley, Ind. Ter.					FIELD NO.		

	NAME	RELATION-SHIP TO PERSON FIRST NAMED	AGE	SEX	BLOOD	TRIBAL ENROLLMENT YEAR	COUNTY	PAGE
1	Colbert, Martin		48	M	1/4	1897	Pontotoc	62
2	" Mattie Zora	Wife	34	F	I.W.	1897	"	80
3	Nichols, Velary Etta	Dau	14	F	1/8	1897	"	62
4	Gooch, Cora Eugenia	"	12	"	1/8	1897	"	62
5	Colbert, Martin Jr.	Son	11	M	1/8	1897	"	62
6	" Benj. Franklin	"	10	"	1/8	1897	"	62
7	" Cecil Calvin	"	8	"	1/8	1897	"	62
8	" Tolbert Ray	"	6	"	1/8	1897	"	62
9	" Mamie Marie	Dau	3	F	1/8	1897	"	62
10	" Luther Carl	Son	2wks	M	1/8			

TRIBAL ENROLLMENT OF PARENTS

	NAME OF FATHER	YEAR	COUNTY	NAME OF MOTHER	YEAR	COUNTY
1	Frank Colbert	Dead	Chickasaw Roll	Martha Colbert	Dead	non citizen
2	John F. Perry	"	non-citizen	*(Illegible)* J. Perry	"	" "
3	No. 1			No. 2		
4	No. 1			No. 2		
5	No. 1			No. 2		
6	No. 1			No. 2		
7	No. 1			No. 2		
8	No. 1			No. 2		
9	No. 1			No. 2		
10	No. 1			No. 2		

(NOTES)

Mattie Zora Colbert and all children admitted by Dawes Com. Case No. 32. No appeal.
No. 2 On Chickasaw Roll as Mattie Z. Colbert *(No. 2 Dawes' Roll No. I.W. 259)*
No. 3 " " " " V.E. " No. 3 now the wife of James L. Nichols non-citizen; Evidence of marriage filed Nov. 28, 1902. *(No. 3 Dawes' Roll No. 4082)*
No. 4 On Chickasaw Roll as C.E. Colbert; No. 4 now the wife of Wesley Dean Gooch non-citizen' Evidence of marriage filed Nov. 7th 1902. *(No. 4 Dawes' Roll No. 4083)*
No. 6 On Chickasaw Roll as B.F. Colbert, Jr. *(No. 5 Dawes' Roll No. 4084)*
No. 7 " " " " C.E. " *(No. 6 Dawes' Roll No. 4085)*
No. 8 " " " " T.R. " *(No. 7 Dawes' Roll No. 4086)*
No. 9 " " " " M.M. " *(No. 8 Dawes' Roll No. 4087)*
No. 10 Enrolled July 9th 1900. *(No. 9 Dawes' Roll No. 1088)* *(No. 10 Dawes' Roll No. 4089)*

Sept. 13/98.

RESIDENCE: Pontotoc COUNTY					CARD NO.		
POST OFFICE: Purcell, Ind. Ter.					FIELD NO.		
NAME	RELATIONSHIP TO PERSON FIRST NAMED	AGE	SEX	BLOOD	TRIBAL ENROLLMENT		
					YEAR	COUNTY	PAGE
1 Criner, Eunice		5	F	1/16	1897	Pontotoc	63

TRIBAL ENROLLMENT OF PARENTS

NAME OF FATHER	YEAR	COUNTY	NAME OF MOTHER	YEAR	COUNTY
1 Joe Criner	1897	Pontotoc	Lizzie Johnson		non-citizen

(NOTES)

Sept. 13th 1898.

RESIDENCE: Pontotoc COUNTY					CARD NO.		
POST OFFICE: Paola, Ind. Ter.					FIELD NO.		
NAME	RELATIONSHIP TO PERSON FIRST NAMED	AGE	SEX	BLOOD	TRIBAL ENROLLMENT		
					YEAR	COUNTY	PAGE
1 Myers, Joseph F.		43	M	I.W.	1897	Pontotoc	81
2 " Eula	Wife	29	F	1/4	1897	"	63
3 Colbert, Elizabeth	Mother in Law	65	"	1/8	1897	"	63

TRIBAL ENROLLMENT OF PARENTS

NAME OF FATHER	YEAR	COUNTY	NAME OF MOTHER	YEAR	COUNTY
1 Abraham Myers	Dead	Non citizen	Jobitha Myers		non citizen
2 Holmes Colbert	"	Panola	Elizabeth Colbert	1897	Pontotoc
3 Henry Love	"	Chickasaw Roll	Sally Love	Dead	Chickasaw Roll

(NOTES)

No. 1 On Chickasaw Roll as J.F. Myers *(No. 1 Dawes' Roll No. 258) (No. 3 Dawes' Roll No. 4081)*
Nos. 1 & 2 Both admitted by Dawes Com. Case No. 105 and No Appeal taken.
Certified copy of marriage license certificate to be furnished. Received Oct. 31/98.

Sept. 13, 1898.

RESIDENCE: Pontotoc COUNTY					CARD NO.		
POST OFFICE: Purcell, Ind. Ter.					FIELD NO.		
NAME	RELATIONSHIP TO PERSON FIRST NAMED	AGE	SEX	BLOOD	TRIBAL ENROLLMENT		
					YEAR	COUNTY	PAGE
1 Goode, C.A.		34	M	I.W.	1897	Pontotoc	81
2 " Ada	Wife	26	F	1/4	1897	"	63
3 " Lila	Dau	8	"	1/8	1897	"	63

TRIBAL ENROLLMENT OF PARENTS

	NAME OF FATHER	YEAR	COUNTY	NAME OF MOTHER	YEAR	COUNTY
1	E.D. Goode		non citizen	Fannie Goode		non citizen
2	John Turnbull	Dead	Choctaw Roll	Lucy Turnbull	Dead	Panola
3	No. 1			No. 2		

(NOTES)

All also admitted by Dawes Commission Case No. 49 and No Appeal taken. *(No. 1 Dawes' Roll No. 257)*
See additional testimony of No. 1 taken *(date illegible)*.

Sept. 13, 1898.

RESIDENCE: Pontotoc ***COUNTY*** ***CARD NO.***
POST OFFICE: Paola, Ind. Ter. ***FIELD NO.***

	NAME	RELATION-SHIP TO PERSON FIRST NAMED	AGE	SEX	BLOOD	TRIBAL ENROLLMENT		
						YEAR	COUNTY	PAGE
1	McCrummen, E.L.		27	M	I.W.	1897	Pontotoc	91
2	" Susie	Wife	23	F	1/16	1897	"	61

TRIBAL ENROLLMENT OF PARENTS

	NAME OF FATHER	YEAR	COUNTY	NAME OF MOTHER	YEAR	COUNTY
1	D.H. McCrummen		Non Citizen	Sally McCrummen		non citizen
2	Jim Dulen (I.W.)	Dead	Pontotoc	Pochantas Dulen	Dead	Pontotoc

(NOTES)

Original marriage license and certificate filed with Dawes Com in 1897; Attach to *(remainder illegible)*.
No. 2 On Chickasaw Roll as Susie Edwards. *(No. 1 Dawes' Roll No. 101)*
Evidence of divorce between No. 2 and her former husband ? A, Edwards filed Jany 14, 190?

Sept. 13/98.

RESIDENCE: Pickens ***COUNTY*** ***CARD NO.***
POST OFFICE: Pauls Valley, Ind. Ter. ***FIELD NO.***

	NAME	RELATION-SHIP TO PERSON FIRST NAMED	AGE	SEX	BLOOD	TRIBAL ENROLLMENT		
						YEAR	COUNTY	PAGE
1	McClure, Imon		26	M	3/4	1897	Pickens	16
2	*(Blank on original)*							
3	" Lillie	Dau	4	F	3/8	1897	Pickens	16
4	" Russ	Son	3	M	3/8	1897	"	16
5	" Imon O.	"	7mo	"	3/8			
6	" John W.	"	4mo	"	3/8			
7	" Lucy Belt	Dau	6mo	F	3/8			
8	McClure, Jennie	Wife	30	F	I.W.	1897	Pickens	83

TRIBAL ENROLLMENT OF PARENTS						
	NAME OF FATHER	YEAR	COUNTY	NAME OF MOTHER	YEAR	COUNTY
1	Tecumseh McClure	1897	Pickens	Mary McClure	Dead	Pickens
2						
3	No. 1			Jennie McClure		White woman
4	No. 1			" "		" "
5	No. 1			" "		" "
6	No. 1			" "		" "
7	No. 1			" "		" "
8	A.J. Casey		Non citizen	Folena Casey	D'd	Non Citizen

(NOTES)

No. 1 On Chickasaw Roll as Iman
No. 1 Husband of Jennie McClure, *(Remainder illegible).*
No. 4 Died May 11th 1902. Proof of Death filed Oct. 5th 1902.
No. 5 Evidence of Birth received and filed Feb. 10th 1902.
No. 6 Enrolled May 24th 1900.
No. 7 Born Aug. 26th 1901. Enrolled Feb. 10, 1902.
No. 7 Died Aug. 31, 1902; Proof of Death filed Oct. 2?, 1902.
No. 8 Transferred from Chickasaw Card No. *(illegible).*

Sept. 15/98.

RESIDENCE: Pontotoc ***COUNTY*** ***CARD NO.***
POST OFFICE: Purcell, Ind. Ter. ***FIELD NO.***

	NAME	RELATION-SHIP TO PERSON FIRST NAMED	AGE	SEX	BLOOD	TRIBAL ENROLLMENT YEAR	COUNTY	PAGE
1	Friend, Retta		23	F	1/32	1897	Pontotoc	63
2	" Alice	Dau	4wks	F	1/64			
3	" Dorset Carter	Son	3mo	M	1/64			
4	" Thomas L.	husband	35	M	I.W.			

	NAME OF FATHER	YEAR	COUNTY	NAME OF MOTHER	YEAR	COUNTY
1	I.F. Williams		non citizen	Elizabeth Williams	Dead	Chickasaw Roll
2	T.L. Friend		white man	No. 1		
3	" " "		" "	No. 1		
4	*(Illegible)* Friend		non citizen	Carley Friend		non citizen

(NOTES)

No. 1 Wife of T.L. Friend, Chickasaw Doubtful Card No. 17
No. 2 Evidence of Birth received and filed April 30th 1902.
No. 3 Enrolled December 14th 1900
No. 4 transferred from Chickasaw Card #D.17. *(No. 4 Dawes' Roll No. 181)*

Sept. 13/98.

RESIDENCE: Pontotoc COUNTY					CARD NO.			
POST OFFICE: Waldon, Ind. Ter.					FIELD NO.			
	NAME	RELATION-SHIP TO PERSON FIRST NAMED	AGE	SEX	BLOOD	TRIBAL ENROLLMENT		
						YEAR	COUNTY	PAGE
1	Waldon, Hosey		32	M	3/4	1897	Pontotoc	64
2	" Susie	Wife	30	F	Full	1897	"	64
3	" Sina	Dau	6	"	7/8	1897	"	64
4	" Ebelene	"	4	"	7/8	1897	"	64
5	" Sadie	"	2	"	7/8	1897	"	64
6	" Hosea Thomas	Son	1/2	M	7/8			
7	" Ja?cy	Dau	6mo	F	7/8			
8	" *(Illegible)*	Son	2mo	M	7/8			

TRIBAL ENROLLMENT OF PARENTS

	NAME OF FATHER	YEAR	COUNTY	NAME OF MOTHER	YEAR	COUNTY
1	Thos. Waldon	1897	Pontotoc	Sophie Waldon	1897	Pontotoc
2	Ephraim Alexander	Dead	"	Jennie Alexander	Dead	"
3	No. 1			No. 2		
4	No. 1			No. 2		
5	No. 1			No. 2		
6	No. 1			No. 2		
7	No. 1			No. 2		
8	No. 1			No. 2		

(NOTES)

No. 6 Evidence of Birth received and filed Feb. 26th 1902
No. 7 Enrolled May 24th 1900
No. 8 Born Dec, 21st 1901; Enrolled Feb 26, 1902
No. 7 died Oct. 15, 1900. Proof of death filed *(remainder illegible)*

Sept. 13/98.

RESIDENCE: Pontotoc COUNTY					CARD NO.			
POST OFFICE: Waldon, Ind. Ter.					FIELD NO.			
	NAME	RELATION-SHIP TO PERSON FIRST NAMED	AGE	SEX	BLOOD	TRIBAL ENROLLMENT		
						YEAR	COUNTY	PAGE
1	Howard, William B.		28	M	I.W	1897	Pontotoc	81
2	" Mary J.	Wife	18	F	3/4	1897	"	65
3	" Harriet May	Dau	2	"	3/8	1897	"	65
4	" William Bryan	Son	10mo	M	3/8			
5	" Allie Viola	Dau	2mo	F	3/8			

6	" Robert Lee	Son	3mo	M	3/8			

TRIBAL ENROLLMENT OF PARENTS

	NAME OF FATHER	YEAR	COUNTY	NAME OF MOTHER	YEAR	COUNTY
1	A.L. Howard	Dead	Pontotoc	May C. Howard		non citizen
2	Joe Wolfe	"	Chickasaw Roll	Harriet Wolfe	Dead	Chickasaw Roll
3	No. 1			No. 2		
4	No. 1			No. 2		
5	No. 1			No. 2		
6	No. 1			No. 2		

(NOTES)

No. 2 On Chickasaw Roll as M.J. Howard *(No. 1 Dawes' Roll No. 8)*
No. 3 " " " " H.M. "
No. 4 Evidence of Birth received and filed March 11th 1902
No. 5 Enrolled June 8th 1899
No. 6 Enrolled May 16, 1901

P.O. Norman, O.T. Sept. 15/1898.

RESIDENCE: Pontotoc ***COUNTY*** ***CARD NO.***
POST OFFICE: Purcell, Ind. Ter. ***FIELD NO.***

	NAME	RELATION-SHIP TO PERSON FIRST NAMED	AGE	SEX	BLOOD	TRIBAL ENROLLMENT		
						YEAR	COUNTY	PAGE
1	Randolph, Elizabeth		30	F	1/8	1897	Pontotoc	63
2	" Joe M.	Son	3	M	1/16	1897	"	63
3	" Fay	Dau	17mo	F	1/16	1897	"	89
4	" Olive E.	"	4mo	"	1/16			
5	" Paul Williams	Son	6wks	M	1/16			
6	" James	husband	23	M	I.W.			

TRIBAL ENROLLMENT OF PARENTS

	NAME OF FATHER	YEAR	COUNTY	NAME OF MOTHER	YEAR	COUNTY
1	Fletcher Williams		Non Citizen	Elizabeth Williams	Dead	Chickasaw Roll
2	James Randolph		White man	No. 1		
3	" "		" "	No. 1		
4	" "		" "	No. 1		
5	" "		" "	No. 1		
6	*(Illegible)* Randolph		Non Citizen	Allie Randolph		Non Citizen

(NOTES)

No. 1 Wife of James Randolph, Chickasaw Doubtful Card No. D.16.
No. 3 Registered under Act of Legislature, July 1st 1897, Chick Roll Page 89
No. 3 Proof of Birth received and filed Oct. 9th 1902 *(No. 3 Dawes' Roll No. 4080)*

No. 4 Enrolled Nov. 3/99.
No. 5 Born Sept. 24th 1901; Enrolled Nov. 24th 1901.
No. 6 transferred from Chickasaw Card #D.16. *(No. 6 Dawes' Roll No. 180)*
See decision of May 5, 1903.

P.O. Paola, I.T. 12/2/04 Sept. 13th 1898.

RESIDENCE: Pickens **COUNTY** **CARD NO.**
POST OFFICE: Davis, Ind. Ter. **FIELD NO.**

	NAME	RELATION-SHIP TO PERSON FIRST NAMED	AGE	SEX	BLOOD	TRIBAL ENROLLMENT		
						YEAR	COUNTY	PAGE
1	Shannon, Daisy		17	F	1/16	1897	Pickens	19
2	Howell, Calvin H.	Bro	14	M	1/16	1897	"	19
3	Shannon, Jesse R. *(difficult to read)*	Hus.	32	M	?			

TRIBAL ENROLLMENT OF PARENTS

	NAME OF FATHER	YEAR	COUNTY	NAME OF MOTHER	YEAR	COUNTY
1	Thomas P. Howell		Choctaw residing in Chickasaw Dist.	Lizzie Grant Howell	Dead	Pickens
2	" " "		" "	" " "	"	"
3	*(Illegible Name)*			*(Illegible Name)*		

(NOTES)

No. 1 is now the wife of Jesse R. Shannon on Chickasaw Card #D.349. 9/3/01
Father of Nos. 1 & 2, on Choctaw Card #111.
(Remainder illegible)

No. 1 lives at Wynnewood Sept. 13/98.

RESIDENCE: Pickens **COUNTY** **CARD NO.**
POST OFFICE: Davis, Ind. Ter. **FIELD NO.**

	NAME	RELATION-SHIP TO PERSON FIRST NAMED	AGE	SEX	BLOOD	TRIBAL ENROLLMENT		
						YEAR	COUNTY	PAGE
1	Grant, Thomas		67	M	I.W.	1897	Pontotoc	78

TRIBAL ENROLLMENT OF PARENTS

	NAME OF FATHER	YEAR	COUNTY	NAME OF MOTHER	YEAR	COUNTY
1	James Grant	Dead	Non-Citizen	Jane Grant	Dead	Non-Citizen

(NOTES)

Married to Mary Jane Love in 1853. *(No. 1 Dawes' Roll No. 256)*
On Choctaw Intermarried Roll, Page 39, *(Remainder illegible)*
Also on Choctaw Roll 1896, Chickasaw Dist. No. 14585 *(remainder illegible)*

Marriet Margaret S. Howell in 1873 on 1818 Annuity roll, Pickens Co, he died in 187?.

Sept. 13th 1898.

RESIDENCE: Pontotoc ***COUNTY*** ***CARD NO.***
POST OFFICE: Wynnewood, Ind. Ter. ***FIELD NO.***

	NAME	RELATION-SHIP TO PERSON FIRST NAMED	AGE	SEX	BLOOD	TRIBAL ENROLLMENT YEAR	COUNTY	PAGE
1	Conrady, Henry		72	M	I.W.	1897	Pontotoc	80

TRIBAL ENROLLMENT OF PARENTS

	NAME OF FATHER	YEAR	COUNTY	NAME OF MOTHER	YEAR	COUNTY
1	Mattie Conrady	Dead	Non-citizen	Mary Conrady	Dead	Non-citizen

(NOTES)

On Chickasaw Roll as Henry Conradey.
Admitted by the Dawes Com. Card No. 31 and No appeal taken.

P.O. Paulo Valley, I.T.

Sept. 16th 1898.

RESIDENCE: Pontotoc ***COUNTY*** ***CARD NO.***
POST OFFICE: Purcell, Ind. Ter. ***FIELD NO.***

	NAME	RELATION-SHIP TO PERSON FIRST NAMED	AGE	SEX	BLOOD	TRIBAL ENROLLMENT YEAR	COUNTY	PAGE
1	Turnbull, C.W.		32	M	1/8	1897	Pontotoc	62
2	" Jettie Lemons	Wife	19	F	I.W.			
3	" Loyd Mertin	Son	3mo	M	1/16			
4	" Clarence Rex	"	1mo	"	1/16			

TRIBAL ENROLLMENT OF PARENTS

	NAME OF FATHER	YEAR	COUNTY	NAME OF MOTHER	YEAR	COUNTY
1	John Turnbull	Dead	Choctaw Roll	Lucy Turnbull	Dead	Chickasaw Roll
2	Henry Lemons	"	Non citizen	Della Waite		Non-Citizen
3	No. 1			No. 2		
4	No. 1			No. 2		

(NOTES)

No. 3 Enrolled Nov. 3rd 1899
No. 4 Born Dec. 20, 1901; Enrolled Jan. 28th 1902.

Sept. 13/98.

RESIDENCE: Pontotoc COUNTY						CARD NO.		
POST OFFICE: Purcell, Ind. Ter.						FIELD NO.		
	NAME	RELATION-SHIP TO PERSON FIRST NAMED	AGE	SEX	BLOOD	TRIBAL ENROLLMENT		
						YEAR	COUNTY	PAGE
1	Sparks, George W.		29	M	I.W.			
2	" Dollie	Wife	22	F	1/4	1897	Pontotoc	62
3	" Richard L.	Son	5	M	1/8	1897	"	62
4	" Ethel	Dau	3	F	1/8	1897	"	62

TRIBAL ENROLLMENT OF PARENTS

	NAME OF FATHER	YEAR	COUNTY	NAME OF MOTHER	YEAR	COUNTY
1	Thos. Sparks		non-citizen	Hannah Sparks	Dead	Non-Citizen
2	John Turnbull	Dead	Choctaw Roll	Lucy Turnbull	"	Chickasaw Roll
3	No. 1			No. 2		
4	No. 1			No. 2		

(NOTES)

No. 1 Admitted as an Intermarried Citizen and *(No. 1 Dawes' Roll No. 255)*
Nos. 2, 3 & 4 as Citizens by blood by Dawes Commission in 1896, On Chickasaw Case #83; No appeal
No. 3 On Chickasaw Roll as R.L. Sparks.

Sept. 13, 1898.

RESIDENCE: Pontotoc COUNTY						CARD NO.		
POST OFFICE: Johnson, Ind. Ter.						FIELD NO.		
	NAME	RELATION-SHIP TO PERSON FIRST NAMED	AGE	SEX	BLOOD	TRIBAL ENROLLMENT		
						YEAR	COUNTY	PAGE
1	Johnston, Albert S.		23	M	1/8	1897	Pontotoc	61

	NAME OF FATHER	YEAR	COUNTY	NAME OF MOTHER	YEAR	COUNTY
1	Thos. Johnston	Dead	non citizen	Elizabeth Johnston	Dead	Pontotoc

(NOTES)

On Chickasaw Roll as A.S. Johnson.

P.O. Waldon, I.T. 6/24/??

Sept. 13, 1898.

RESIDENCE: Pontotoc COUNTY						CARD NO.		
POST OFFICE: Wynnewood, Ind. Ter.						FIELD NO.		
	NAME	RELATION-SHIP TO PERSON FIRST NAMED	AGE	SEX	BLOOD	TRIBAL ENROLLMENT		
						YEAR	COUNTY	PAGE
1	Murray, J.A.		42	M	1/8	1897	Pontotoc	61

2	" Cora	Wife	29	F	I.W.			
3	" Frankie Lee	Dau	9	F	1/16	1897	Pontotoc	61
4	" Henry C.	Son	6mo	M	1/16			

TRIBAL ENROLLMENT OF PARENTS

	NAME OF FATHER	YEAR	COUNTY	NAME OF MOTHER	YEAR	COUNTY
1	Frank Murray		non citizen	Margaret Murray	Dead	Chickasaw Roll
2	D.M. Carr	Dead	non citizen	Ella Carr		non citizen
3	No. 1			Cora Murray		white woman
4	No. 1			" "		" "

(NOTES)

No. 1 Husband of Cora Murray, Chickasaw Card No. D.85. *(No. 2 Dawes' Roll No. 254)*
No. 3 On Chickasaw Roll as Frankie Murray
No. 4 Evidence of Birth received and filed Feby. 10th 1902
No. 2 Transferred from Chickasaw card #D.85.
See decision of March 5, 1904. March 28, 1904.

Sept. 13/1898.

RESIDENCE: Pontotoc ***COUNTY*** ***CARD NO.***
POST OFFICE: Johnson, Ind. Ter. ***FIELD NO.***

	NAME	RELATIONSHIP TO PERSON FIRST NAMED	AGE	SEX	BLOOD	TRIBAL ENROLLMENT		
						YEAR	COUNTY	PAGE
1	Mitchell, Rilla		20	F	1/16	1897	Pontotoc	61
2	" Jessie Pauline	Dau	17mo	"	1/32			
3	" George	Son	3mo	M	1/32			
4	" Mantie	"	7wks	"	1/32			
5	" Gaines A.	Husband	31	M	I.W.			

TRIBAL ENROLLMENT OF PARENTS

	NAME OF FATHER	YEAR	COUNTY	NAME OF MOTHER	YEAR	COUNTY
1	Josh Davis	Dead	Non citizen	Laura Davis	Dead	Pontotoc
2	G.A. Mitchell		" "	No. 1		
3	" " "		" "	No. 1		
4	" " "		" "	No. 1		
5	Wm Mitchell		" "	Carann Mitchell	Dead	non citizen

(NOTES)

No. 1 On Chickasaw Roll as Perilla Mitchell.
No. 1 Wife of G.A. Mitchell, U.S. Citizen.
No. 1 is wife of Gaines A. Mitchell on Chickasaw Card D.229
No. 2 Evidence of Birth received and filed April 4th 1902
No. 3 Enrolled Mar. 6th 1899,
No. 4 Enrolled August 31st 1901

No. 5 transferred from Chickasaw Card #D.229 March 29, 1903. *(No. 5 Dawes' Roll No. 7)*
See decision of March 13, 1903.

Sept. 13/98.

RESIDENCE: Pontotoc ***COUNTY***					***CARD NO.***			
POST OFFICE: Wynnewood, Ind. Ter.					***FIELD NO.***			
	NAME	RELATION-SHIP TO PERSON FIRST NAMED	AGE	SEX	BLOOD	TRIBAL ENROLLMENT		
						YEAR	COUNTY	PAGE
1	Stewart, Josephine		43	F	3/8	1897	Pontotoc	60
2	" Wiley	Son	18	M	3/16	1897	"	60
3	" Frank	"	16	M	3/16	1897	"	60
4	" John	"	14	"	3/16	1897	"	60
5	" Carl	"	12	"	3/16	1897	"	60
6	" Addie	Dau	6	F	3/16	1897	"	60

TRIBAL ENROLLMENT OF PARENTS

	NAME OF FATHER	YEAR	COUNTY	NAME OF MOTHER	YEAR	COUNTY
1	J.D. Harris	Dead	Chickasaw Roll	Julia Harris	Dead	Chickasaw Roll
2	Charles F. Stewart		Choctaw Residing in Chickasaw Dist.	No. 1		
3	" " "		" "	No. 1		
4	" " "		" "	No. 1		
5	" " "		" "	No. 1		
6	" " "		" "	No. 1		

(NOTES)

No. 1 is wife of Charles F. Stewart on Choctaw Card #98.
No. 2 On Chickasaw Roll as Willie

Sept. 13/98.

RESIDENCE: Pontotoc ***COUNTY***					***CARD NO.***			
POST OFFICE: Johnson, Ind. Ter.					***FIELD NO.***			
	NAME	RELATION-SHIP TO PERSON FIRST NAMED	AGE	SEX	BLOOD	TRIBAL ENROLLMENT		
						YEAR	COUNTY	PAGE
1	Johnston, Lem		27	M	1/8	1897	Pontotoc	61
2	" Orin A.	Son	3	"	1/16	1897	"	61
3	" Cora E.	Dau	2	F	1/16	1897	"	61
4	" Clarence F.	Son	4mo	M	1/16			
5	" Elsie May	Dau	3mo	F	1/16			

6	" Eva Pearl	"	1mo	"	1/16			

TRIBAL ENROLLMENT OF PARENTS

	NAME OF FATHER	YEAR	COUNTY	NAME OF MOTHER	YEAR	COUNTY
1	Thos. Johnston	Dead	non citizen	Elizabeth Jounston	Dead	Pontotoc
2	No. 1			Etta Johnston		U.S. Citz.
3	No. 1			" "		" " "
4	No. 1			" "		" " "
5	No. 1			" "		" " "
6	No. 1			" "		" " "

(NOTES)

No. 1 Certificate of marriage between No. 1 and Etta Johnston Dec. 20 Satisfactory but not *(illegible)*, to be filed. Returned.
No. 1 On Chickasaw Roll as Lem Johnson
No. 2 " " " " O.C. "
No. 3 " " " " C.E. "
No. 4 Evidence of Birth received and filed March 13th 1902
No. 5 Enrolled May 25th 1900
No. 6 Born Decr. 29, 1901; Enrolled Feb. 13, 1902.

Sept. 12/1898.

RESIDENCE: Pontotoc ***COUNTY*** ***CARD NO.***
POST OFFICE: Johnson, Ind. Ter. ***FIELD NO.***

	NAME	RELATION-SHIP TO PERSON FIRST NAMED	AGE	SEX	BLOOD	TRIBAL ENROLLMENT		
						YEAR	COUNTY	PAGE
1	Johnston, Isaac		25	M	2/8	1897	Pontotoc	61

TRIBAL ENROLLMENT OF PARENTS

	NAME OF FATHER	YEAR	COUNTY	NAME OF MOTHER	YEAR	COUNTY
1	Thos. Johnston	Dead	non citizen	Elizabeth Johnston	Dead	Pontotoc

(NOTES)

On Chickasaw Roll as Isaac Johnson.

Sept. 12/1898.

RESIDENCE: Pontotoc ***COUNTY*** ***CARD NO.***
POST OFFICE: Wynnewood, Ind. Ter. ***FIELD NO.***

	NAME	RELATION-SHIP TO PERSON FIRST NAMED	AGE	SEX	BLOOD	TRIBAL ENROLLMENT		
						YEAR	COUNTY	PAGE
1	Walner, John H.		39	M	1/4	1897	Pontotoc	60

	Tribal Enrollment of Parents					
	Name of Father	Year	County	Name of Mother	Year	County
1	Wm Walner	Dead	Non Citizen	Sysab Cartas	Dead	Panola

(Notes)

No. 1 On Chickasaw Roll as J.H. Walner.
Husband of Lula Walner, Choctaw Roll, Card 91.

Residence: Pickens *County* *Card No.*

Post Office: Purdy, Ind. Ter. *Field No.*

	Name	Relationship to Person First Named	Age	Sex	Blood	Tribal Enrollment		
						Year	County	Pag
1	Gibson, Minnie		33	F	Full	1897	Pickens	24
2	" Mitchell	Son	14	M	1/2	1897	"	24
3	" Jane	"	9	"	1/2	1897	"	24
4	" Lucy	Dau	3	F	1/2	1897	"	24
5	" Mississippi	"	4mo	"	1/2			
6	" Josiah	Son	2mo	M	1/2			

	Tribal Enrollment of Parents					
	Name of Father	Year	County	Name of Mother	Year	County
1	*(Illegible Name)*	Dead	Chickasaw Roll	She-minth-a	Dead	Pickens
2	Silas Gibson		Choctaw residing in Chickasaw Dist.	No. 1		
3	" "		" "	No. 1		
4	" "		" "	No. 1		
5	" "		" "	No. 1		
6	" "		" "	No. 1		

(Notes)

No. 1 Wife of Silas Gibson on Choctaw Roll Card No. 84.
No. 1 On Chickasaw Roll as Minnie Gipson
No. 2, 3 & 4 " " " " Gipson.
No. 5 Evidence of Birth filed July 16th 1902
No. 6 Enrolled Sept 27th 1901

Sept. 12th 1898.

RESIDENCE: Pontotoc	**COUNTY**		**CARD NO.**					
POST OFFICE: Dibble, Ind. Ter.			**FIELD NO.**					
	NAME	**RELATIONSHIP TO PERSON FIRST NAMED**	**AGE**	**SEX**	**BLOOD**	**TRIBAL ENROLLMENT**		
						YEAR	**COUNTY**	**PAGE**
1	Reynolds, Zack		38	M	1/2	1897	Pontotoc	39

TRIBAL ENROLLMENT OF PARENTS

	NAME OF FATHER	YEAR	COUNTY	NAME OF MOTHER	YEAR	COUNTY
1	Tom Reynolds	Dead	Panolal	Lida Reynolds	Dead	Panola

(NOTES)

On Chickasaw Roll as Jack Reynolds.

Sept. 12/1898.

RESIDENCE: Pontotoc	**COUNTY**		**CARD NO.**					
POST OFFICE: Walker, Ind. Ter.			**FIELD NO.**					
	NAME	**RELATIONSHIP TO PERSON FIRST NAMED**	**AGE**	**SEX**	**BLOOD**	**TRIBAL ENROLLMENT**		
						YEAR	**COUNTY**	**PAGE**
1	Brown, Sisy		50	F	Full	1897	Pontotoc	41

TRIBAL ENROLLMENT OF PARENTS

	NAME OF FATHER	YEAR	COUNTY	NAME OF MOTHER	YEAR	COUNTY
1	Ton-a-tub-by	Dead	Chickasaw Roll	Ka-nok-ke	Dead	Chickasaw Roll

(NOTES)

On Chickasaw Roll as Sissy Brown.

Sept. 12/98.

RESIDENCE: Pontotoc	**COUNTY**		**CARD NO.**					
POST OFFICE: Walker, Ind. Ter.			**FIELD NO.**					
	NAME	**RELATIONSHIP TO PERSON FIRST NAMED**	**AGE**	**SEX**	**BLOOD**	**TRIBAL ENROLLMENT**		
						YEAR	**COUNTY**	**PAGE**
1	Brown, Annie		65	F	Full	1897	Pontotoc	41
2	" Sarah	Dau	21	"	"	1897	"	41
3	Rodgers, Nora	Gr Dau	9	"	1/2	1897	"	41
4	Brown, Loman	Son	19	M	Full	1893	"	P.R.#2 53

TRIBAL ENROLLMENT OF PARENTS

	NAME OF FATHER	YEAR	COUNTY	NAME OF MOTHER	YEAR	COUNTY
1	Johnie	Dead	Chickasaw Roll	Sha-tha-he-cha	Dead	Chickasaw Roll

2	Chi-ki-ke Brown	"	Pontotoc	No. 1		
3	Hugh Rodgers		Non citizen	Lottie Brown	Dead	Pontotoc
4	Chi-ki-ke Brown	Dead	Pontotoc	Annie Brown	1897	"

(NOTES)

No. 1 Died March 28, 1901; Proof of Death filed June 14th 1901
No. 4 On Chickasaw Pay Roll as Lomand Che ki ky

Sept. 15/98.

RESIDENCE: Pickens COUNTY CARD NO.
POST OFFICE: Pauls Valley, Ind. Ter. FIELD NO.

	NAME	RELATION-SHIP TO PERSON FIRST NAMED	AGE	SEX	BLOOD	TRIBAL ENROLLMENT		
						YEAR	COUNTY	PAGE
1	Barr, A.D.		37	M	I.W.	1897	Pontotoc	80
2	" Emma	Wife	18	F	Full	1897	"	61
3	" Alta	Dau	2	"	1/2	1897	"	62
4	" Ethel	"	1	"	1/2	1897	"	90
5	" Addie	"	14	"	1/2	1897	"	61
6	" Ema	"	12	"	1/2	1897	"	61
7	" Maddie May	"	9	"	1/2	1897	"	61
8	" Sam T.	Son	7	M	1/2	1897	"	62

TRIBAL ENROLLMENT OF PARENTS

	NAME OF FATHER	YEAR	COUNTY	NAME OF MOTHER	YEAR	COUNTY
1	Samuel Barr	Dead	Non-Citizen	Johanna Barr		Non Citizen
2	Holder	"	Chickasaw Roll	Matilda Land	1897	Pontotoc
3	No. 1			No. 2		
4	No. 1			No. 2		
5	No. 1			Laura Barr	Dead	Pontotoc
6	No. 1			" "	"	"
7	No. 1			" "	"	"
8	No. 1			" "	"	"

(NOTES)

No. 3 On Chickasaw Roll as Alty Barr. *(No. 1 Dawes' Roll No. 99)*
No. 2 Died March 23rd 1900. Proof of Death filed Oct. 30th 1902.
Evidence of marriage etween No. 1 and the motherNos. 5, 6-7 and 8 *(remainder illegible)*
No. 5 On Chickasaw Roll as Eddie Barr
No. 4 Died March 24th 1900; Proof of Death filed Oct. 23rd 1902
No. 7 On Chickasaw Roll as Mattie M.

P.O. Sulphur Springs, I.T. 5/20/02. Sept. 12/98.

RESIDENCE: Pontotoc	***COUNTY***	***CARD NO.***	
POST OFFICE: Iona, Ind. Ter.		***FIELD NO.***	

	NAME	RELATION-SHIP TO PERSON FIRST NAMED	AGE	SEX	BLOOD	TRIBAL ENROLLMENT		
						YEAR	COUNTY	PAGE
1	Thomas, Willie		10	M	1/2	1897	Pontotoc	49
2	Goodall, Mary	Mother	33	F	I.W.	1897	"	80

TRIBAL ENROLLMENT OF PARENTS

	NAME OF FATHER	YEAR	COUNTY	NAME OF MOTHER	YEAR	COUNTY
1	Billy Thomas	Dead	Chickasaw Roll	Mary Goodall (I.W.)	1897	Pontotoc
2	Jordon	Dead	non citizen	Martha Jordon		non citizen

(NOTES)

No. 1 is the som of Mary Goodall, on Chickasaw Care #D.12
See Chickasaw Card #D.12 Dec - 1 - 99
No. 2 is the wife of John Goodall, admitted by U.S. Court Southern Dist. Case #100 and denied by C.C.C.C.
John Goodall, husband of No. 2 is on Choctaw card #4963.
No. 2 formerly the wife of William Thomas, a recognized citizen by blood of the Chickasaw Nation.
He died in 1898.
No. 2 originally opted for enrollment on Chickasaw card D.12 - Sept. 12/18??
transferred to this card Feb. 5, 1905. *(Remainder illegible)*

Sept. 12th 1898.

RESIDENCE: Pontotoc	***COUNTY***	***CARD NO.***	
POST OFFICE: McGee, Ind. Ter.		***FIELD NO.***	

	NAME	RELATION-SHIP TO PERSON FIRST NAMED	AGE	SEX	BLOOD	TRIBAL ENROLLMENT		
						YEAR	COUNTY	PAGE
1	Jones, Burney		45	M	3/4	1897	Pontotoc	48
2	" Jane	Wife	45	F	Full	1897	"	48
3	" Joseph	Son	16	M	7/8	1897	"	48
4	" Mary	Dau	8	F	7/8	1897	"	48
5	~~Strickland, Hannah~~	~~niece~~	~~18~~	~~"~~	~~3/4~~	~~1897~~	~~"~~	~~61~~

TRIBAL ENROLLMENT OF PARENTS

	NAME OF FATHER	YEAR	COUNTY	NAME OF MOTHER	YEAR	COUNTY
1	Edman Jones	Dead	Chickasaw Roll	*(Illegible)* Jones	Dead	Chickasaw Roll
2	Ma-ta-ho-mey	"	" "	Ta-la-he	"	" "
3	No. 1			No. 2		
4	No. 1			No. 2		
5	~~Charles Strickland~~	~~Dead~~	~~Chickasaw Roll~~	~~Elizabeth Strickland~~	~~Dead~~	~~Chickasaw Roll~~

(NOTES)

3/20/99 No. 5 No. 5 Married to Louis Nichols and *(remainder illegible)*

P.O. Davis, I.T. 7/24/?? Sept. 12/1898.

RESIDENCE: Pontotoc ***COUNTY***				***CARD NO.***				
POST OFFICE: Johnson, Ind. Ter.				***FIELD NO.***				

	NAME	RELATION-SHIP TO PERSON FIRST NAMED	AGE	SEX	BLOOD	TRIBAL ENROLLMENT		
						YEAR	COUNTY	PAGE
1	Strickland, Tom		20	M	1/8	1897	Pontotoc	61
2	" Jettie	Wife	15	F	I.W.			
3	" Glassey	Dau	7wks	"	1/16			
4	" C.W.	Son	2mo	M	1/16			

TRIBAL ENROLLMENT OF PARENTS

	NAME OF FATHER	YEAR	COUNTY	NAME OF MOTHER	YEAR	COUNTY
1	Charles Strickland	Dead	Chickasaw Roll	Elizabeth Strickland	Dead	Chickasaw Roll
2	John Grider		non citizen	Mattie Grider		Non citizen
3	No. 1			No. 2		
4	No. 1			No. 2		

(NOTES)

No. 2 Enrolled March 20/99 *(No. 2 Dawes' Roll No. 98)*
No. 3 Enrolled Dec. 6th 1900
No. 4 Born April 18th 1902; Enrolled June 24th 1902
No. 4 Given names are Charles William. See letter *(remainder illegible)*

Sept. 12/98.

RESIDENCE: Pontotoc ***COUNTY***				***CARD NO.***				
POST OFFICE: McGee, Ind. Ter.				***FIELD NO.***				

	NAME	RELATION-SHIP TO PERSON FIRST NAMED	AGE	SEX	BLOOD	TRIBAL ENROLLMENT		
						YEAR	COUNTY	PAGE
1	Cash, A.P.		29	M	I.W.	1897	Pontotoc	91
2	" Alice	Wife	18	F	3/4	1897	"	48
3	" Patterson Shi	Son	1mo	M	3/8			
4	" Tyree	"	2mo	"	3/8			
5	" Elpha	Dau	2wks	F	3/8			

	TRIBAL ENROLLMENT OF PARENTS					
	NAME OF FATHER	YEAR	COUNTY	NAME OF MOTHER	YEAR	COUNTY
1	O.B. Cash	Dead	non citizen	Camilla Cash		non citizen
2	B.M. Jones	1897	Pontotoc	Jane Jones	1897	Pontotoc
3	No. 1			No. 2		
4	No. 1			No. 2		
5	No. 1			No. 2		

(NOTES)

No. 2 On Chickasaw Roll as Alice Jones *(No. 1 Dawes' Roll No. 97)*
No. 3 Enrolled Dec. 17, 1898
No. 4 Enrolled Aug. 6, 1900
No. 5 Born March 20, 1902; Enrolled April 3, 1902.

Sept. 12/98.

RESIDENCE: Pontotoc ***COUNTY*** ***CARD NO.***
POST OFFICE: Wynnewood, Ind. Ter. ***FIELD NO.***

	NAME	RELATION-SHIP TO PERSON FIRST NAMED	AGE	SEX	BLOOD	TRIBAL ENROLLMENT		
						YEAR	COUNTY	PAGE
1	Lael, Noah		49	M	I.W.	1897	Pontotoc	89
2	" Eddie C.	Son	18	"	1/2	1897	"	49
3	" Rushie	Dau	16	F	1/2	1897	"	49

	TRIBAL ENROLLMENT OF PARENTS					
	NAME OF FATHER	YEAR	COUNTY	NAME OF MOTHER	YEAR	COUNTY
1	Jacob Lael	Dead	Non Citizen	Susan Lael	Dead	Non citizen
2	No. 1			Lucy Lael	"	Tishomingo
3	No. 1			Lucy Lael	"	"

(NOTES)

No. 1 On Chickasaw Roll as Noah Leal *(No. 1 Dawes' Roll No. 96)*
No. 2 " " " " Eddie "
No. 3 " " " " Ruth "
See testimony of No. 1 taken Oct. 20, 1902.
Evidence of divorce between Lucy Hamilton and James H. Hamilton filed Feby. 16, 1903.

Sept. 12, 1898.

RESIDENCE: Pontotoc	**COUNTY**				**CARD NO.**			
POST OFFICE: Waldon, Ind. Ter.					**FIELD NO.**			
	NAME	**RELATIONSHIP TO PERSON FIRST NAMED**	**AGE**	**SEX**	**BLOOD**	**TRIBAL ENROLLMENT**		
						YEAR	**COUNTY**	**PAGE**
1	Pikey, Katie		35	F	Full	1897	Pontotoc	65
2	" Mollie	Dau	14	"	3/4	1897	"	65
3	" Minerva	"	13	"	3/4	1897	"	65
4	" Sophia	"	12	"	3/4	1897	"	65
5	" Montford J.	Son	7	M	3/4	1897	"	65
6	" Thos. Benson	"	4	"	3/4	1897	"	65
7	" Catherine	Dau	5wks	F	3/4			
8	" Delila	"	2	F	1/2			

TRIBAL ENROLLMENT OF PARENTS

	NAME OF FATHER	**YEAR**	**COUNTY**	**NAME OF MOTHER**	**YEAR**	**COUNTY**
1	Stemontubby	Dead	Pontotoc	Siley	Dead	Pontotoc
2	Ben Pikey	"	"	No. 1		
3	" "	"	"	No. 1		
4	" "	"	"	No. 1		
5	" "	"	"	No. 1		
6	" "	"	"	No. 1		
7	Illegitimate			No. 1		
8	Illegitimate			No. 1		

(NOTES)

No. 1 On Chickasaw Roll as Hattie Pikey *(No. 2 Dawes' Roll No. 4073) (No. 3 Dawes' Roll No. 4074)*
No. 5 " " " " M.J. " *(No. 4 Dawes' Roll No. 4075) (No. 5 Dawes' Roll No. 4076)*
No. 6 " " " " J. Berry " *(No. 6 Dawes' Roll No. 4077) (No. 7 Dawes' Roll No. 4078)*
No. 7 Evidence of Birth filed July 15, 1902 *(No. 8 Dawes' Roll No. 4963)*
Affidavits of No. 1 and Thomas Walden as to the degree of Chickasaw blood of No's 1 to 6 inclusive
No. 8 Born Jany 15, 1901; Application rec'd May 31, 1905, under Act of Congress approved March 3, 1905.
Sept. 12/1898.

RESIDENCE: Pontotoc	**COUNTY**				**CARD NO.**			
POST OFFICE: Dibble, Ind. Ter.					**FIELD NO.**			
	NAME	**RELATIONSHIP TO PERSON FIRST NAMED**	**AGE**	**SEX**	**BLOOD**	**TRIBAL ENROLLMENT**		
						YEAR	**COUNTY**	**PAGE**
1	Higgins, Thos. H.		26	M	I.W.			
2	" Frances	Wife	19	F	Full	1897	Pontotoc	65
3	" Nebby C.	Son	2	M	1/2			

4	" Thomas Nebbe	"	2wk	"	1/2			
5	" Patsey Ann	Dau	2mo	F	1/2			

TRIBAL ENROLLMENT OF PARENTS

	NAME OF FATHER	YEAR	COUNTY	NAME OF MOTHER	YEAR	COUNTY
1	Jack Higgins	Dead	Non-Citizen	Hester Higgins	Dead	Non-Citizen
2	Ben Pikey	"	Chickasaw Roll	Kissie Pikey	1897	Pontotoc
3	No. 1			No. 2		
4	No. 1			No. 2		
5	No. 1			No. 2		

(NOTES)

No. 2 On Chickasaw Roll as Francies Higgins *(No. 1 Dawes' Roll No. 95)*
No. 3 " " " " Nebby C. " *(remainder illegible)* *(No. 3 Dawes' Roll No. 4071)*
No. 3 Proof of Birth received and filed Oct. 23, 1902.
No. 4 Enrolled Decr 13/98; Died Feb. 15, 1899. Proof of Death filed Oct. 26th 1902.
No. 5 Born July 30, 1902; Enrolled Oct. 23, 1902. *(No. 5 Dawes' Roll No. 4972)*

P.O. Tuttle 10/16/04

Sept. 12/98.

RESIDENCE: Pontotoc ***COUNTY*** ***CARD NO.***
POST OFFICE: Iona, Ind. Ter. ***FIELD NO.***

	NAME	RELATIONSHIP TO PERSON FIRST NAMED	AGE	SEX	BLOOD	TRIBAL ENROLLMENT		
						YEAR	COUNTY	PAGE
1	Vanderslice, Robert J.		37	M	I.W.	1897	Pontotoc	80
2	" Mary	Wife	32	F	Full	1897	"	48
3	" Minnie	Dau	10	F	1/2	1897	"	48
4	" Walter	Son	7	M	1/2	1897	"	48
5	" Jacob	"	5	"	1/2	1897	"	48
6	" Maulsee Bula	Dau	1	F	1/2	1897	"	90
7	Edwards, David	St. Son	14	M	1/2	1897	"	48
8	" Nannie	" Dau	13	F	1/2	1897	"	48
9	" Sam I	" Son	15	M	1/2	1893	Pickens	P.R.#1 138
10	Vanderslice, Eliza	Dau	1mo	F	1/2			

TRIBAL ENROLLMENT OF PARENTS

	NAME OF FATHER	YEAR	COUNTY	NAME OF MOTHER	YEAR	COUNTY
1	Jacob Vanderslice	Dead	Non-Citizen	Louisam Sanders		Non Citizen
2	Isum Chigter	"	Chickasaw Roll	Molsie Benton Chigter	Dead	Chickasaw Roll
3	No. 1			No. 2		
4	No. 1			No. 2		

5	No. 1			No. 2		
6	No. 1			No. 2		
7	Charlie Edwards	Dead	Non-Citizen	No. 2		
8	" "	"	" "	No. 2		
9	" "	"	" "	No. 2		
10	No. 1			No. 2		

(NOTES)

No. 1 See decision of June 21, '04. *(No. 1 Dawes' Roll No. 383)*
No. 1 is now the Husband of Laura C. Mersersmith on Choctaw Card No. 2206, April 26th 1902.
No. 2 Died May 15, 1899. Proof of Death filed May 4th 1902.
No. 3 Died July 20, 1902. Proof of Death filed Nov. 21, 1902. *(No. 6 Dawes' Roll No. 4070)*
No. 6 On Chickasaw Roll as Malissa B. Vanderslice; Proof of Birth received and filed Oct. 2, 1902.
No. 9 On Chickasaw Pay Roll No. 1 as Sam Edwards; Enrolled Sept. 27th 1899.
No. 10 Enrolled June 16th 1899.

Sept. 12/1898.

RESIDENCE: Pontotoc ***COUNTY*** ***CARD NO.***
POST OFFICE: Purcell, Ind. Ter. ***FIELD NO.***

	NAME	RELATION-SHIP TO PERSON FIRST NAMED	AGE	SEX	BLOOD	TRIBAL ENROLLMENT		
						YEAR	COUNTY	PAGE
1	Poff, Maggie May		12	F	1/2	1897	Pickens	22

TRIBAL ENROLLMENT OF PARENTS

	NAME OF FATHER	YEAR	COUNTY	NAME OF MOTHER	YEAR	COUNTY
1	Old Man Poff	Dead	Non-Citizen	Serena Tushasahy	Dead	Chickasaw Roll

(NOTES)

No. 1 On Chickasaw Roll as Maggie Mary Poff.

Sept. 12/98.

RESIDENCE: Tishomingo ***COUNTY*** ***CARD NO.***
POST OFFICE: Regan, Ind. Ter. ***FIELD NO.***

	NAME	RELATION-SHIP TO PERSON FIRST NAMED	AGE	SEX	BLOOD	TRIBAL ENROLLMENT		
						YEAR	COUNTY	PAGE
1	Keel, Lewis		56	M	Full	1897	Tishomingo	35
2	" Maulsie	Wife	54	F	"	1897	"	35

TRIBAL ENROLLMENT OF PARENTS

	NAME OF FATHER	YEAR	COUNTY	NAME OF MOTHER	YEAR	COUNTY
1	Tish-ap-a-le-tubby	Dead	Chickasaw Roll	Ste-ma-ke-cha	Dead	Chickasaw Roll
2	Cha-tub-by	"	" "	*(Name Illegible)*	"	" "

(NOTES)

No. 1 Died March 24th 1902; Proof of Death filed April 17, 1902.
No. 2 is a full-blood - See affidavit filed Sept. 26th 1902. *(No. 2 Dawes' Roll No. 4069)*

Sept. 29th 1898.

RESIDENCE: Pontotoc **COUNTY** **CARD NO.**
POST OFFICE: Pauls Valley, Ind. Ter. **FIELD NO.**

	NAME	RELATIONSHIP TO PERSON FIRST NAMED	AGE	SEX	BLOOD	TRIBAL ENROLLMENT YEAR	COUNTY	PAGE
1	Strickland, Charles Guy	NAMED	12	M	1/4	1897	Pontotoc	61
2	" Wm Douglass	Bro	5	"	1/4	1897	"	61

	NAME OF FATHER	YEAR	COUNTY	NAME OF MOTHER	YEAR	COUNTY
1	Charles Strickland	Dead	Chickasaw Roll	Sarah Strickland Bullock		White woman
2	" "	"	" "	" " "		" "

(NOTES)

No. 1 On Chickasaw Roll as C.G. Strickland.
No. 2 " " " " W.D. "
Sarah Strickland Bullock, on Chickasaw Doubtful Card No. 9

Sept. 12, 1898.

RESIDENCE: Pontotoc **COUNTY** **CARD NO.**
POST OFFICE: Roff, Ind. Ter. **FIELD NO.**

	NAME	RELATIONSHIP TO PERSON FIRST NAMED	AGE	SEX	BLOOD	TRIBAL ENROLLMENT YEAR	COUNTY	PAGE
1	Land, C.M.C.	NAMED	48	M	I.W.	1897	Pontotoc	80
2	" Maulda Folsom	Wife	34	F	3/4	1897	"	49
3	" Oscar Lee	Son	15	M	3/8	1897	"	49
4	" Hiram	"	13	"	3/8	1897	"	49
5	" Lula	Dau	11	F	3/8	1897	"	49
6	" Alice	"	9	"	3/8	1897	"	49
7	" Kitty	"	7	"	3/8	1897	"	49

TRIBAL ENROLLMENT OF PARENTS

	NAME OF FATHER	YEAR	COUNTY	NAME OF MOTHER	YEAR	COUNTY
1	Hiram Land		Non Citizen	Sally Ann Land	Dead	Non Citizen
2	Sampson Fulsom	Dead	Chickasaw Roll	Kittie Fulsom	"	Chickasaw Roll
3	No. 1			No. 2		
4	No. 1			No. 2		
5	No. 1			No. 2		

6	No. 1			No. 2		
7	No. 1			No. 2		

(NOTES)

All on Chickasaw Roll as Laud.
No. 2 " " " " Marilda Laud
No. 3 " " " " Oscar "

P.O. Roff, I.T. 9/25/02.

Sept. 12, 1898

RESIDENCE: Pontotoc COUNTY CARD NO.
POST OFFICE: Paola, Ind. Ter. FIELD NO.

	NAME	RELATIONSHIP TO PERSON FIRST NAMED	AGE	SEX	BLOOD	TRIBAL ENROLLMENT YEAR	COUNTY	PAGE
1	Yoakum, John J.		22	M	1/16	1897	Pontotoc	66
2	" Bertha B.	Dau	15mo	F	1/32	1897	"	89
3	" Minnie A.	Wife	21	"	I.W.			
4	" Beulah Pearl	Dau	2mo	"	1/32			
5	" Uana Lee	"	1wk	"	1/32			

TRIBAL ENROLLMENT OF PARENTS

	NAME OF FATHER	YEAR	COUNTY	NAME OF MOTHER	YEAR	COUNTY
1	M.M. Yoakum		Non citizen	Fannie Yoakum	Dead	Pontotoc
2	No. 1			Minnie Yoakum		non citizen
3	G.A. Bennett		Non citizen	Mary E. Bennett		non citizen
4	No. 1			No. 3		
5	No. 1			No. 3		

(NOTES)

M.M. Yoakum father of No. 1 on Chickasaw D.280.
No. 2 Registered under Act of Legislature, July 31/1897; Chick Roll Page 89
No. 2 Died Sept 21, 1898. See Copy of letter from No. 1 filed Sept 12th 1902; Proof of Death filed Oct. 13th 1902.
No. 3 Enrolled March 20/99 *(No. 3 Dawes' Roll No. 93)*
No. 4 Enrolled May 25th 1900
No. 5 Born Decr 1901; Enrolled Dec. 31st 1901

Sept. 12th 1898.

RESIDENCE: Pontotoc ***COUNTY***				***CARD NO.***				
POST OFFICE: Paola, Ind. Ter.				***FIELD NO.***				
	NAME	**RELATION-SHIP TO PERSON FIRST NAMED**	**AGE**	**SEX**	**BLOOD**	**TRIBAL ENROLLMENT**		
						YEAR	**COUNTY**	**PAGE**
1	Yoakum, George H.		20	M	1/16	1897	Pontotoc	66
2	" William	Bro	17	"	1/16	1897	"	66
3	" Leonard	"	14	"	1/16	1897	"	66
4	" Mary B.	Sister	13	F	1/16	1897	"	66

TRIBAL ENROLLMENT OF PARENTS

	NAME OF FATHER	**YEAR**	**COUNTY**	**NAME OF MOTHER**	**YEAR**	**COUNTY**
1	M.M. Yoakum	Dead	Non Citizen	Fannie Yoakum	Dead	Pontotoc
2	" " "	"	" "	" "	"	"
3	" " "	"	" "	" "	"	"
4	" " "	"	" "	" "	"	"

(NOTES)

No. 1 On Chickasaw Roll as D.H. Yoakum
No. 2 Died Feb. 16, 1899. Proof of Death filed Sept. 12, 1902.
No. 4 On Chickasaw Roll as M.B. Yoakum
M.M. Yoakum father of Nos 1 to 4 inclusive, on Chickasaw Card #D.280.

Sept. 12, 1898.

RESIDENCE: Pontotoc ***COUNTY***				***CARD NO.***				
POST OFFICE: Jett, Ind. Ter.				***FIELD NO.***				
	NAME	**RELATION-SHIP TO PERSON FIRST NAMED**	**AGE**	**SEX**	**BLOOD**	**TRIBAL ENROLLMENT**		
						YEAR	**COUNTY**	**PAGE**
1	Fulsome, Osaac		50	M	3/4	1897	Pontotoc	49

TRIBAL ENROLLMENT OF PARENTS

	NAME OF FATHER	**YEAR**	**COUNTY**	**NAME OF MOTHER**	**YEAR**	**COUNTY**
1	Sampson Fulsom	Dead	Chickasaw Roll	Kittie Fulsome	Dead	Chickasaw Roll

(NOTES)

P.O. *(Illegible)*

Sept. 12, 1898.

RESIDENCE: Pontotoc	**COUNTY**	**CARD NO.**	
POST OFFICE: Johnson		**FIELD NO.**	

	NAME	RELATION-SHIP TO PERSON FIRST NAMED	AGE	SEX	BLOOD	TRIBAL ENROLLMENT		
						YEAR	COUNTY	PAGE
1	Bunch, Joseph S.		41	M	I.W.	1897	Pontotoc	91
2	" Emma	Wife	33	F	1/4	1897	"	61
3	" Thomas P.	Son	7	M	1/8	1897	"	61
4	" Maudie M.	Dau	6	F	1/8	1897	"	61
5	" Albert C.	Son	4	M	1/8	1897	"	61
6	" Joseph Douglas	"	3mo	"	1/8	DIED PRIOR TO SEPTEMBER 20, 1902		

TRIBAL ENROLLMENT OF PARENTS

	NAME OF FATHER	YEAR	COUNTY	NAME OF MOTHER	YEAR	COUNTY
1	N.P. Bunch	Dead	Non Citizen	Nancy M. Bunch		Non-Citizen
2	T.B. Johnston (I.W.)	"	Pontotoc	Elizabeth Johnston	Dead	Pontotoc
3	Joseph S. Bunch	1897	" (No. 1)	No. 2		
4	" " "	1897	" (No. 1)	No. 2		
5	" " "	1897	" (No. 1)	No. 2		
6	No. 1			No. 2		

(NOTES)

No. 2 is the wife of Joseph S. Bunch a white man *(No. 1 Dawes' Roll No. 92)*
No. 2 On Chickasaw Roll as Ema Bunch
No. 3 " " " " J.B. "
No. 4 " " " " M.M. "
No. 5 " " " " A.C. "
No. 6 Enrolled May 24th 1900
No. 6 Died June 18, 1902; Proof of Death filed Nov. 13, 1902.
Evidence of divorce between No. 1 and his former wife Joanna L. Bunch filed Jany. 14, 1902.
See affidavit of J. Brown filed Feby 13, 1900.

Sept. 12, 1898.

RESIDENCE: Pontotoc	**COUNTY**	**CARD NO.**	
POST OFFICE: Purcell, Ind. Ter.		**FIELD NO.**	

	NAME	RELATION-SHIP TO PERSON FIRST NAMED	AGE	SEX	BLOOD	TRIBAL ENROLLMENT		
						YEAR	COUNTY	PAGE
1	Morris, Joseph E.		34	M	I.W.	1897	Pickens	87
2	" Annie	Wife	32	F	3/4	1897	Pontotoc	63
3	White, Willie	St. Son	15	M	3/8	1897	"	63
4	" James	" "	7	"	3/8	1897	"	63

TRIBAL ENROLLMENT OF PARENTS						
	NAME OF FATHER	**YEAR**	**COUNTY**	**NAME OF MOTHER**	**YEAR**	**COUNTY**
1	Joseph Morris	Dead	Non-Citizen	Ellen C. Morris	Dead	Non-Citizen
2	John Billie	"	Chickasaw Roll	Julia Haynes	1897	Pontotoc
3	John White		Non-Citizen	No. 2		
4	" "		" "	No. 2		

(NOTES)

No. 2 On Chickasaw Roll as Annie White.

P.O. Davis, I.T. 10/30/02.

Sept. 12/1898.

RESIDENCE: Pickens ***COUNTY*** ***CARD NO.***

POST OFFICE: Pauls Valley, Ind. Ter. ***FIELD NO.***

	NAME	**RELATION-SHIP TO PERSON FIRST NAMED**	**AGE**	**SEX**	**BLOOD**	**TRIBAL ENROLLMENT**		
						YEAR	**COUNTY**	**PAGE**
1	McClure, Tecumseh		68	M	1/2	1897	Pickens	16
2	" Ed	Son	22	"	3/4	1897	"	16
3	Paul, Abby	Dau	18	F	3/4	1897	"	16
4	" Dewey	G. Son	3mo	M	5/8			
5	McClure, Tecumseh, Jr.	" "	9	"	3/8	1897	Pickens	16
6	" Amanda	" Dau	8	F	3/8	1897	"	16
7	" Tamsey	" "	7	"	3/8	1897	"	16
8	Hutchins, Hattie O.	Dau of No 3	2 1/2	"	3/8			
9	" Daisy May	" " " "	8mo	"	3/8			

TRIBAL ENROLLMENT OF PARENTS						
	NAME OF FATHER	**YEAR**	**COUNTY**	**NAME OF MOTHER**	**YEAR**	**COUNTY**
1	McClure		non-citizen	El-ta-jah	Dead	Chickasaw Roll
2	No. 1			Mary McClure	"	Pickens Co
3	No. 1			" "	"	" "
4	Wm Paul	1897	Pickens	No. 3		
5	Jenson McClure	Dead	"	Battie McClure	Dead	Non-Citizen
6	" "	"	"	" "	"	" "
7	" "	"	"	" "	"	" "
8	George Hutchins		Non citizen	No. 3		
9	" "		" "	No. 3		

(NOTES)

No. 1 Died March 13th 1902; Proof of Death filed Oct. 14th 1902.

No. 3 is now the wife of George Hutchins, non citizen. Evidence of marriage filed Nov. 11th 1902

No. 4 Died June 27th 1898; Proof of Death filed Oct. 14th 1902.

No. 8 Born March 1, 1900. Enrolled Oct. 11, 1902.
No. 9 Born Feb. 21, 1902. Enrolled Oct. 25th 1902.

Sept. 12/98.

RESIDENCE: Choctaw Nation **COUNTY** **CARD NO.**
POST OFFICE: Coalgate, Ind. Ter. **FIELD NO.**

	NAME	RELATIONSHIP TO PERSON FIRST NAMED	AGE	SEX	BLOOD	TRIBAL ENROLLMENT YEAR	COUNTY	PAGE
1	Mishontombby, Aaron		23	M	Full	1897	Chick. residing in Choctaw N. 3rd Dist.	74

TRIBAL ENROLLMENT OF PARENTS

	NAME OF FATHER	YEAR	COUNTY	NAME OF MOTHER	YEAR	COUNTY
1	Mishontaumby	1897	Chick. residing in Choctaw N. 3rd Dist.	Liza Mishontaumby	1897	Chick. residing in Choctaw N. 3rd Dist.

(NOTES)

On Chickasaw Roll as Aaron Anderson.

Sept. 8, 1898.

RESIDENCE: Pontotoc **COUNTY** **CARD NO.**
POST OFFICE: Viola, Ind. Ter. **FIELD NO.**

	NAME	RELATIONSHIP TO PERSON FIRST NAMED	AGE	SEX	BLOOD	TRIBAL ENROLLMENT YEAR	COUNTY	PAGE
1	Anolitubby, Shosha		60	F	Full	1893	Pontotoc	32
2	Lumpka, Markey	St. Dau	43	"	"	1897	"	55
3	Dyer, Tecumseh	Gr. Son	18	M	"	1897	Pickens	18
4	Neal, Oliver	" "	8	"	"	1897	Pontotoc	55

TRIBAL ENROLLMENT OF PARENTS

	NAME OF FATHER	YEAR	COUNTY	NAME OF MOTHER	YEAR	COUNTY
1	Cha-fah	Dead	Chickasaw Roll	Ste-ma-ho-te	Dead	Chickasaw Roll
2	A-me-a-stubby	"	" "	No-ye	"	" "
3	Suffron Dyer	"	Pontotoc	Lizzie Dyer	"	Pontotoc
4	Silas Neal	1897	Chick. residing in Choctaw N. 1st Dist.	Lottie Harris	1897	"

(NOTES)

No. 1 On 1893 Chickasaw Pay Roll No. 2 as Shosha Amolitubby
No. 2 Died June 5, 1899. Proof of Death filed Oct. 14th 1902.
No. 4 On Chickasaw Roll as Oliver Harris.
No. 3 now husband of Mattie Dyer.

Sept. 8, 1898.

RESIDENCE: Pontotoc ***COUNTY*** ***CARD NO.***
POST OFFICE: Viola, Ind. Ter. ***FIELD NO.***

	NAME	RELATIONSHIP TO PERSON FIRST NAMED	AGE	SEX	BLOOD	TRIBAL ENROLLMENT YEAR	TRIBAL ENROLLMENT COUNTY	TRIBAL ENROLLMENT PAGE
1	Burris, George		24	M	Full	1897	Pontotoc	55

TRIBAL ENROLLMENT OF PARENTS

	NAME OF FATHER	YEAR	COUNTY	NAME OF MOTHER	YEAR	COUNTY
1	John Burris	Dead	Pontotoc	Sophie Burris	Dead	Pontotoc

(NOTES)

Sept. 8th 1898.

RESIDENCE: Pontotoc ***COUNTY*** ***CARD NO.***
POST OFFICE: Viola, Ind. Ter. ***FIELD NO.***

	NAME	RELATIONSHIP TO PERSON FIRST NAMED	AGE	SEX	BLOOD	TRIBAL ENROLLMENT YEAR	TRIBAL ENROLLMENT COUNTY	TRIBAL ENROLLMENT PAGE
1	Frazier, Jim		26	M	Full	1897	Tishomingo	29
2	" Lottie	Wife	23	F	"	1897	Pontotoc	55
3	" Jackson	Son	6mo	M	"			

	NAME OF FATHER	YEAR	COUNTY	NAME OF MOTHER	YEAR	COUNTY
1	Galloway Frazier	1897	Tishomingo	Phoebe Frazier	1897	Tishomingo
2	Hollie Nolatubby	Dead	Pontotoc	Susie Harris	1897	Pontotoc
3	No. 1			No. 2		

(NOTES)

No. 2 On Chickasaw Roll as Lottie Harris.
No. 3 Enrolled July 18th 1901
No. 3 Died Oct. 6th 1901; Proof of Death filed Jan. 25th 1902.

P.O. Connerville, I.T. 5/19/04.

Sept. 8, 1898.

RESIDENCE: Pontotoc ***COUNTY*** ***CARD NO.***
POST OFFICE: Jeff, Ind. Ter. ***FIELD NO.***

	NAME	RELATIONSHIP TO PERSON FIRST NAMED	AGE	SEX	BLOOD	TRIBAL ENROLLMENT YEAR	TRIBAL ENROLLMENT COUNTY	TRIBAL ENROLLMENT PAGE
1	Ayahakatubby, Amy		44	F	Full	1897	Pontotoc	94
2	Willis, Johnson	Son	22	M	"	1897	"	57
3	Ayahakatubby, Emanuel	G. Son	9	"	"	1893	"	110

TRIBAL ENROLLMENT OF PARENTS

	NAME OF FATHER	YEAR	COUNTY	NAME OF MOTHER	YEAR	COUNTY
1	Ayahakatubby	Dead	Chickasaw Roll	On-ho-ye	Dead	Chickasaw Roll
2	Willis	"	" "	No. 1		
3	Davis Ayakatubby	"	Pontotoc	Malinda	Dead	Pontotoc

(NOTES)

No. 1 On Chickasaw Roll as Annie Iyokotubby

Nos. 1 & 3 On 1893 Chickasaw Pay Roll No. 2 as Amy and Emanuel Iyakatubby

No. 3 Died Decr 5th 1901; Proof of Death filed Oct. 18th 1902.

No. 2 is husband of Minnie Anderson on *(remainder illegible)*

Sept. 8/98.

RESIDENCE: Pontotoc ***COUNTY*** ***CARD NO.***

POST OFFICE: Center, Ind. Ter. ***FIELD NO.***

	NAME	RELATION-SHIP TO PERSON FIRST NAMED	AGE	SEX	BLOOD	TRIBAL ENROLLMENT YEAR	COUNTY	PAGE
1	Perry, J.M.		39	M	3/4	1897	Pontotoc	39

TRIBAL ENROLLMENT OF PARENTS

	NAME OF FATHER	YEAR	COUNTY	NAME OF MOTHER	YEAR	COUNTY
1	Johnson Perry	Dead	Chickasaw Roll	Liley Perry	Dead	Chickasaw Roll

(NOTES)

Sept. 8th 1898.

RESIDENCE: Choctaw Nation ***COUNTY*** ***CARD NO.***

POST OFFICE: Coalgate, Ind. Ter. ***FIELD NO.***

	NAME	RELATION-SHIP TO PERSON FIRST NAMED	AGE	SEX	BLOOD	TRIBAL ENROLLMENT YEAR	COUNTY	PAGE
1	Anderson, Wallace		15	M	Full	1897	Chick. residing in Choctaw N. 3rd Dist.	74

TRIBAL ENROLLMENT OF PARENTS

	NAME OF FATHER	YEAR	COUNTY	NAME OF MOTHER	YEAR	COUNTY
1	John Anderson	1897	Chick. residing in Choctaw N. 3rd Dist.	Liza Anderson	1897	Chick. residing in Choctaw N. 3rd Dist.

(NOTES)

Sept. 8th 1898.

RESIDENCE: Choctaw Nation		**COUNTY**			**CARD NO.**			
POST OFFICE: Coalgate, Ind. Ter.					**FIELD NO.**			
	NAME	**RELATIONSHIP TO PERSON FIRST NAMED**	**AGE**	**SEX**	**BLOOD**	**TRIBAL ENROLLMENT**		
						YEAR	**COUNTY**	**PAGE**
1	Mishontaumbby, Jincy		18	F	Full	1897	Chick. residing in Choctaw N. 3rd Dist.	74
2	" Jackson	Son	2	M	"	1896	" "	74
3	" Iba	Dau	1	F	1/2			

TRIBAL ENROLLMENT OF PARENTS

	NAME OF FATHER	YEAR	COUNTY	NAME OF MOTHER	YEAR	COUNTY
1	Mishontombby	1897	Chick. residing in Choctaw N. 3rd Dist.	Liza Mishontombby	1897	Chick. residing in Choctaw N. 3rd Dist.
2	Illegitimate			No. 1		
3	Illegitimate			No. 1		

(NOTES)

No. 2 born March 2, 1893. Proof of birth filed March 11, 04. *(No. 1 Dawes' Roll No. 4066)*
No. 3 born September 3, 1901. Application received March 7, 1905 *(No. 2 Dawes' Roll No. 4788)*
under Act of Congress approval March ?, 1905. *(No. 3 Dawes' Roll No. 4962)*

Sept. 8, 1898.

RESIDENCE: Choctaw Nation		**COUNTY**			**CARD NO.**			
POST OFFICE: Coalgate, Ind. Ter.					**FIELD NO.**			
	NAME	**RELATIONSHIP TO PERSON FIRST NAMED**	**AGE**	**SEX**	**BLOOD**	**TRIBAL ENROLLMENT**		
						YEAR	**COUNTY**	**PAGE**
1	Mishontombby		80	M	Full	1897	Chick. residing in Choctaw N. 3rd Dist.	74
2	" Liza	Wife	80	F	"	1897	" "	74

TRIBAL ENROLLMENT OF PARENTS

	NAME OF FATHER	YEAR	COUNTY	NAME OF MOTHER	YEAR	COUNTY
1	*(Blank)*	Dead	Chickasaw Roll	*(Illegible)*	Dead	Chickasaw Roll
2	*(Blank)*	"	" "	*(Illegible)*	"	" "

(NOTES)

Sept. 8, 1898.

RESIDENCE: Choctaw Nation COUNTY CARD NO.
POST OFFICE: Guertie, Ind. Ter. FIELD NO.

	NAME	RELATIONSHIP TO PERSON FIRST NAMED	AGE	SEX	BLOOD	TRIBAL ENROLLMENT YEAR	COUNTY	PA
1	Leader, Susan		26	F	Full	1897	Chick. residing in Choctaw N. 3rd Dist.	
2	" Emily	Dau	1	"	1/2			
3	" Morris	Sopn	1wk	M	1/2			

	NAME OF FATHER	YEAR	COUNTY	NAME OF MOTHER	YEAR	COUNTY
1	Mishontaumbby	1897	Chick. residing in Choctaw N. 3rd Dist.	Liza	1897	Chick. residing Choctaw N. 3rd D
2	Morris Leader		Atokabo Choctaw Nation	No. 1		
3	" "		" "	No. 1		

(NOTES)

No. 1 Wife of Morris Leader, Choctaw Roll, Card No. 72.
No. 2 Evidence of Birth received and filed Feb. 26th 1901. *(No. 2 Dawes' Roll No. 4750)*
No. 3 Evidence of Birth received and filed Feb. 26th 1902.
See addidavits of No. 1 and Elum Anderson as to exact date of the birth of No. 2. Died July 15, 1903.
Sept. 8/9

RESIDENCE: Pontotoc COUNTY CARD NO.
POST OFFICE: Stonewall, Ind. Ter. FIELD NO.

	NAME	RELATIONSHIP TO PERSON FIRST NAMED	AGE	SEX	BLOOD	TRIBAL ENROLLMENT YEAR	COUNTY	PAGE
1	Cass, Wall DEAD		38	M	Full	1897	Pontotoc	52
2	" Lizzie	Wife	31	F	"	1897	"	52
3	" Lem DEAD	Son	11	M	"	1897	"	52
4	" Benjamin	"	8	"	"	1897	"	52
5	Killcrease, Minnie	Step Dau	16	F	"	1897	"	52
6	" Lettie	" "	14	"	"	1897	"	52
7	" Annie	" "	11	"	"	1897	"	52
8	Carter, Watson	Ward	11	M	"	1897	"	54
9	Brown, Victoria May	Dau of No. 5	1 1/2	F	"			

TRIBAL ENROLLMENT OF PARENTS

	NAME OF FATHER	YEAR	COUNTY	NAME OF MOTHER	YEAR	COUNTY
1	Lewis Cass	Dead	Pontotoc	Maulsie Wall	Dead	Pontotoc
2	Johnson Perry	"	"	*(Illegible)* Perry	"	"

3	No. 1			*(Illegible)* Cass	1897	"
4	No. 1			" "	1897	"
5	Eastman? Killcrease	1897	Pontotoc	No. 2		
6	" "	1897	"	No. 2		
7	" "	1897	"	No. 2		
8	Robert Carter	Dead	Chick. residing in Choctaw N. 1st Dist.	Liza Ann	Dead	Chick residing in Choctaw N. 1st Dist.
9	Culberson Brown		Chick card #141	No. 5		

(NOTES)

No. 2 is now the wife of Benjamin Gilmore
No. 1 Died Feby 16, 1902' Proof of Death filed July 8th 1902.
No. 3 Died Feby 23rd 1902; Proof of Death filed July 8th 1902.
No. 9 Born April 12, 1901; Evidence of Birth filed Dec. 23, 1902.

No. 5 P.O. Hogan, I.T. 12/23/02.
P.O. of Nos. 2-6-7-8 Jesse I.T. 1/29/04.

Sept. 8, 1898.

RESIDENCE: Choctaw Nation ***COUNTY*** ***CARD NO.***
POST OFFICE: Oconee, Ind. Ter. ***FIELD NO.***

	Name	Relationship to Person First Named	Age	Sex	Blood	Tribal Enrollment Year	County	Page
1	Perkins, Jane		23	F	Full	1897	Chick residing in Choctaw N. 3rd Dist.	75

TRIBAL ENROLLMENT OF PARENTS

	Name of Father	Year	County	Name of Mother	Year	County
1	William James	1897	Pontotoc	Annie James	1897	Pontotoc

(NOTES)

Also on Page 94 as Jane James.
Wife of Albert Perkins Chickasaw Roll Card No. 69.

Sept. 8, 1898.

RESIDENCE: Pontotoc ***COUNTY*** ***CARD NO.***
POST OFFICE: Ada, Ind. Ter. ***FIELD NO.***

	Name	Relationship to Person First Named	Age	Sex	Blood	Tribal Enrollment Year	County	Page
1	Perry Houston		28	M	Full	1897	Pontotoc	42

	TRIBAL ENROLLMENT OF PARENTS					
	NAME OF FATHER	YEAR	COUNTY	NAME OF MOTHER	YEAR	COUNTY
1	Johnson Perry	Dead	Pontotoc	Annie *(Illegible)*	1897	Pontotoc

(NOTES)

No. 1 is now the husband of No. 1 on Chickasaw Card #1269
See letter of No. 1 filed *(remainder illegible)*

Sept. 8, 1898.

RESIDENCE: Tishomingo ***COUNTY*** ***CARD NO.***
POST OFFICE: Ravia, Ind. Ter. ***FIELD NO.***

	NAME	RELATIONSHIP TO PERSON FIRST NAMED	AGE	SEX	BLOOD	TRIBAL ENROLLMENT		
						YEAR	COUNTY	PAGE
1	John, McKinney		26	M	Full	1897	Pickens	22

	TRIBAL ENROLLMENT OF PARENTS					
	NAME OF FATHER	YEAR	COUNTY	NAME OF MOTHER	YEAR	COUNTY
1	Levison John	Dead	Pickens	Shum-ah-te-cha	Dead	Pickens

(NOTES)

Sept. 5/98.

RESIDENCE: Pontotoc ***COUNTY*** ***CARD NO.***
POST OFFICE: Center, Ind. Ter. ***FIELD NO.***

	NAME	RELATIONSHIP TO PERSON FIRST NAMED	AGE	SEX	BLOOD	TRIBAL ENROLLMENT		
						YEAR	COUNTY	PAGE
1	Lanham, Perry G.		31	M	I.W.	1897	Pontotoc	80
2	" Mary Jane	Wife	27	F	3/4	1897	"	47
3	" Jimmie	Son	9	M	3/8	1897	"	47
4	" Charles H.	"	6	"	3/8	1897	"	47
5	" Amanda	Dau	3	F	3/8	~~1897~~	~~"~~	~~47~~
6	" Bessie	"	1	"	3/8			
7	" Manley	Son	7wks	M	3/8			

	TRIBAL ENROLLMENT OF PARENTS					
	NAME OF FATHER	YEAR	COUNTY	NAME OF MOTHER	YEAR	COUNTY
1	*(Illegible)* Lanham	Dead	Non Citizen	Amanda Lanham		Non citizen
2	Houston *(Illegible)*	"	Chickasaw Roll	Betsey *(Illegible)*	Dead	Pontotoc
3	No. 1			No. 2		
4	No. 1			No. 2		
5	No. 1			No. 2		

6	No. 1			No. 2		
7	No. 1			No. 2		

(NOTES)

No. 1 On Chickasaw Roll as P.J. Lanham. *(No. 1 Dawes' Roll No. 91)*
No. 2 " " " " Mary G. Lanham.
No. 3 " " " " Jemmie "
No. 5 Died in April 1899. Proof of Death filed *(Illegible date)*1902.
No. 6 Evidence of Birth received and filed March 11th 190?
No. 7 Born June 25th 1902. Enrolled Aug. 7th 190?

Sept. 8th 1898.

RESIDENCE: Pontotoc **COUNTY** **CARD NO.**
POST OFFICE: Center, Ind. Ter. **FIELD NO.**

	NAME	RELATION-SHIP TO PERSON FIRST NAMED	AGE	SEX	BLOOD	TRIBAL ENROLLMENT YEAR	COUNTY	PAGE
1	Tyson, Ed		24	M	Full	1897	Pontotoc	48

TRIBAL ENROLLMENT OF PARENTS

	NAME OF FATHER	YEAR	COUNTY	NAME OF MOTHER	YEAR	COUNTY
1	Cub-brish Tyson	Dead	Pontotoc	Betsy Tyson	Dead	Pontotoc

(NOTES)

P.O. Maxwell, IT

Sept. 8th 1898.

RESIDENCE: Choctaw Nation **COUNTY** **CARD NO.**
POST OFFICE: Star, Ind. Ter. **FIELD NO.**

	NAME	RELATION-SHIP TO PERSON FIRST NAMED	AGE	SEX	BLOOD	TRIBAL ENROLLMENT YEAR	COUNTY	PAGE
1	DeArmon, Laura		18	F		1897	Chick residing in Choctaw N. 1st Dist.	91
2	" Ester Lee	Dau	1wk	"				
3	" Ora-?nay	"	2m	"				

TRIBAL ENROLLMENT OF PARENTS

	NAME OF FATHER	YEAR	COUNTY	NAME OF MOTHER	YEAR	COUNTY
1	Albert W. Perry	1897	Chick residing in Choctaw N 1st Dist.	Tabitha Perry	Dead	Non citizen
2	J.E. DeArmon			No. 1		
3	" " "			No. 1		

(NOTES)

(All notations illegible)
P.O. Iron Bridge, I.T. 11/24/02.

Sept. 8th 1898.

RESIDENCE: Pontotoc **COUNTY**					**CARD NO.**			
POST OFFICE: Wayne, Ind. Ter.					**FIELD NO.**			

	NAME	RELATIONSHIP TO PERSON FIRST NAMED	AGE	SEX	BLOOD	TRIBAL ENROLLMENT		
						YEAR	COUNTY	PAGE
1	Colbert, Joe E.		41	M	3/8	1897	Pontotoc	64
2	" Elizabeth Unora	Wife	29	F	I.W.	1897	"	81
3	" Annie R.	Dau	13	"	3/16	1897	"	64
4	" Nancy Laura	"	10	"	3/16	1897	"	64
5	" Henry Jattle	Son	7	M	3/16	1897	"	64
6	" Lottie M	Dau	5	F	3/16	1897	"	64
7	" Joseph E.	Son	3mo	M	3/16			

TRIBAL ENROLLMENT OF PARENTS

	NAME OF FATHER	YEAR	COUNTY	NAME OF MOTHER	YEAR	COUNTY
1	Henry Colbert	Dead	Chickasaw Roll	Louisa Patterson	1897	Tishomingo
2	*(Illegible)* Ingram		Non-Citizen	Nannie Ingram		Non-Citizen
3	No. 1			No. 2		
4	No. 1			No. 2		
5	No. 1			No. 2		
6	No. 1			No. 2		
7	No. 1			No. 2		

(NOTES)

Nos. 1 to 6 Admitted by Dawes Com. Case 36.
No. 2 On Chickasaw Roll as Norah Colbert *(No. 2 Dawes' Roll No. 253)*
No. 3 " " " " A.R. "
No. 4 " " " " Lula "
No. 5 " " " " H.C. "
George R. Collins, of Stonewall, I.T. testifies under oath that he was present at the marriage of Joe E. Colbert and Elizabeth Elnora Ingram and that he heard the minister read the license. William E. Byrd of Stonwall, I.T. states that he knows the marriage license was issued in accordance with the Chickasaw law and the license money paid. See testimony of No ? as to status of No. 2 as an intermarried citizen Sept 24 1902 taken at Pauls Valley I.T. Oct. 21 1902.

Sept. 8 1898.

RESIDENCE: Choctaw Nation 1st Dist. **COUNTY**					**CARD NO.**			
POST OFFICE:					**FIELD NO.**			

	NAME	RELATIONSHIP TO PERSON FIRST NAMED	AGE	SEX	BLOOD	TRIBAL ENROLLMENT		
						YEAR	COUNTY	PAGE
1	Dilbert, Luella		19	F	1/2	1897	Chick residing in Choctaw Nat 1st Dist.	91

2	" Leester Bel	Son	1mo	M	1/4			
3	" Elord Edward	"	1mo	"	1/4			

TRIBAL ENROLLMENT OF PARENTS

	NAME OF FATHER	YEAR	COUNTY	NAME OF MOTHER	YEAR	COUNTY
1	Albert W. Perry	1897	Chick residing in Choctaw N 1st Dist.	Tabitha Perry	Dead	Non-Citizen
2	Frank Dilbert		Non Citizen	No. 1		
3	Frank Dilbert		" "	No. 1		

(NOTES)

(All notations illegible)

P.O. Dolberg, IT 10/15/02

Sept. 8, 1898.

RESIDENCE: Choctaw Nation **COUNTY** **CARD NO.**

POST OFFICE: Wilburton, Ind. Ter. **FIELD NO.**

	NAME	RELATIONSHIP TO PERSON FIRST NAMED	AGE	SEX	BLOOD	TRIBAL ENROLLMENT YEAR	COUNTY	PAGE
1	Isheatubby		58	M	Full	1897	Chick residing in Choctaw N. 1st Dist.	78

TRIBAL ENROLLMENT OF PARENTS

	NAME OF FATHER	YEAR	COUNTY	NAME OF MOTHER	YEAR	COUNTY
1	*(Illegible Name)*	Dead	Chickasaw Roll	Ah-ah-na-*(illegible)*	Dead	Chickasaw Roll

(NOTES)

Sept. 8, 1898.

RESIDENCE: Pontotoc **COUNTY** **CARD NO.**

POST OFFICE: Stonewall, Ind. Ter. **FIELD NO.**

	NAME	RELATIONSHIP TO PERSON FIRST NAMED	AGE	SEX	BLOOD	TRIBAL ENROLLMENT YEAR	COUNTY	PAGE
1	Owens, Mattie M.		15	F	Full	1897	Pontotoc	37

TRIBAL ENROLLMENT OF PARENTS

	NAME OF FATHER	YEAR	COUNTY	NAME OF MOTHER	YEAR	COUNTY
1	*(Illegible Name)*	Dead	Pontotoc	*(Illegible Name)*	1897	Pontotoc

(NOTES)

(All notations illegible)

Sept. 8 1898.

RESIDENCE: Pontotoc COUNTY					CARD NO.		
POST OFFICE: Stonewall, Ind. Ter.					FIELD NO.		
NAME	RELATIONSHIP TO PERSON FIRST NAMED	AGE	SEX	BLOOD	TRIBAL ENROLLMENT		
					YEAR	COUNTY	PAGE
1 Underwood, William		21	M	Full	1897	Pontotoc	59

TRIBAL ENROLLMENT OF PARENTS

NAME OF FATHER	YEAR	COUNTY	NAME OF MOTHER	YEAR	COUNTY
1 Wallace Underwood	Dead	Pontotoc	*(Illegible)* Underwood	1897	Pontotoc

(NOTES)

(All notations illegible)

Sept. 8th 1898.

RESIDENCE: Pontotoc COUNTY					CARD NO.		
POST OFFICE: Viola, Ind. Ter.					FIELD NO.		
NAME	RELATIONSHIP TO PERSON FIRST NAMED	AGE	SEX	BLOOD	TRIBAL ENROLLMENT		
					YEAR	COUNTY	PAGE
1 Patterson, Agnes		78	F	Full	1897	Pontotoc	56
2 Columbus, Etta	G. Dau	15	"	"	1897	"	56
3 Duke, Curtis	G. Son	14	M	"	1897	"	56
4 " Dora	G. Dau	12	F	"	1897	"	56

TRIBAL ENROLLMENT OF PARENTS

NAME OF FATHER	YEAR	COUNTY	NAME OF MOTHER	YEAR	COUNTY
1 Mo-so-tubby	Dead	Chickasaw Roll	She-ma-le-key	Dead	Chickasaw Roll
2 Walt Columbus	"	Pontotoc	Julia Columbus	"	Pontotoc
3 Billie Duke	1897	"	Nancy Duke	"	"
4 " "	1897	"	" "	"	"

(NOTES)

No. 1 Died May 24th 1899. Proof of Death filed Nov. 14th 1902.
No. 2 On Chickasaw Roll as Etta Duke.
No. 3 Died July 14th 1901. Evidence of Death filed Sept. 11, 1901.

Sept. 8, 1898.

RESIDENCE: Pontotoc COUNTY					CARD NO.		
POST OFFICE: Viola, Ind. Ter.					FIELD NO.		
NAME	RELATIONSHIP TO PERSON FIRST NAMED	AGE	SEX	BLOOD	TRIBAL ENROLLMENT		
					YEAR	COUNTY	PAGE
1 Durin, Wesley		26	M	Full	1897	Pontotoc	56

TRIBAL ENROLLMENT OF PARENTS						
	NAME OF FATHER	YEAR	COUNTY	NAME OF MOTHER	YEAR	COUNTY
1	Richard Durin	1897	Pontotoc	Agnes Patterson	1897	Pontotoc

(NOTES)

Sept. 8th 1898.

RESIDENCE: Pontotoc COUNTY									
POST OFFICE: Waupunuka, Ind. Ter.									

CARD NO.
FIELD NO.

	NAME	RELATION-SHIP TO PERSON FIRST NAMED	AGE	SEX	BLOOD	TRIBAL ENROLLMENT		
						YEAR	COUNTY	PAGE
1	Maytubby, Eastman		36	M	Full	1897	Pontotoc	56
2	" Minnie	Wife	22	F	"	1897	"	56
3	" Franklin	Son	5	M	"	1897	"	56

TRIBAL ENROLLMENT OF PARENTS						
	NAME OF FATHER	YEAR	COUNTY	NAME OF MOTHER	YEAR	COUNTY
1	Hogan Maytubby	Dead	Pontotoc	Lucy Maytubby	Dead	Pontotoc
2	Richard Durin	1897	"	Agnes Patterson	1897	"
3	No. 1			No. 2		

(NOTES)

Sept. 8th 1898.

RESIDENCE: Pontotoc COUNTY									
POST OFFICE: Stonewall, Ind. Ter.									

CARD NO.
FIELD NO.

	NAME	RELATION-SHIP TO PERSON FIRST NAMED	AGE	SEX	BLOOD	TRIBAL ENROLLMENT		
						YEAR	COUNTY	PAGE
1	Hennerson, Mollie		20	F	Full	1897	Pontotoc	42
2	Scott, Mary	Dau	4	"	3/4	1897	"	42
3	" Wilburn	Son	11mo	M	3/4			

	NAME OF FATHER	YEAR	COUNTY	NAME OF MOTHER	YEAR	COUNTY
1	Jim Hennerson	Dead	Tishomingo	Benis Colbert	1897	Pontotoc
2	Houston Scott		Chick Freedman	No. 1		
3	" "		" "	No. 1		

(NOTES)

No. 1 On Chickasaw Roll as Mollie Anderson
No. 3 Evidence of Birth received and filed May 13th 1902.
(Remainder illegible.)

Sept. 8, 1898.

RESIDENCE: Pontotoc COUNTY					CARD NO.		
POST OFFICE: Stonewall, Ind. Ter.					FIELD NO.		
NAME	RELATION-SHIP TO PERSON FIRST NAMED	AGE	SEX	BLOOD	TRIBAL ENROLLMENT		
					YEAR	COUNTY	PAGE
1 Colbert, Benis		45	F	Full	1897	Pontotoc	42
2 Robeson, Jane	Dau	15	"	"	1897	Pontotoc	42
3 Colbert, Lucy	"	7	"	"	1897	"	42
4 " Nancy	"	5	"	"	1897	"	42
5 " Cubby	Son	3	M	"	1897	"	42
6 " Jim	"	10	"	"	1897	"	42
7 Henderson, John	"	21	"	"	1897	"	42
8 Robeson, Eliza	Gr. Dau	5mo	F	1/2			

TRIBAL ENROLLMENT OF PARENTS

NAME OF FATHER	YEAR	COUNTY	NAME OF MOTHER	YEAR	COUNTY
1 A-wah-tub-by	Dead	Chickasaw Roll	Shun-pol-e-cha	Dead	Chickasaw Roll
2 Adam Lewis	"	Pontotoc	No. 1		
3 Cubby Colbert	"	"	No. 1		
4 " "	"	"	No. 1		
5 " "	"	"	No. 1		
6 " "	"	"	No. 1		
7 Jim Henderson	"	Tishomingo	No. 1		
8 Joe Robinson	1896	Atoka	No. 1		

(NOTES)

No. 2 On Chickasaw Roll as Jane Colbert.

No. 2 Is wife of Joe Robinson on Chickasaw card #3279. Evidence of marriage filed July 25th 1902. The surname of her husband appears to be Robeson. See letter 11,904 - 1902 G.O. Files

No. 7 On Chickasaw Roll as John Colbert.

No. 8 Born Feby 1, 1902; Enrolled July 25, 1902.

Sept. 8, 1898.

RESIDENCE: Pontotoc COUNTY					CARD NO.		
POST OFFICE: Pontotoc, Ind. Ter.					FIELD NO.		
NAME	RELATION-SHIP TO PERSON FIRST NAMED	AGE	SEX	BLOOD	TRIBAL ENROLLMENT		
					YEAR	COUNTY	PAGE
1 Cravatt, Forbus		30	M	Full	1897	Pontotoc	51
2 " Lena	Wife	27	F	"	1897	"	51
3 " Amanda	Dau	10	"	"	1897	"	51
4 " Stella	"	2	"	"	1897	"	51

5	McCurtain, Edmon	Ward	18	M	"	1897	Pickens	18
6	" Humphrey	"	17	"	"	1897	"	18
7	Cravatt, Overton	Son	7mo	"	"			

TRIBAL ENROLLMENT OF PARENTS

	NAME OF FATHER	YEAR	COUNTY	NAME OF MOTHER	YEAR	COUNTY
1	Henderson Cravatt	Dead	Chickasaw Roll	Melvina Cravatt	Dead	Chickasaw Roll
2	Robert Sewell	"	" "	Se-le-an	"	Pontotoc
3	No. 1			Lucy Cravatt	"	"
4	No. 1			No. 2		
5	Eastman McCurtain	Dead	Pontotoc	Kissie	Dead	Pontotoc
6	" "	"	"	Se-le-an	"	"
7	No. 1			No. 2		

(NOTES)

No. 1 Enrolled Decr 13/99.

Sept. 8, 1898.

RESIDENCE: Choctaw Nation		*COUNTY*			*CARD NO.*			
POST OFFICE: Guertie, Ind. Ter.					*FIELD NO.*			
	NAME	RELATION-SHIP TO PERSON FIRST NAMED	AGE	SEX	BLOOD	TRIBAL ENROLLMENT		
						YEAR	COUNTY	PAGE
1	Lewis, Thompson		13	M	1/2			
2	" Dickson	Bro	8	"	1/2			

TRIBAL ENROLLMENT OF PARENTS

	NAME OF FATHER	YEAR	COUNTY	NAME OF MOTHER	YEAR	COUNTY
1	John Lewis		Atoka Co. Choctaw Nation	Al-lich-ta Lewis		
2	" "		" "	" "		

(NOTES)

Nos. 1 & 2 On Choctaw Census Record No. 2 Page 343 transferred to Chickasaw Roll by Dawes Com.
Father of Nos. 1 & 2 is John Lewis, on Choctaw Card #4941.
Allichta Lewis acknowledges to be a full blood Chickasaw but name not found on Chickasaw Roll, Sept. 8/98.

No. 1 On Choctaw Roll 1896 at Atoka County No. 3344.

No. 2 " " " 1896 " " " " 3345 as *(Name illegible)*

Nos. 1 & 2 *(Illegible)*

RESIDENCE: Choctaw Nation		**COUNTY**			**CARD NO.**			
POST OFFICE: Owl, Ind. Ter.					**FIELD NO.**			
	NAME	**RELATIONSHIP TO PERSON FIRST NAMED**	**AGE**	**SEX**	**BLOOD**	**TRIBAL ENROLLMENT**		
						YEAR	**COUNTY**	**PAGE**
1	Bond, Alice		22	F	Full			
2	" Jesse	Son	2	M	1/2			

TRIBAL ENROLLMENT OF PARENTS

	NAME OF FATHER	YEAR	COUNTY	NAME OF MOTHER	YEAR	COUNTY
1	Lawson Roberts	Dead	Chickasaw Roll	Klicy Roberts	1897	Chick residing in Choctaw N 3rd Dist.
2	*(Illegible)* Bond		Atoka County Choctaw Roll	No. 1		

(NOTES)

(All Notations Illegible)

Sept. 8, 1898.

RESIDENCE: Pontotoc		**COUNTY**			**CARD NO.**			
POST OFFICE: Pontotoc, Ind. Ter.					**FIELD NO.**			
	NAME	**RELATIONSHIP TO PERSON FIRST NAMED**	**AGE**	**SEX**	**BLOOD**	**TRIBAL ENROLLMENT**		
						YEAR	**COUNTY**	**PAGE**
1	Sealy, Willis		28	M	Full	1897	Pontotoc	50
2	" Henry	Son	4	"	"	1897	"	50
3	" George	"	5mo	"	"			

TRIBAL ENROLLMENT OF PARENTS

	NAME OF FATHER	YEAR	COUNTY	NAME OF MOTHER	YEAR	COUNTY
1	Joseph Sealy	Dead	Pontotoc	Mary Ann Sealy	1897	Pontotoc
2	No. 1			Alice Sealy	1897	"
3	No. 1			" "	1897	"

(NOTES)

Proper name of Alice Sealy, above is Alice Ayakatubby.
No. 1 Wife and one child on Chickasaw Card #747?.
No. 1 Died Nov. 3 1900. Proof of Death filed July 15 1901.
(This notation illegible).
No. 3 Died Nov. 3, 1900. Proof of Death filed July 15 1901.
No. 3 Enrolled Nov. 3/99.

Sept. 8/98.

RESIDENCE: Choctaw Nation 3rd Dist. **COUNTY** **CARD NO.**
POST OFFICE: Guertie, Ind. Ter. **FIELD NO.**

	NAME	RELATIONSHIP TO PERSON FIRST NAMED	AGE	SEX	BLOOD	TRIBAL ENROLLMENT YEAR	COUNTY	PAGE
1	Pusley, Susan		40	F	Full			

TRIBAL ENROLLMENT OF PARENTS

	NAME OF FATHER	YEAR	COUNTY	NAME OF MOTHER	YEAR	COUNTY
1	Aaron Frazier	Dead	Chickasaw Roll	Malinda Frazier	Dead	Chickasaw Roll

(NOTES)

On Chickasaw Census Record No. 2 Page 403, transferred to Chickasaw Roll by Dawes Com.
Also on Choctaw Roll 1896, Atoka County, No. 10545 as Susan Pusley.

Sept. 7/98.

RESIDENCE: Pontotoc **COUNTY** **CARD NO.**
POST OFFICE: Pontotoc, Ind. Ter. **FIELD NO.**

	NAME	RELATIONSHIP TO PERSON FIRST NAMED	AGE	SEX	BLOOD	TRIBAL ENROLLMENT YEAR	COUNTY	PAGE
1	Sealy, Mary Ann		52	F	Full	1897	Pontotoc	50
2	" Ben	Son	25	M	"	1897	"	50
3	" Viney	G. Dau	5	F	"	1897	"	50

TRIBAL ENROLLMENT OF PARENTS

	NAME OF FATHER	YEAR	COUNTY	NAME OF MOTHER	YEAR	COUNTY
1	Ma-to-ho-mey	Dead	Chickasaw Roll	Ta-la-che	Dead	Chickasaw Roll
2	Joseph Sealy	Dead	Pontotoc	No. 1		
3	Willis "	1897	"	Alice Sealy	1897	Pontotoc

(NOTES)

No. 1 On Chickasaw Roll as Morgan Sealy.
No. 1 Died Decr 17th 1899. Proof of Death filed July 15th 1901.
Proper name of Alice Sealy, above is Alice Ayakatubby.

Sept. 7/98.

RESIDENCE: Chocyaw Nation **COUNTY** **CARD NO.**
POST OFFICE: Coalgate, Ind. Ter. **FIELD NO.**

	NAME	RELATIONSHIP TO PERSON FIRST NAMED	AGE	SEX	BLOOD	TRIBAL ENROLLMENT YEAR	COUNTY	PAGE
1	Sullivan, Daniel		42	M	I.W.	1897	Chick. residing in Choctaw N. 3rd Dist.	82

2	" Rachel	Wife	35	F	1/2	1897	" " " "	73
3	" Michael Jos.	Son	16	M	1/4	1897	" " " "	73
4	~~" Mary B.~~	~~Dau~~	~~14~~	~~F~~	~~1/4~~	~~1897~~	~~" " " "~~	~~73~~
5	" Edward A.	Son	10	M	1/4	1897	" " " "	73
6	" Ellen	Dau	8	F	1/4	1897	" " " "	73
7	" Anna L.	"	6	"	1/4	1897	" " " "	73
8	" Robert E.	Son	3	M	1/4	1897	" " " "	73
9	" Florence	Dau	1	F	1/4			

TRIBAL ENROLLMENT OF PARENTS

	NAME OF FATHER	YEAR	COUNTY	NAME OF MOTHER	YEAR	COUNTY
1	Mike Sullivan	Dead	Non-Citizen	Margaret Sullivan	Dead	Non-Citizen
2	Toney Maytubby	"	Chickasaw Roll	Mandy Maytubby	"	Chickasaw Roll
3	No. 1			No. 2		
4	No. 1			No. 2		
5	No. 1			No. 2		
6	No. 1			No. 2		
7	No. 1			No. 2		
8	No. 1			No. 2		
9	No. 1			No. 2		

(NOTES)

No. 1 Will mail marriage license and certificate to Dawes Commission. Received Sept. 22 1898.
No. 2 Died Jan 19 1899, Proof of Death filed May 10 1902.
No. 1 Married white non-citizen Aug 28/99 - Sept. 11/99
No. 3 On Chickasaw Roll as Mike J. Sullivan
No. 4 Transferred to Card #553 *(remainder illegible)*
No. 9 Evidence of Birth received and filed May 24th 1902.

Sept. 7th 1898.

RESIDENCE: Choctaw Nation ***COUNTY*** ***CARD NO.***
POST OFFICE: Star, Ind. Ter. ***FIELD NO.***

	NAME	RELATION-SHIP TO PERSON FIRST NAMED	AGE	SEX	BLOOD	TRIBAL ENROLLMENT YEAR	COUNTY	PAGE
1	Rucker, Rutha		16	F	1/8	1897	Chick residing in Choctaw N. 1st Dist.	91
2	" Albert W.	Son	2mo	M	1/16			
3	" Mamie Arenia	Dau	3mo	F	1/16			

	TRIBAL ENROLLMENT OF PARENTS					
	NAME OF FATHER	YEAR	COUNTY	NAME OF MOTHER	YEAR	COUNTY
1	Albert W. Perry	1897	Chick residing in Choctaw N. 1st Dist.	Tabitha Perry	Dead	Non citizen
2	Welch Rucker		Non-Citizen	No. 1		
3	Wilton Rucker		" "	No. 1		

(NOTES)

No. 1 Registered under Act of Legislature July 31st 1897, Chickasaw Roll Page *(illegible)*
(Remainder illegible) *(No. 2 Dawes' Roll No. 252)*

P.O. Cowlington, I.T. Sept. 7/98.

RESIDENCE: Choctaw Nation COUNTY CARD NO.
POST OFFICE: Star, Ind. Ter. FIELD NO.

	NAME	RELATIONSHIP TO PERSON FIRST NAMED	AGE	SEX	BLOOD	TRIBAL ENROLLMENT		
						YEAR	COUNTY	PAGE
1	Perry, Albert W.		39	M	1/4	1897	Chick residing in Choctaw N. 1st Dist.	91
2	" Annie M.	Wife	25	F	I.W.	1897	" " " "	91
3	" Emma J.	Dau	2	"	1/8	1897	" " " "	91
4	" *(Illegible)* D.	Son	3wks	M	1/8			
5	" Ida Fay	Dau	13	F	1/8	1897	Chick residing in Choctaw N. 1st Dist.	91
6	" Maude	"	10	"	1/8	1897	" " " "	91
7	" Allen *(Illegible)*	Son	5mo	M	1/8			

	TRIBAL ENROLLMENT OF PARENTS					
	NAME OF FATHER	YEAR	COUNTY	NAME OF MOTHER	YEAR	COUNTY
1	Chas. Perry	Dead	Non citizen	Susan Perry	Dead	Chickasaw Roll
2	*(Illegible)* Dodd		" "	*(Illegible)* Dodd	"	non citizen
3	No. 1			No. 2		
4	No. 1			No. 2		
5	No. 1			*(Illegible information)*		
6	No. 1			*(Illegible information)*		
7	No. 1			No. 2		

(NOTES)

(All notations illegible)

Sept. 7/98.

RESIDENCE: Choctaw Nation	COUNTY				CARD NO.		
POST OFFICE: Allen, Ind. Ter.					FIELD NO.		
NAME	RELATIONSHIP TO PERSON FIRST NAMED	AGE	SEX	BLOOD	TRIBAL ENROLLMENT		
					YEAR	COUNTY	PAGE
1 Wolfe, Moses		57	M	Full	1897	Pontotoc	44

TRIBAL ENROLLMENT OF PARENTS

NAME OF FATHER	YEAR	COUNTY	NAME OF MOTHER	YEAR	COUNTY
1 *(Illegible Name)*	Dead	Chickasaw Roll	*(Illegible Name)*	Dead	Chickasaw Roll

(NOTES)

(All notations illegible)

Sept. 7/98.

RESIDENCE: Choctaw Nation	COUNTY				CARD NO.		
POST OFFICE: Stewart, Ind. Ter.					FIELD NO.		
NAME	RELATIONSHIP TO PERSON FIRST NAMED	AGE	SEX	BLOOD	TRIBAL ENROLLMENT		
					YEAR	COUNTY	PAGE
1 Ott, Eliza Wade		22	F	1/2	1897	Chick residing in Choctaw N. 1st Dist.	60
2 " Johnson	Son	10mo	M	1/4			
3 " Jack	"	5mo	M	1/4			

TRIBAL ENROLLMENT OF PARENTS

NAME OF FATHER	YEAR	COUNTY	NAME OF MOTHER	YEAR	COUNTY
1 Joe *(Illegible)*	Dead	Choctaw Roll	*(Illegible Name)*	1897	Chick residing in Choctaw N. 1st Dist.
2 Carney Ott		" "	No. 1		
3 " "		" "	No. 1		

(NOTES)

Wife of Carney Ott, Choctaw Roll Card No. 66
(Statement illegible)
No. 2 Enrolled Aug. 8th 1899
No. 3 Born March 1st 1902; Enrolled Aug. ? 1902
No. 2 Died April 7, 1902; Proof of death filed Dec. 24 1902.

Sept. 7/98.

RESIDENCE: Pontotoc COUNTY					CARD NO.		
POST OFFICE: Stonewall, Ind. Ter.					FIELD NO.		
NAME	RELATION-SHIP TO PERSON FIRST NAMED	AGE	SEX	BLOOD	TRIBAL ENROLLMENT		
					YEAR	COUNTY	PAGE
1 Allen, Charley		29	M	Full	1897	Pontotoc	51
2 " Lizzie	Wife	33	F	"	1897	"	51
3 Allen, Melton *(Illegible Name)*	Son	3	M	"	1897	"	51
4 Allen, Paralee	Dau	10m	F	"			
5 " Clara	"	?mo	"	"			

TRIBAL ENROLLMENT OF PARENTS

	NAME OF FATHER	YEAR	COUNTY	NAME OF MOTHER	YEAR	COUNTY
1	Charley Brown	Dead	Tishomingo	Malinda Brown	Dead	Tishomingo
2	E-mo-nubby	"	Pontotoc	*(Illegible Name)*	1897	Pontotoc
3	No. 1			No. 2		
4	No. 1			No. 2		
5	No. 1			No. 2		

(NOTES)

No. 2 On Chickasaw Roll as Lizzie Reed. *(No. 3 Dawes' Roll No. 4053)*
(Remainder illegible)

Sept. 7/98.

RESIDENCE: Pontotoc COUNTY					CARD NO.		
POST OFFICE: Ada, Ind. Ter.					FIELD NO.		
NAME	RELATION-SHIP TO PERSON FIRST NAMED	AGE	SEX	BLOOD	TRIBAL ENROLLMENT		
					YEAR	COUNTY	PAGE
1 Harris, Joe		23	M	Full	1897	Pontotoc	?
2 " Ema	Wife	18	F	"	1897	"	?
3 " Flalis	Son	5mo	M	"			

TRIBAL ENROLLMENT OF PARENTS

	NAME OF FATHER	YEAR	COUNTY	NAME OF MOTHER	YEAR	COUNTY
1	*(Illegible Name)*	Dead	Chickasaw Roll	Emily Dalton	1897	Pontotoc
2	*(Illegible)* Fulsom	1897	Pontotoc	*(Illegible)* Fulsom	Dead	"
3	No. 1			No. 2		

(NOTES)

No. 2 *(Statement illegible)*
No. 3 Born Jan 24th 1902; Enrolled *(remainder illegible)*

Sept. 7/98.

RESIDENCE: Pontotoc COUNTY					CARD NO.		
POST OFFICE: Stonewall, Ind. Ter.					FIELD NO.		
NAME	RELATIONSHIP TO PERSON FIRST NAMED	AGE	SEX	BLOOD	TRIBAL ENROLLMENT YEAR	COUNTY	PAGE
1 Byrd, William L.		54	M	1/4	1897	Pontotoc	39

TRIBAL ENROLLMENT OF PARENTS

	NAME OF FATHER	YEAR	COUNTY	NAME OF MOTHER	YEAR	COUNTY
1	*(Illegible Name)*	Dead	*(Illegible)*	*(Illegible Name)*	Dead	Pontotoc

(NOTES)

(All notations illegible.)

Sept. 7/98.

RESIDENCE: Choctaw Nation COUNTY					CARD NO.		
POST OFFICE: Stewart, Ind. Ter.					FIELD NO.		
NAME	RELATIONSHIP TO PERSON FIRST NAMED	AGE	SEX	BLOOD	TRIBAL ENROLLMENT YEAR	COUNTY	PAGE
1 Fulsom, Tennissee		25	F	3/4	1897	Chick residing in Choctaw N. 1st Dist.	69
2 Wade, Lizzie	Dau	5	"	7/8	1897	" " " "	69
3 ~~Perry, William~~	~~"~~	~~1~~	~~"~~	~~7/8~~			
4 Choate, Willie	Son	1	M	7/8			

TRIBAL ENROLLMENT OF PARENTS

	NAME OF FATHER	YEAR	COUNTY	NAME OF MOTHER	YEAR	COUNTY
1	Solomon Fulsom	Dead	Chickasaw Roll	Libby Fulsom	Dead	Chickasaw Roll
2	*(Illegible)* Wade	"	" "	No. 1		
3	*(Illegible)* Perry		Chick residing in Choctaw N. 1st Dist.	No. 1		
4	James Choate	1896	Pontotoc	No. 1		

(NOTES)

No. 3 Died Aug. 13, 1899. Proof of death fled Aug. 6/03. *(No. 4 Dawes' Roll No. 4961)*
No. 4 born Nov. 6, 1901; Application received April 8, 1905, under Act of Congress, approved *(date illegible)*.

RESIDENCE: Choctaw Nation COUNTY					CARD NO.		
POST OFFICE: Stewart, Ind. Ter.					FIELD NO.		
NAME	RELATIONSHIP TO PERSON FIRST NAMED	AGE	SEX	BLOOD	TRIBAL ENROLLMENT YEAR	COUNTY	PAGE
1 Wade, Alemos H.		40	M	1/2			

TRIBAL ENROLLMENT OF PARENTS						
	NAME OF FATHER	YEAR	COUNTY	NAME OF MOTHER	YEAR	COUNTY
1	*(Illegible Name)*	Dead	Choctaw Roll	*(Illegible Name)*	Dead	Chickasaw Roll

(NOTES)

(All notations illegible)

Sept. ?/98.

RESIDENCE: Choctaw Nation **COUNTY** **CARD NO.**
POST OFFICE: Owl, Ind. Ter. **FIELD NO.**

	NAME	RELATIONSHIP TO PERSON FIRST NAMED	AGE	SEX	BLOOD	TRIBAL ENROLLMENT		
						YEAR	COUNTY	PAGE
1	Benton, Earnest		20	M	Full	1897	Pontotoc	42
2	" Hattie Adeline	Dau	4mo	F	1/2			
3	" Davis	Son	2mo	M	1/2			
4	" Maggie	Wife	24	F	I.W.			

TRIBAL ENROLLMENT OF PARENTS						
	NAME OF FATHER	YEAR	COUNTY	NAME OF MOTHER	YEAR	COUNTY
1	Davis Benton	Dead	Pontotoc	Louisa Benton	1897	Pontotoc
2	No. 1			Maggie Benton		Non citizen
3	No. 1			" "		" "
4	James *(Illegible)*		Non Citz	Louisa *(Illegible)*		

(NOTES)

No. 2 Enrolled June 23rd, 190? *(No. 3 Dawes' Roll No. 4052)*
No. 3 Born Sept. 17th 1902. Enrolled Nov. 1st 1902. *(No. 4 Dawes' Roll No. 544)*

Sept. 7/98.

RESIDENCE: Choctaw Nation **COUNTY** **CARD NO.**
POST OFFICE: Owl, Ind. Ter. **FIELD NO.**

	NAME	RELATIONSHIP TO PERSON FIRST NAMED	AGE	SEX	BLOOD	TRIBAL ENROLLMENT		
						YEAR	COUNTY	PAGE
1	~~Benton, Louisa~~		~~43~~	~~F~~	~~Full~~	~~1897~~	~~Pontotoc~~	~~42~~

TRIBAL ENROLLMENT OF PARENTS						
	NAME OF FATHER	YEAR	COUNTY	NAME OF MOTHER	YEAR	COUNTY
1	~~*(Illegible Name)*~~	~~Dead~~	~~Chickasaw Roll~~	~~Sophia *(Illegible)*~~	~~Dead~~	~~Chickasaw Roll~~

(NOTES)

No. 1 Died Sept 24th 1900. Proof of Death filed Nov. 13th 1902.

Sept. 7/98.

RESIDENCE: Pontotoc COUNTY					CARD NO.		
POST OFFICE: Stonewall, Ind. Ter.					FIELD NO.		
NAME	RELATIONSHIP TO PERSON FIRST NAMED	AGE	SEX	BLOOD	TRIBAL ENROLLMENT		
					YEAR	COUNTY	PAGE
1 Wilson, Kate		21	F	Full	1897	Pontotoc	49
2 Underwood, Intolubby	Son	3	M	"	1897	"	49

TRIBAL ENROLLMENT OF PARENTS

NAME OF FATHER	YEAR	COUNTY	NAME OF MOTHER	YEAR	COUNTY
1 George Wilson	1897	Pontotoc	Adeline Wilson	Dead	Pontotoc
2 *(Illegible)* Underwood	Dead	"	No. 1		

(NOTES)

No. 1 now wife of Henderson Brown, on Chick *(remainder illegible).*

Sept. 7/98.

RESIDENCE: Pontotoc COUNTY					CARD NO.		
POST OFFICE: Stonewall, Ind. Ter.					FIELD NO.		
NAME	RELATIONSHIP TO PERSON FIRST NAMED	AGE	SEX	BLOOD	TRIBAL ENROLLMENT		
					YEAR	COUNTY	PAGE
1 ~~Wilson, Lem~~		~~30~~	~~M~~	~~Full~~	~~1897~~	~~Pontotoc~~	~~87~~

TRIBAL ENROLLMENT OF PARENTS

NAME OF FATHER	YEAR	COUNTY	NAME OF MOTHER	YEAR	COUNTY
1 ~~George Wilson~~	~~1897~~	~~Pontotoc~~	~~Adeline Wilson~~	~~Dead~~	~~Pontotoc~~

(NOTES)

No. 1 On 1893 Chickasaw Pay Roll No. 2 Page 227.
No. 1 Died August 17, 1900. Enrollment cancelled by *(remainder illegible).*

Sept. 7/98.

A-ME-A-STUBBY 178
A-WAH-TUB-BY 190
ABEL, JR 55
ABRAM
Amanda 31
Bula May 31
Edward 31
Elward 31
Riva Ann 31
Tom Garritt 31
Vina Maude 31
ADAMS
Alice 101
John 101
John C 101
Lucinda 144
Lucinda Brittain 101, 144
R A
ADKINS
Charles Richard 48
Edna Ellen 48
Elander 48
Evelina 48
H G 48
Harvey G 48
Israel Earnest 48
L P 47
AH-AH-NA-*(ILLEGIBLE)* 187
AH-CO-NA-HE 96
AH-HA-KA-TUBBY 19
ALDRIDGE
Robt 90
ALEXANDER
Arch 59
Baby 59
Bob 59
Caroline 120
Charles F 59
Chilly 120
Cornelia Garret 59
D A 59
Della 59
Ephraim 156
Gipson 1
J A 59
James Arthur 59
Jennie 59, 156
Lucy 1
Mattie E 59
Pierce 1
W V 59
Whit Hyden 59
ALLEN
Charley 197
Clara 197
Lizzie 197
Melton *(Illegible)* 197
Nancy 128
Paralee 197
Samuel 128
ALLIE 77
ALLISON
? W 103
Janey 103
Josie 103
Nancy 103
Wade 103
Will 103
AMALITUBBY
Shosha 178
AMANDA 77
ANALITUBBY
Shosha 178
ANDERSON
Aaron 178
Elum 182
John 180
Liza 180
Mary M 7
Minnie 180
Mollie 189
W A 7
Wallace 180
ANGLEN
Lucy O 38
ANGLIN
Albert Thomas 38
Annie May 38
Lillie Rhoda 38
Lucy Obedient 38
Sydney C 38
W A 39
ANNA I 108
ARCHEERSON

Janey 85
ARIVAN 32
ARNOLD
Cyndie 105
James 122
Sam 105
ASBERRY
A S 132
Douglas 132
Sallie 132
ASBURY
Alice 132
Allen S 132
David F. 132
Edgar Allen 132
Eula 132
Mary 132
Myrtle 132
Nellie 132
Rual D 132
Wm Douglas 132
ATKINS
Charles 48
Edna 48
Harvey 48
Isreal 48
AUTRY
Fred A 1
AYAHAKATUBBY 180
Amy 179
Emanuel 179
AYAKATUBBY
Alice 193
Davis 180
AYEKATUBBY
Alice 192
B M 98
BAILEY
Annie 108
Annie L 108
E S 108
Furman 108
Jewel 108
O S 108
O W 108
P 108
Pontotoc P 108
Richard Furman 108
Sarah E 108
BAKER
Angeline 128
H F 128
H T 128
Mary H 128
Saml D 128
Susan Stacey 121
BALL
Ada C 38
Ada Clifford 38
Albert P 39
M F 38
Mary A 39
Millard F 38, 39
Myrtle V 38
Myrtle Virginia 38
Rhoda L 39
BANKS
John 11
Mary 11
BARNES
John F 54
Viture 54
BARNETT
Benj 1
Mary 1
BARR
A D 165
Addie 165
Alta 165
Alty 165
Eddie 165
Ema 165
Emma 165
Ethel 165
Johanna 165
Laura 165
Maddie May 165
Sam 165
Samuel 165
BASS
Howell 55
Jerry 55
Margaret 55
Rhoda N 55

BAUGH
Ann 43
Ete 43
BELK
Belle 35
George 36
BELL
A G 138
Alta Pearl 135
Anna 135
Charles D 135
Delila Lucinda 138
Eliza 138
Emma O 138
Grant 138
J E 135
J S 135
James Smith 135
Joe Edgar 135
BENNETT
G A 174
Mary E 174
BENNIE 66
BENTON
Davis 199
Earnest 199
Hattie Adeline 199
Louisa 199
Maggie 199
BESSIE 119
BILLEE
John 80
BILLIE
Ah-lawecha 9
Alexander 9
John 177
BLACK
Annie Lee 33
Camelia 33
Charley 95
Henretta 33
Ida 33
John 34
John Dechard 33
Kissie 95
Kizzi 95
Mamie 96
Mamie Wilbert 95
Overton 33
Sam 33, 34
Sophia E 34
Sophia Ellen 33
Sophie A 34
BLACKWOOD
A C 147
Amelia C 147
Andrew C, Jr 147
Georgia M 147
Jemima C 147
John 147
Mary 147
Nobe? G 147
Nora I 147
BLAKE
Callie 44
John Y 45
John Y F 45
BLEVINS
Lemuel 121
Robert Earl 121
Susie 121
Susie P 121
Toad 121
Willie 121
Wirtie Clyde 121
BOHANAN
Joseph 12
BOHANNAN
Silas W 11
BON
Rhoda E 109
Thos W 109
BOND
Adelaide 22
Alice 192
Cornelius 9
Eliza 9
Emeline 9
Esther 9
Henry 10
Henry J 10
(Illegible) 192
Jesse 9, 10, 192
Lizzie 10

Mary 9, 10
Sallie Ann 9
Sally Ann 10
BONNER
Flora 37
Freeman 56
Iszoda 37
John A 56
Susan 56
Susan E 37
Whitmel Francis 37
Wm F 37
Z A 37
Zadok Augustus 37
BOOKER
Dave 99
BOURLAND
Ben 107
Bessie 107
Charles Howard 107
Clemmie 107
Frances Emma 107
Francis 108
Henry 98, 107
Mandy 107
William 107
BOX
Rhoda Fulsom 38
W T 38
BOYD
Callie 97
James 89
Nancy Love 89
R L 89
Sallie 97
Sarah 57
Thos C T 57
BRADLEY
Clara Hicks 3
Earnest 3
Francis 4
Frank Colbert 3
Holmes 3
Nellie 3
Pressley 4
Texanna 4
Winter P 3, 4
BRADY
Bridget 135
Caroline 135
John 135
M N 135
Mike N 135
BRAILEY
Nettie 28
BRANUM
Ellen 147
Mattie 147
Merritt 147
T C 147
BRENNAN
Nannie E 27
Thomas 27
BRITON
Lucenda 101
BRITTAIN
Eveline 144
Frank 144
Lucinda 101
M B 101
M L 144
BRITTENBURG 119
Alice M 119
Don A 119
James B 119
Maria 119
Mary Ann 119
Norma S 119
BROWN
A J 109
A-co-ead-le 122, 123
A-cu-id-ley 110
Aaron 53, 97
Adaline 85
Annie 110, 165
Benson 122
C H 7
Calvin 98
Catherine 7
Charley 197
Chi-ki-ke 165
Cleo 123
Culberson 183
Cyrus Harris 6, 7

Douglas Cooper 23
Elizabeth 24
Elsie 97
Ethel 7
Frances 110
Frances V 7, 74
Francis 111
Guy 7, 53
Hattie 68, 85
Henderson 200
Henry 68
Hepsey 72
Houston 86
I B 7
Ida Belle 6
J 176
J L 7
James 27
James Lewis 7
Jennie 86
Jesse 86
Joe 53
Joe, Sr 7
John 68
Josiah 7, 74
Kate 7
Leonard 85
Liza 122
Loman 165
Lottie 165
Lou 74
Louis L 7
Lucy 110
Malinda 197
Martha 23
Martha Josephine 7
Mary 53
Millie 53
Minerva 110, 123
Minerva Lee 122
Myrtle 86
N J 7
Nancy 110
Otto 68
Pinkney 72
Quidley 136
Roberson 85
Rolia 53, 54
Sarah 165
Sissy 165
Sisy 165
Susan 20
Victoria May 182
Virginia Catherine 7
W J 7
W M 136
William 24, 110
William Josiah 6
Wm 23
BROWNING
Albert 6
Anna 6
Annie 6
Bula B 6
Joe 6
Josiah 6
Lovie Ann 6
Lower 6
Lucy 6
Samuel W 6
Samuel Winston 6
William H 6
Wm Henry 6
BRYD
Benjamin Franklin 100
John 100
Mary Moore 100
BUCHANAN
Henry 128
BULLOCK
Sarah Strickland 173
BUNCH
A C 176
Albert C 176
Ema 176
Emma 176
J B 176
Joanna L 176
Joseph Douglas 176
Joseph S 176
M M 176
Maudie M 176
N P 176
Nancy M 176

Thomas P....176
BURD 101
BURKS
Benj G 134
Dr 134
Hanna 126
John 126
Johnie Wenona....126
Johnnie....126
Rayden....125
Roma 126
Rowena....126
Roy 126
Susan 134
Susan D....134
Vera 125
Verra 126
William....125
William D....134
BURNEY
Blanch 52
Clay P 52
Clefford....52
Clefford C 52
Clifford C....52
David 52
David E....134
Douglas Johnson....52
Eliza 52
Emily 52
Julian 51
Lucy 134
Minnie 52
Una 51
Valey 52
Vessie 52
W B 51
BURRIS
Bessie 94
Colbert A....2
Dewit 94
Eastman....78, 94, 103
Emily 2
George 179
George Washington....2
John 179
Laura A 2
Lemuel Colbert....2
Lena 78
Letha 94
Lillie 94
Liney 94, 103
Melton 94
Robert Lee....94
Sophie 179
Zula 2
BURSSI
G W 2
L C 2
BYARS
Alice Ophelia....63
C P 63
Catherine....62, 64
Charlie T....63
H 63
Jim Jones....63
Katie 63
Katie May....63
Katie, Jr....63
Lizzie E, Jr....63
N H 63
Nancy 63
Nancy E....63
Nathan 64
Nathan H....62
Roy N 63
S F 63
Samuel T....63
T N 63
Thomas N....62
W C 63
William C....63
BYNUM
B M 54
E 54
Effie 54
Mary F 54
Willis 54
BYRD 123
??olsie Colbert....101
B F 100
George Franklin....100
Hattie Zelma....100
Lonnie E....100

Lula May 100
Mamie 100
Mrs B F 101
Nannie Watson 100
Roy Neal 100
William E 186
William F, Jr 100
William L 198
CABB
Richard T 128
CALHOUN
Emily 5
Johnson 5
Louisa 5
CAMPBELL
J M 104
Michael 22
Viona S 73
CANIFAN
Jasper 112
Mattie 112
CARLTON
Frances 56
George R 56
Guy 56
Josie 56
Pearlie 56
Roberson 55
Sarah 55
CARR
D M 161
Ella 161
CARTAS
Sysab 164
CARTER
Ada Gertrude 89
Ada Gertrude Carter 89
B W 89
Benjamin W 89
C D 89
Italy Cecil 89
John 70
John E 70
Julia 89
Julia Josephine 89
Robert 183
Serena 89, 90
Stella F 89
Stella Laflore 89
Watson 182
CARTUBBY
Butch 74, 75
CASEY
A J 155
Andrew J 114
Charles Calvin 114
Effie May 114
F A 143
Folena 155
Folina 143
Lula 114
Newt F 114
CASH
A P 168
Alice 168
Camilla 169
D B 169
Elpha 168
Patterson 168
Patterson Shi 168
Tyree 168
CASS
Benjamin 182
(Illegible) 183
Lem 182
Lewis 182
Lizzie 182
Wall 182
CATE
J S 98
CECIL
Italy 89
CHA-FAH 178
CHA-TUB-BY 172
CHASE
A D 57
Abel 55
Abel D 44, 45
Abel D, Jr 54
Abel D, Sr 44
Emma 44
Emmet 54
Grove 54
Gussie 54

Lennie Mabel 54
Nancy 44, 55, 57
Roxie 54
CHIGTER
Isum 171
Molsie Benton 171
CHISHOLM
Cora 131
Wm 131, 132
CHOATE
James 198
Willie 198
CHUMMUTTIE 19
Tennessee 19
CLAYTON
Benj F 122
Indianola D................................ 122
Indola 122
Lockie S 122
Paul Sharpe 122
Rebecca 122
Tamsey 122
Tamsey A 122
W S 121
William Herbert 122
CO-IK-KE 2
COCHANTUBBY
Cubby 75
COFFEE
Charley 87
Minnie 87
COFFEY
Amanda Virginia.......................... 76
Anderson Wolford........................ 76
Charley 87
Earnest 76
Ella 87
Hillary 87
Ivy 73
M P 71
M W 71, 77
Mary Alverta 76
Melton W 76
Merritt Price 76
Mint 73
Nancy 77
Sale 76, 77
Taylor Overton..............................76
Walter 76
William Lee 76
COLBERT
A R 186
Annie R......................................186
B F, Jr 152
Benis 189, 190
Benj Franklin 152
C E 152
Calvin C.....................................109
Cecil Calvin 152
Cubby 190
Czarina...30
Czarina M 30
E F 45
Ed 19
Ed F 45
Elizabeth 153
Elizabeth Unora 186
Elsie 19, 83
Elzira Oxberry...............................87
Emma F.....................................109
Frank 152
H C 186
Henrietta.......................................30
Henry 71, 186
Henry Jattle 186
Holmes.......................................153
Jane 190
Jim 190
Joe E 186
John 190
Joseph 87
Joseph E 186
Leonidus.......................................53
Lottie M 186
Louisa 71
Lucy 190
Lula 186
Luther Carl..................................152
M M 152
Mamie Marie...............................152
Martha 152
Martin 152
Martin, Jr....................................152
Mary 45, 147

Mattie Z 152
Mattie Zora 152
Nancy 190
Nancy Laura 186
Norah 186
Sam 45
T R 152
Tolbert Ray 152
Vann 83
Walter 30
Walter Cevera 30
COLEMAN
Aaron 18
Arian 18
Bertha Marie 18
Bessie 18
Bessie Neva 18
Donie B 21
Henry L 18
Marie 18
Ola Gladys 18
Riley 21
Riley Buford 21
Riley L 21
Ruby Almedia 21
Sarah Gaddy 21
COLEY 11
Rhoda 11
COLLINS
Andy 61
Audry B 61
George 61, 91
George H 61
George R 186
Hettie 61
J P 61
J R 61
James 61, 147
James P 61
John 61, 91
Louisa 61
Theodore 61
COLSON
J M 104
COLUMBUS 66
Etta 188
Julia 188
Walt 188
CONDER
James 52
Victoria 52
CONRADEY
Henry 159
CONRADY
Henry 159
Mary 159
Mattie 159
CONWAY
Elizabeth J 17
COOK
Ananias 131
C C 131
Cabey Celess 131
Charles 131
Cleo 131
Levera 131
Mary 131
Stella 131
W V 131
William Nye 131
William V 131
COOPER
Beckie 12
Becky 11
Frances 11, 12
Francis 12
Henry 11
Isreal 12
Mary 11
Maude 11
Norris 11
Robert 11
COPELAND
Betty 35
L G 35
COURTNEY
Mary Ann 119
COX
Ada 46
Ada E 46
Hewitt 86
Ida 46
Mary 46
Robert 42

Sarah 86
William R 46
Wm 46
Wm R 46
COYLE
Ake 66
Albert 67
Albert Pike 66
Bee 67
Benjamin Harrison 67
Clara 66
Earl 67
Earnest Earl 67
James Thomas 66
Jim 67
Lillie Audry 67
Mabel Pearl 67
Pearl 67
Pike 67
Violet Teresa 67
CRAVATT
Amanda 190
Forbus 190
Henderson 191
Lena 190
Lucy 191
Melvina 191
Overton 191
Stella 190
CRINER
Alva 43
Ben 43
Bob 43
Buck 43
Charles Cook 43
Dolphus 44
Etta 43
Eunice 153
Frank 43
Franklin 43
George 43, 44, 127, 129, 130
Hazel 44
Joe 44, 153
Joe W 127
Joe William 43
John 43, 44
John Adolphus 43
Laura 43
Lizzie 127
Matilda 127, 129, 130
Matilda Love 43
Minnie 44
Mollie 43, 44
Norma 44
CROSBY
Thomas 106
CROW
A J 62
Annie 62
P C 62
CURR
P N 114
DALTON
Emily 197
DAORS
Lonnie 128
DAVIS
Benjamin 36
D S 36
Daniel 105
Dora Stella 36
Elizabeth 36
James R 36
James Russell 36
John 36
John Henry 36
Josh 161
Julia 36
Laura 161
Lavina 90
Nicey 105
Nora B 36
Nora Belle 36
DEARMAN
J E 185
DEARMON
Ester Lee 185
Laura 185
Ora-?nay 185
DECHARD 106
DECHERD
Eugenia 106
Frances 106
N G 106

P S 106
DENNIS
Sarah 137
DICKERSON
J N 30
DILBERT
Elord Edward 187
Frank 187
Lester Bel 187
Luella 186
DOAK
Dudley 81
Dudley Nail 81
Elizabeth 81
Henry Love 81
Lorre Lee 81
Love Lee 81
DODD
(Illegible) 195
DOUGLAS
Nancy L 121
DRAWNGUESS
Albert 66
Eliza 66
Mary 66
DUKE
Billie 188
Curtis 188
Dora 188
Egga 188
Nancy 188
DULEN
Jim 154
Pochantas 154
DULIN
Janie May 137
Jim 137
Ola Lee 137
Pocahontas 137
Simpson 137
DURIN
Richard ....
Wesley 188
DURODERIGO 67
Albert Franklin 66
Eliza 66
Jane 66
Osavior 33, 66
DUTTON
Harriet 107
Henry 107
DYER
Lizzie 178
Mattie 178
Suffron 178
Tecumseh 178
E-MO-NUBBY 197
EARNEST 110
EASTON
James 46
Margaret 46
EBISCH
C A F 50
C A Frederick 49
C F 50
Christian Frederick 49
Christianna 49
Fred 49, 50
Liddia 49
Mattie 49, 50
May 49
W F Ernest 49
Wagoner 49
EDDINGTON
N A 42
Sarah 42
EDWARD
Abram 32
EDWARDS
A 154
Charlie 172
David 171
Nannie 171
Sam 172
Sam I 171
Susie 154
EL-TA-JAH 177
ELK 91
ELKIN
B T 3
Tempey 3
ELLIOTT
Hannah 125
J C 126

John Cyrus 125
Martha 126
Olivia 126
ELONZO 119
EMA 84
EMILY C 148
ERNIE 55
ESAU 115
EUGINE 106
F G 130
FALLEY 113
FITCH
D H 53
Daniel 53
Eliza Easter 52
Joe 52
Mary Ellen 52
Maude 52
FITZHUGH
Ida 81
John 81
John M 81
Katie 81
Love Lee 81
Robt 81
FLEETWOOD
Emily 87
Emly 87
FLERCHER
Mary Ester 27
FLETCHER
Peter 27
FLORDELIO 48
FLORE
Mary A 50
FOLSOM
Arnold 26
Charlotte 14
Clarence 26
Cleveland 26
Delena 15
Dennis 14
Edler 14, 15
Edlin 15
Elias 14
Frank 14
Hettie 17, 18, 22, 24
Irene 14
Katie 16
Lela 26
Leora 22
Lewis F 26
Leyca 26
Lizzie 26
Lloyd Ray 22
Nathan 17
Olen William 22
Prudence 26
Vera 14
Walker 17, 18, 22, 24
Walter 22
Walter W 22
Willie 14
Willis 14, 15, 16, 26
Winnie 26
FOLSUM
Nathan 17
FOSTER
Florence 80
George 80
Henry C 80
Hewlett 81
Lizzie 80
William 80
FRANK 130
FRAZIER
Aaron 193
Galloway 179
Jackson 110, 179
Jim 179
Lottie 179
Malinda 193
Phoebe 179
Sarah 110
FRIEND
Alice 155
Carley 155
Dorset Carter 155
Retta 155
T L 155
Thomas L 155
FRY
Jeff 90
Sammie J 90

Sophia 90
Sophie 90
FRYREAR
A M 136
Annie May.. 136
Elizabeth.. 136
Ema 136
Emet 136
Emma 136
Frank 136
Robert D.. 136
Roda 136
S B 136
S Burl 136
FULSOM
(Illegible).. 197
Kittie 173
Libby 198
Mr 58
Rhoda 16
Sampson..173, 175
Soloman 198
Tennissee.. 198
FULSOME
Kittie 175
Osaac 175
FURMAN
Annie R 38
Vinnie Beam 38
G B 126
G C 130
G M 98, 130
GADDIS
Bill 42
Georgia.. 42
Georgia A.. 42
John Dewey.. 42
Melvina Love 42
William 42
William B.. 42
William Manuel 42
GADDY
Adeline.. 21
Aley 21
Arch 21
Sarah 21
GALLATIN
A G 109
Elizabeth 109
Minnie 109
Perry 109
GALLATON
Perry 109
GARDNER
Edna D 142
Grant 143
GARLAND
Jake 58
Lucy 56, 58
Mich 58
GARRY
Lillie 21
GAY
Lexas A 117
GEO F 101
GEORGE 91
GEORGIA 123, 148
GIBBONS
Amelia J 67
Elizabeth 68
Emely J 68
James 68
James E 67, 68
M C 68
Margaret C 67
Migs E 67
Murray 67
GIBSON
Calvin 138, 139
Douglas..138
Jane 164
Johnie 138
Johnnie..139
Josiah 164
Louisa 138
Lucy 164
Minnie 164
Mississippi..164
Mitchell..164
Nancy 138, 139
Silas 164
GILMORE
Benjamin..183
GIPSON 164

Minnie ... 164
GODFREY
Louisa ... 5
Nellie ... 5
Wesley Calhoun ... 5
GOINS
Ruder ... 114
Susan ... 114
GOLDSBY
Nancy Ann ... 101
P R ... 101
GOOCH
Wesley Dean ... 152
GOOCH
Cora Eugenia ... 152
GOODALL
John ... 167
Mary ... 167
GOODE
Ada ... 153
C A ... 153
E D ... 154
Fannie ... 102, 154
Lige ... 102
Lila ... 153
GORDON
Emily ... 87
Nancy ... 87
Richard ... 87
Richard J D ... 87
GRACIE C ... 142
GRAHAM
Minerva J ... 45
GRANT
? F ... 146
C F ... 146
C J ... 146
Carrie L ... 146
James ... 158
Jane ... 146, 158
Mattie C ... 146
Nora J ... 146
Thomas ... 158
Thos ... 146
Tom ... 146
GRAY
Adam ... 101
Elsie ... 101
GREENLEE
F M ... 22
V E ... 22
GREENWOOD
Benj ... 85
Betsey ... 74
Betty ... 85
George ... 19
Myrtle ... 85
Pearl ... 74
Samuel A ... 85
Simeon ... 19
Susie ... 19
GRIDER
John ... 168
Mattie ... 168
GROVE ... 55
GRUNDY
Mattie ... 47
GUY
Angeline ... 4
Angeline Elizabeth ... 4
Douglas ... 101
Douglas D ... 100
Jan McGee ... 4
Jane ... 90
Maggie J ... 4
Serena ... 4
Serena Josephine ... 4
William ... 4, 90
William Malcolm ... 4
Wm M ... 4
HALL
George J ... 91
Henrietta ... 91
John W ... 91
Malinda ... 6
Mary E ... 91
Walton ... 6
HAMILTON
Alex ... 27
James H ... 169
Lucy ... 169
Lutitia ... 27
HAMM
Charles S ... 116

Charles Wesley 116
Mattie L 116
HAMPTON
Fannie 35
Marion 35
Mr 58
HANNIE 41
HARDIE 92
HARDWICK
Joe 83
HARDY
Amanda 91
Charles R 91
Dewey 91
Jennetta 91
Reuben 91
Vinnie 91
Walter 91
HARE
F M 31
Francis 37
Laura J 31
Samuel I 31
Samuel J 31
Sarah 31, 37
Zoda 37
HARLIN
Belton 86
George 86
Mary 86
Pearl 86
Ruth G 86
HARMON
John 127
Laura 127
HARNEY
Sison 96
HARRIS
Amanda 23
Ben 73
Bennie 73
Bertie 23
Culberson 10
Cyrus 24, 25, 30
Daisy 73
Ema 197
Flalis 197
Hattie 24
Helen 28
Henderson 10
Hettie 23, 24
Irene 10
J D 162
James M 24
James W 23
Joe 197
John 23
Julia 162
Lottie 178, 179
Lucretia 23
Lucy 28
Mary 28
Nancy 25, 30
Oliver 178
R W 28
Serena 73
Susie 179
Tammie 28
Tennie 23
V S 73
Viney 10
William 23
HATTIE H 101
HAWKINS
J C 87
Joseph Walter 87
Mandy 87
Minnie 87
HAYES
Rose 3
Thomas 3
HAYNES
Julia 80, 177
HAYS
Alexander 3
Annetta 3
Benton Orthella 3
Emma E 109
J S 109
J W 109
Jennetta 3
Jennie 3
John S 109
Lizie 109

Rose 3
Thomas... 3
Thomas Wesley 109
HAZE
Emma E...................................... 109
Thomas W 109
HE???
Stella 126
HEALD
Belle 65, 66
Benjamin 65
C H 65
Charles H...................................... 65
Eliza Jane Guy.............................. 65
William 65
HEEL
C H 70
Hobart 91
Jane 91
HENDERSON
Addie Ruth 83
C W 60, 82, 83
Charles Colbert............................. 83
Charley 83
Ella 83
Grover 83
Grover Cleveland 83
Jim 190
John 93, 190
John Thomas 83
Johnnie 83
Louisa 60, 83
Luella 83
Thelma 83
HENNERSON
Jim 189
Mollie ....
HENRY
Elizabeth....................................... 55
Zeke 55
HEREFORD
John 45
Tibbie 45
HERNDON
Clyde Elwood............................... 71
Ellwood 71, 72
Elwood 71
J M ....
John Milton...................................71
Lafavorite......................................72
Mirtie 72
Myrtle Gale 71
Otto A 71
HEWITT
Julius 125
Louvina.......................................125
Nora 125
Sam 125
Saml 125
Stella 125
Thomas 125
HICKMAN
Chester 13
E A 13
Edwin L...13
Eugene A.......................................13
Frank 13
Frankie 13
Gertie 13
Hester 13
Josephine.......................................13
Lad 13
Lucy 13
Manie 13
Serena 13
Willis 13
HIGGINS
Frances...170
Francies..171
Hester 171
Jack 171
Nebby C 170, 171
Patsey Ann 171
Thomas Nebbe 171
Thos H 170
HILL
Harry Vernon 112
Jas A 112
John Edgar 112
John T 112
Mary A...112
Susie 112
Susie E 112
Thomas J 112

U de 112
Wm Riley 112
HILLHOUSE
Easter 53
HISER
Mincis Willis 54
HOFFMAN
Jesse 113
HOGUE
Beulah 127, 128
Henry 127, 128
HOLDER 165
B J 106
HOLLIS
Joe 40
HOSEA
Georgia 93
HOWARD
A L 157
Allie Viola 156
Frank 128
H M 157
Harriet May 156
Kitty 128
M J 157
Mary J 156
May C 157
Robert Lee 157
William B 156
William Bryan 156
HOWELL
Brunetta 118
Calvin H 158
Jane Colbert 118
John T 118
Lizzie 111
Lizzie Grant 158
Margaret S 159
T P 111
Thomas P. 158
HUDDLESTON
L M 51
Me 51
HULER
Foster 144
HULL
Belle Langdon 142
Bessue 143
Flora 143
Jesse 142
Joseph K. 142
Lucian 143
Lucius Irvin 143
Mary 143
Nelvie 79
Sippey 79, 142
Sippia 143
Sippie 122
Theodore 143
W M 143
William 143
William Jesse 142
Wm 79, 142, 143
HUME
Charlie 30
HUMES
Alfred 60
Buck 83
Jennie 60
HUNA
Mary E 30
HUNTER
Sophie 2
HUTCHINS
Daisy May 177
George 177
Hattie O 177
I-A-PA-HUBBY 96
I-AH-NE-AH 55, 56
IDONUBBY
Ginsey 96
(ILLEGIBLE)
Betsey 184
Houston 184
James 199
Joe 196
Louisa 199
Sophia 199
IMAN 155
IMPSON
William 12
INGRAM
Clytie 70
Eliza Gile 70

Elizabeth Elnora ... 186
Gertie ... 70
Hettie ... 70
Lyda ... 70
Martha ... 70
Mollie ... 70
Nannie ... 186
Ruby ... 70
Tony ... 70
W R ... 70
William Hobart ... 70
William St ... 70
IOTONTUBBY ... 96
Ginsy ... 96
ISHEATUBBY ... 187
IYAKATUBBY
Amy ... 180
Emanuel ... 180
IYOKATUBBY
Annie ... 180
J E ... 113
JACKSON
Hattie ... 68
JAMES
Annie ... 183
Celey ... 19
Elsie Gaines ... 133
George ... 122, 123
Jane ... 183
Joe ... 19
Lou ... 19
Lucy ... 19
Martin ... 123
Simon J ... 133
William ... 183
JENKINS
Boyd ... 78
James ... 78
Jennie ... 78
Minnie ... 78
Peter ... 78
JENNIE ... 123
JESSIE ... 86
JOEL
Alice ... 88
Ella ... 88
Lee ... 88
Solomon ... 88
JOHN ... 91
Levison ... 184
McKinney ... 184
JOHNIE ... 165
JOHNSON
Ben ... 42
C E ... 163
Elba ... 72
Elizabeth ... 63
Emely ... 72
Emly ... 72
Frances ... 72
Geo W ... 72
George ... 27, 40, 82
Henry Z ... 105
Isaac ... 163
John ... 72
Laura L ... 42
Lem ... 163
Lizzie ... 153
Lola M ... 72
Lola Maude ... 72
Lucretia ... 104
Lucy ... 40, 82
Maybell ... 72
O C ... 163
Sam ... 43
Six Shooter ... 72
Thos ... 63
Wesley R ... 72
Wesley W ... 72
William A ... 43
William M ... 72
Willie M ... 72
Zella Marigold ... 72
JOHNSTON
Albert S ... 160
Annie ... 1
Clarence F ... 162
Cora E ... 162
Dellena ... 1
Elizabeth ... 160, 163, 176
Elsie May ... 162
Etta ... 163
Eva Pearl ... 163
Georgia ... 120

Georgianna 1
Georianna 1
Isaac 163
L L 1, 120
Laura 120
Lawrence Lister 1
Lem 162
Lizzie 1
Maggie 1
Maggie May 1
Orin A 162
T B 176
Thos 163
Thos B 1
Willie 1
JOLLY
C C 128
JONES
Alice 169
B M 169
Burney 167
Eaman Mays 151
Edman 167
Eliza 151
Erin Marray 151
Jane 167, 169
Joseph 167
Mary 167
Mary Ella 151
Mary Waite 139
N B 151
Winfield Scott 151
JORDAN
Anneta 34
Jesse L 34
Jessie 34
Jos H 34
Martha 34
Mollie 34
Sally 34
JORDON 167
Martha 167
JOUNSTON
Elizabeth 163
JOURDAN
Mollie 34
JUDE 125
JUZAN
Alevia 30
Alex 30
Alexia 30
KA-NOK-KE 165
KANEY
Alice ....
Amos 85
Billie 84
Eastman 84
Guyamy 85
Harmon 2, 96
Joanna 85
Lafayette 2
Lottie 84
Lucy 84
Margaret 84
Mary 96
Robert Harmon 96
KANY
Harmon 96
KEEL
Cecil 29
Guy 29, 98
Jane 85
Johnson 29
Lewis 172
Lewis Colbert 29
Lula 29, 86
Maulsie 172
Overton 29, 85
William Simon 29
Winona 29
KEMP
Elizabeth Minerva 16
J C 16
Joel 16
Joel Carr 16
Maria 16
KENNEL
Jos 149
Mamie 149
KERNAL
George 96
KERNEL
Amy Parker 95
Charley 95

George 95
Joe 95
Joseph 95
KERR
Irene 114
Lockhart B.. 114
Perry N.. 114
Phoebe 114
Rita 114
W F 114
Waite Tecumseh.. 114
KILLCREASE
Annie 182
Eastman.. 183
Lettie 182
Minnie 182
KIMBERLIN
Eliza 110
Elizabeth..51, 117
G W 110
Ira Earnest 110
Izaah J 51
Lizzie 51, 110
R S 110
W G 51, 110, 117
William G.. 110
William H.. 110
Zudie 51
KING
Callie Boyd 97
Clemmie Lelia.. 97
F J 97
Marie Boyd 97
KINNEY
Amanda.. 25
Ida 25
James 25
Jesse 25
Jessie 25
John H 25
Levi 25
Lillie 25
Ludie 25
Margaret.. 25
Minnie 25
Osceola.. 25
Oscola 25
Patrick 25
KIRKWOOD
Lige 56
Susan 56
KISSIE 191
KREBBS
Elizabeth 94
Nathaniel..94
Robt C 94
L M 123
LA-DITCHA..93
LAEL
Eddie 169
Eddie C 169
Jacob 169
Lucy 169
Noah 169
Rushie 169
Ruth 169
Susan 169
LAFLON
Charles 49
Mary A..49
LAFLORE
Charles 50
LAMBERT
Emily 151
Hiram 151
LAND
Alice 173
C M C 173
Hiram 173
Kitty 173
Lula 173
Marilda..174
Matilda..165
Maulda Folsom 173
Oscar 174
Oscar Lee 173
Sally Ann 173
LANGDON
Joe 142
Libbie 142
LANHAM
Amanda..184
Bessie 184
Charles H 184

Jemmie ... 185
Jimmie ... 184
Manley ... 184
Mary G ... 185
Mary Jane ... 184
P J ... 185
Perry G ... 184
LANNOM
Annie Myrtle ... 137
Bertha ... 137
Cordelia ... 137
R T ... 137
Samantha J ... 137
William R ... 137
LASATER
Corinne ... 140
Geo M ... 141
Milas ... 140, 141
Sarah ... 140, 141
Sophronia ... 141
LAVINA ... 79
LAW
Adolphus H ... 39
Elizabeth ... 39
Margaret Elizabeth ... 39
LAWINEY ... 96
LAWRENCE
Anne ... 138
Azzie Anna ... 138
Eliza ... 138
Osborne ... 138
LAWT ... 123
LEADER
Billie ... 97
Emily ... 182
Jim ... 98
Morris ... 182
Susan ... 182
LEE
Biddie ... 129
J J ... 104
Kate ... 129
Sam ... 129
Sam S ... 129
LEMONS
Henry ... 159
LESTER
America ... 29
E W ... 29
Ella ... 29
Moran S. ... 99
Wesley ... 99
LEWIS ... 26
Adam ... 190
Al-lich-ta ... 191
Allichta ... 191
Benj ... 21
Benjamin ... 20
Bill ... 77
Blunt ... 20
Dickson ... 191
Eliza Love ... 77
Hepsie ... 20
Jennis ... 20
John ... 191
Lena ... 20
Louisa ... 21
Mary ... 26
Polly ... 2
Sholika ... 20
Thompson ... 191
LINDSAY ... 123
LINDSEY ... 4
Pam ... 4
LIZA ... 182
LIZA ANN ... 183
LIZZIE ... 41
LO-AH-TE ... 92
LONG
Jane ... 96
Marshall ... 96
LOVE
Alvia ... 62
Annie ... 123
Betty ... 62
Buck ... 130
Calvin S. ... 98
Cary Ann ... 123
Clara M ... 51
Clara Maude ... 51
Clarence ... 124
Elizabeth ... 130
Frank ... 62
Frank C ... 130

G W 123
George 62, 123, 124
George C 130
Grace E.. 130
Hattie Simpson............................. 130
Henry 153
Joe 130
Judge 58
Lafayette...................................... 121
Lauta Overton............................... 123
Lena B 51
Lena Belle 50
Lizzie Melvina 124
Lottie Lillian 62
Martha 34
Mary H.. 51
Mary Hazel.................................... 51
Mary Jane..................................... 158
Mary M 50
Melvina 62, 123, 124
Nona 124
Nona E 130
Overton 34
Pearl G 130
R F, Jr 130
R J 130
Robert B 130
Robert H..................................51, 106
Robert Howard.............................. 51
Robt H 51
Ruby Jewel................................... 124
Sallie 51
Sallie G.. 130
Sally 106, 153
Sam 124
Sarah 98
Thomas B 50
W E 62
Will E 62
William 130
Wm 123

LOWRANCE
Charles Orrick 27
Charley 27
Eleanor 27
John 27
Mary Easter.................................... 27
May A 27
Oscar 27
Oscar K 27
Robert H..27
Robt A 27
Willis B 27

LULA M 101

LUMPKA
Markey..178

LYDIA 70

LYNN
J C 98

MA-KO-E-CHA..................................20
MA-SA-TUBBY 188
MA-TA-HO-MEY 167
MA-TO-HO-MEY 193

MCALESTER
Joe 44
Kate 44

MCCANN
Harris 27

MCCAULEY
Bryan 58
C T 32
Elmer 58
James 58, 61
Jennie 33
Junie 32
Margaret..58
Peachie..32
Richie 32
Susan 58, 61
Susie 32
William 33
Wm Walkins 32

MCCLURE 177
Amanda...177
Battie 177
Ed 177
Imon 154
Imon D..154
Jennie 154, 155
Jenson 177
John W 154
Lillie 154
Lucy Belt.......................................154
Mary 117, 149, 155, 177

Russs 154
Tamsey 177
Tecumseh 117, 149, 155, 177
Tecumseh, Jr 177
MCCOY
James 27, 44
Nanny 27
Sibby 44
MCCRUMMEN
D H 154
E L 154
Sally 154
Susie 154
MCCURTAIN
Ben 15
Clara 16
Eastman 191
Edmon 191
Green 16
Humphrey 191
Randolph 15
MCCURTAISS
Clara 16
MCDANIEL
Cammie 16
Ed 16
James 15
Lula 15
Marvin 15
Mitchell 15
Ruth 15
Susan 46
Thomas 15
MCDONELL
Cleveland 40
Eliza Jane 40
Isaac 40
Josephus 40, 41
Nicodemus 40
Nona 40
Norval 40
Susan 40
W R 40
MCGEE
Arch 69
Cornelius 41
Dora 69
Jessie 69
Liza 41
Martha 68
Nancy 69
MCGLASSON
Emma 52
James 53
Jesse 52
Lula 52
MCGLOSSAN
Eliza 53
Ema 53
Kessoe 53
Marvelton 53
MCKINNEY
Henry 91
Sally Harris 91
MCLANE
Harrison 92
Labon 21
Margaret 123
Mary Jane Callahan 92
Tom 20
Willie 92
Willie B 92
MCLISH
Esther 18
James N 119
Jerry J 69
Jirry 70
John 23
Julia 131, 132
Nancy Love 69
Otwell 69
Polly Ann 119
R H 70
Richard 69, 70
Richard H 69
Richard R 69
Rosa 69
Rose 69
MCMAHON
Frances 67
John 67
MCMILLAN
Alva 98
Alva Linzie 97

Bertha 98
Bertha Frances.............................. 97
Edward 97
George 98
George W 97
Joseph T 97
Lillian Ethel................................. 97
MCMILLAN
Lillie Myrtle 66
MCMILLAN
Mary 66
Millie 97
Nancy 97
Rosie 98
Rosie Rena 97
Sarah 97
MCMILLAN
W A 66
MCMILLAN
W A 66
MALINDA 93, 180
MAMIE 28
MANWELL...............................106, 107
Louisa 106, 107
MARKER
Fannie Grove 14
G G 14
MARRIET 77
MARTIN
Ida 117
Ida M 117
Ida R 117
Sam H 117
Tom 117
Tom F 117
Tom G 117
Tom S 117
Verbeth..................................... 117
Verlinda.................................... 117
MARY 119
MARY F 98
MASON
Sarah A.. 12
MATTHEWS
W D 111
MATTIE M 166
MAUDE 125
MAUPIN
Charles Stuart.................................49
Laurina P..49
Melinda..49
Milton 49
MAYER
Amanda.......................................105
Betsie 105
George 105
Henry 105
Mary 105
MAYS
Clarence 150
Dave 150
David 145, 150, 151
Mrs 134
Sally 150
Susan 150
Susan E 145, 150, 151
Susan Wilson 118
T G 150
Willie 150
MAYTUBBY
Eastman......................................189
Franklin......................................189
Hogan 189
Lucy 189
Mandy 194
Minnie 189
Toney 194
MCBEE
Millie 12
MCCARTY
Claudie Eugene 8
James William................................8
Jas 9
Jefferson Odie L.............................8
Jennie Lou Mittie 8
Jim 9
Mary 9
Mary Elizabeth...............................8
Mary L 9
Nettie 8
Samp 9
Sampie 8
William 8
MCCLATCHY

James 2
Lucy 2
MCDANIEL
Mary 15
MCGEE
Amos 8
Lottie 8
MCKINNEY
Jincey 13
Peter 13
MELTON 72
MERCHANT
E E 79
Ellen 79
Fannie 79
Harry 79
Irene 79
James S W 79
Malvina 79
Victoria 79
MERSERSMITH
Laura C 172
MILLER
Margaret E 10
Winton W 10
MINNIE MAY 84
MISHONTAUMBBY 182
Iba 181
Jackson 181
Jincy 181
MISHONTAUMBY 178
Liza 178
MISHONTOMBBY 181
Aaron 178
Liza 181
MITCHELL
Carann 161
G A 161
Gaines A 161
George 161
Jane 150
Jessie Pauline 161
Joe 150
Mantie 161
Perilla 161
Rilla 161
Wm 161
MOBLEY
B E 41
Gerald Farley 41
Helen Louise 41
Tennie 41
MOBLY
Benj E 42
MOLLARDY
Mollie 31
MOLLISH 19
MONTRAY 78
Liza 78
M G 78
Perry 78
MOORE
Carrie Imogene 148
Catherine 115, 135
Christopher 115, 135
E L 144
E M 148
Elisha 148
Elizabeth 115, 116
Gracie 144
Helen Foster 144
J B 115
James E 115
Jennie 99, 115
Jessie E 148
Lillie 144
Mary Jennie 115
Nancy E 115
Willie 144
Wm 99
MORAN
S 99
MORRIS
Annie 34, 176
Caline 148
Ellen 149
Ellen C 177
Frank 149
Joe 149
Joseph 177
Joseph E 176
Salina 149
Selina 148
Susie 149

William Franklin 148
Wm H 34
MOSELEY
Joseph 104
MOSS
Jeff 9
Sarah 9
MULKEY
Bettie 60
Charles S 60
Elsie 60
H S 60
John C 60
MURRAY
Carrie 80
Cora 161
Eph 80, 93
Frank 161
Frankie 161
Frankie Lee 161
H T 67
Henry C 161
J A 160
Laura 93
Margaret 67, 161
MYERS 105
Abraham 153
Eula 153
George 93
Jobitha 153
John 93
Joseph F 153
Malinda 93
Maude 93
Patsey 80, 93
Thomas David 93
Winfield S 119
NEAL
Oliver 178
Silas 178
NEWBURY
Emily 107
Sampson 107
NEWTON
Calvin 57
Ed 57
Evaline 57
Marion 57
Ruthie V 57
Seith 57
W C 57
William Calvin 57
Willie 57
Willie Ida 57
NICHOLAS
Lena 35
Maggie 35
NICHOLS
A 32, 35
A M 89
Alexander 88
Bob 89
Clyde 89
Clyde Cleveland 88
Daisy 88
Elizabeth 89
George 89
Jewel 35
Joe 103
Joe B 102
Lee 102
Lena 35
Lottie 103
Louis 168
M Brenda 35
Maggie B 35
Mildred 103
R L 102
Robert H 88
Robt J 103
Sarah Lottie 102
Stanwaite 35
Susan 32, 89
Susan M 35, 88
Velary Etta 152
Wait 35
Waitie 35
Walter 88
Winnie 103
Winnie Elsie 102
NO-YE 178
NOLATUBBY
Hollie 179
NOLEN

Bob 108
NORA I 148
NORMA 119
NORMAN
Belinda 74
Catherine 74
Dan 74
Daniel S 74
Katie 74
Wm W 74
NORRIS
James 46
Josephine 45
Josie 46
Margaret A L 46
Maude 45
Minnie 45
Myrtie 45
T 45
Thomas 46
Tom 45
V I 46
NORTON
Bud 74
Henry 74
O-NAH-HE 33
OLIPHANT
Belle 140
Claude Waite 140
Jennie 140
Lucile M 140
Oscar Paul 140
Ruth D 140
Sam R 140
W D 140
Willie 140
ON-HO-YE 180
OSAVIOR
Dollie 33
Frank 33
OTH-TO-HI-YE 21
OTT
Carney 196
Eliza Wade 196
Jack 196
Johnson 196
OVERTON 77
OWENS
Jessie 75
Laura Vaginia 74
Mattie M 187
PALMER
Bud 8
Elizabeth M 8
Jane 8
Joe 8
Joseph 8
Lafayette 8
Lafeate 8
Rhoda 8
Thomas L 8
PARIS
Jack 108
Rachael Owens 108
PARKER
Benny 75
Charles Benjamin 75
Charley 75
Governor 93
Guy 75
John 47
John T 75
Laura 75
Laura B 76
Laura Belle 75
Mary C 75
Sophie 75
Thomas 75
Thos 75
Victoria 75
Victoria Sophronia 75
William 75
William Guy 75
Wilson 75
PATTERSON
Agnes 188, 189
Louisa 186
PAUL
Abby 177
Buck 133
Dewey 177
E O 143
Ellen 143
Jennie 127

S W 133
Sam 49, 132
Samuel Jackson 142
Sarah J 132, 151
Smith 143
Smith W 132, 143
Wm 177
Wm H 132

PENNA
Amanda... 31
Charley... 31
Cyrus 31

PENNER
Amanda... 30
Augustus....................................... 30
Charley... 30
Cyrus 30
Felix 30
Pauline 30

PERKINS
Albert 183
Hardin 17
Jane 183
Katie 17

PERRY
? J 152
Albert W.......................185, 187, 195
Allen *(Illegible)* 195
Annie M 195
Chas 195
Emma J....................................... 195
Houston 183
Ida Fay 195
(Illegible).................................... 198
(Illegible) D................................ 195
J M 180
John F 152
Johnson 180, 182, 184
Liley 180
Maude 195
Susan 195
Tabitha 185, 187, 195
William 198

PETTENRIDGE
C 136
Charley...................................... 136
John 136

PICKENS
Ed 14
Edmon 14
Edmon Jr..14
Fannie Grove...................................14

PIKEY
Ben 170, 171
Catherine.....................................170
Delila 170
Hattie 170
J Berry 170
Katie 170
Kissie 171
M J 170
Minerva.......................................170
Mollie 170
Montford J...................................170
Sophia 170
Thos Benson 170

POE
George 137

POFF
Maggie Mary...............................172
Maggie May................................172
Old Man......................................172

POKE
?raat 59
Mary 59

POLK
Henry T..................................25, 26
Oscar Alinton...............................25

POLLARD
Jake 55
Margaret.......................................55

POTTS
Sophia 29
W A 29

POYNER
Mrs I J 82

PRICE
Alice 61
Ben 61
Benj 60
Benjamin Franklin 60
Betsey 60
Beulah 60
Bisey 60

C C 71
Ellis 60
Erie 71
Guy 71
Jennie 61
Jennie Belle 60
John 71
Louisa 71
Mollie 71
Nathan 61
Sweet 71
Therean Bogart 71
Thomas Guy 71
W N 60

PRIEST
Delena 15

PUSLEY
Susan 193

PYBAS
Boy 149
Daisy 149
Dora 149
E C 149
Fannie Belle 149
K M 149
Lee Winston 149
Nellie H 149
Pat 149

PYBES
Dora 150
F B 150
Nellie H 150

R B 130
R R 126

RANDOLPH
Allie 157
Elizabeth 157
Fay 157
James 157
James M 116
Joe M 157
Olive E 157
Paul Williams 157
Sadie 148
Sarah 116
Tabitha 116
W C 116, 148

REAGAB
Stella 78

REAGAN
Walker 78

REAM
Annie Guy 37
Robt L 37

REED
Lizzie 197

REEL
Dan 112
Daniel 112
Ida 112
Pearl 112

REER
Isena 114
Jackshort 114

RENNIE
Alexander 22
Catherine Rooks 126
Cecil 23
Cecil C 22
Claude 23
Claude C 22
Geo B 125
George Burney 126
James 126
Jessie 23
Jessie D 22
M E 23
Mary Adeline 22
Mary Ellen 22
Mary M 22
May 23
Nora 22
William 22

REYNOLDS
Jack 165
Lida 165
Tom 165
Zack 165

ROBERT J 148

ROBERTS
Jacob 7
Klicy 192
Lawson 192
Margaret M 7

ROBESON 190
Eliza 190
Jane 190
ROBINSON
Joe 190
ROBISON
Addie L 39
Altai E 40
Hattie 40
Hattie Adeline 39
(Illegible).. 40
W F 40
ROBRTSON
Frank 56
Joseph 56
Sarah 56
RODGERS
Hugh 165
Nora 165
ROOSEVELT.. 5
ROXIE 55
RUCKER
Albert W.. 194
Mamie Arenia.. 194
Rutha 194
Welch 195
Wilton 195
RYLE
Emma 84
Jessie Lee 84
M D 84
Mattie 84
Nancy 84
Nannie May.. 84
W H 84
Whitmill A 84
S C 113
SADDLER 120
SADLER
Ginsey 120
Joseph 120
Lavina 120
Louvina 120
Wm 120
SANDERS
Louisam.. 171
SANER
Boss D 93
SCHOEPPE
Christine..90
Elizabeth 90
Fred L 90
John 90
SCOTT
Houston..189
Louisa 20
Mary 189
Wilburn..189
William 21
SE-LE-AN 191
SEALY
Acey 106
Albert 111
Alice 53, 192, 193
Annie 5
Ben 193
Charley..87
Charlie 106
Clarence 53
Daily 111
Dave 5, 115
Eli 115
Ely 5
Esau 115
George 40, 192
Henry 192
Holmes..53
Jewel 53
Joseph 192, 193
Josephine..40
Julia 5
Julie 5
Limond..5
Lottie 53, 115
Maggie 115
Mary Ann..192, 193
Morgan..193
Pey oh kia..111
Phoebi 5
Stephen 5, 111
Viney 193
Wilburn..5
Willis 192, 193
SEIFRIED

Julia 139
Mary L 139
William 139
Wm 139
Wm F 139
SENA 74, 75
SEWELL
Robert 191
SHA-PE-YA-KE 2
SHA-THA-HE-CHA 165
SHANNON
Annie 145
Annie Laura.. 145
Charley.. 145
Charlie Foster.. 145
Daisy 158
Ida Estella.. 145
J R 129
James R 129
Jesse R 158
Jim 129
Joseph Scott.. 145
Laura G 145
Lee 145
Murphy Lena.. 145
Nora 129
Robert Lee.. 145
S E 145
Sarah 129
Scott 145
T F 145
Thressa 145
Thressa May 145
William 145
William T 144
Willie Inez.. 145
SHARP
J M 19
Mary Gladys.. 19
Sallie 19
SHE-MA-HO-GA.. 128
SHE-MA-LE-KEY 188
SHE-MINTH-A.. 164
SHE-NO-KA-CHA..55, 56
SHE-NO-KE-CHA 75
SHEPPA
Elizabeth.. 90
SHIPMAN
Buck 88
D C 88
Kieth 88
Lena 93
Willie Augustus 88
SHOEPPE
Fred 90
SHUM-AH-TE-CHA 184
SHUN-POL-E-CHA..190
SIL-LE-A 12
SILEY 170
SIM-CHA-CHE..14
SIM-E-CHA-CHE..15
SIN-E-CHA-CHE..16
SMITH
? A 76
A M 64
Alfred M 64
E S 64
J A 65
Lillian Estelle..64
Mary A..64
Nancy 65, 76
Sophrona..75
W D 75
SOUSE
Dory 92
Georgia 92
Hix 92
Hosea 93
John 92
Lina 92
Lind 93
Lula 92
SPAIN
David M..133
Georgia 133
Georgia D..126, 133
Jessie 133
McKnightie..133
Mary E 133
Sallie P 133
SPAINE
Georgia 133
Georgia D..133
Jessie 133

McKnight 133
Mary 133
SPARKS
Dollie 160
Ethel 160
George W 160
Hannah 160
R L 160
Richard L 160
Thos 160
SPEAR
E R 141
Mary 141
SPEED
Annie 146
Charles J 146
J L 146
James L 145
Mary 146
Sam 146
Samuel J 146
Willie G 146
Willie Grant 146
STANTON
R D 115
STAPLETON
Mary 33
R H 33
STATEN
Elijah 120
STATON
Elijah 120
Laura 120
Ludie David 120
Nita May 120
Ruthie 120
Will 120
Wm 120
STE-MA-HO-TE 178
STE-MA-KE-CHA 172
STEMONTUBBY 170
STEPHENSON
Ivry 68
Philip 68
Steve 31
Victoria 68
Wayne 68
STEVENSON
John 117
John F 117
John H 116
Lees 117
Malinda 116, 117
Mary 116, 117
STEWART
Addie 162
B M 103
Ben 98
Ben M 98
Carl 162
Charles F 162
Eugene 98
Frances 103
Frank 162
Gertrude M 98
John 162
Josephine 121, 162
Mary Frances 98
Sarah 98
Wiley 162
STIDLER
Adeline 24
STIGLER
Edward 24
Edward Buckley 24
Hettie Lee 24
J S 24
Joseph S 24
Lela H 25
Mary 24, 25
Willie 25
Willie Grady 24
STONE
Bill 65
James B 65
Josephine 65
Josie 65
Lacy 65
Mary 65
Sophia 65
William 65
William C 65
STORY
Elijah 95

Sam 95
STRICKLAND
C G 173
C W 168
Charles 167, 168, 173
Charles Guy 173
Elizabeth 167, 168
Glassey 168
Hannah 167
Jettie 168
Martha 90
Tom 168
W D 173
Wm Douglass 173
SU??ATT
Lee 104
Sarah 104
SULLIVAN
Anna L 194
Daniel 193
Edward A 194
Ellen 194
Florence 194
Margaret 194
Mary B 194
Michael Jos 194
Mike 194
Mike J 194
Rachel 194
Robert E 194
SULPHIE 96
TA-LA-CHE 193
TA-LA-HE 167
TALLEY
Agnes 113
Allen D 113
Elisabeth 113
Fannie 113
Sudie B 113
Thomas P 113
William 113
Willis N 113
Wm 113
TAMSEY P 113
TAYLOR
John 68
Joseph 45
Lena 45
Tora 68
TEL-LO-NECK-KA 12
THOMAS
Amanda 83
Billy 167
C D 32
Charles Cruce 32
Charles W 32
Charley 32
Eliza 83
Isaac 35, 36, 83
Isaac Alva 35
Margaret 32
Minnie 32
Russell Gardner 32
William 167
Willie 167
THOMASON
Cyntha 5
William 5
THORNTON
Anita 79
Carrie Murray 79
G G 80
M A 80
Robert 79
W D 80
William D 80
Wm D 80
TILLOWER
Liney 60
TISH-A-HAM-BEY 20
TISH-AP-A-LE-TUBBY 172
TISH-E-OF-TA 92
TO-KA-THLAN-KE 20
TO-KA-THLON-CHE 20
TO-YAH-HE-NA 20
TOLBERT
Danl 127
Laura 127
TOM 32, 125
TOMS
Becky 36
Creek 36
TON-A-TUB-BY 165
TROOP

Addie Jewel 47
Cecil Gordon 47
Franklin 47
Jesse L 47
Laura May 47
Laure 47
Mahala Jane 47
Myrtle 47
Myrtle Jane 47
Newel 47
TURMAN
Annie Ream 37
Louis Brudinot 37
Louis M 38
Louis N 37
Martha E 37
Thos J 37
Vinnie Hoxie 37
Vinnie Ream 37
TURNBULL
Adel 102
C W 159
Clarence Rex 159
Claude 102
Dick 102
Fannie 102
Jettie Lemons 159
John 64, 102, 154, 159, 160
Lottie 64
Loyd Martin 159
Lucy 64, 102, 154, 159, 160
Maude 102
Roy 64
Ryan 64
Virgil Oster 64
TUSHASAHY
Serena 172
TYE
Elizabeth 111
Geo W 111
TYSON
Betsy 185
Cub-brish 185
Ed 185
UNDERWOOD
(Illegible) 200
Intalubby 200
Wallace 188
William 188
VAIL 28
Jinsey Colbert 28
Rebecca 28
Vergie 28
Willie 28
VANDERSLICE
Eliza 171
Jacob 171
Malissa B 172
Mary 171
Maulsee Bula 171
Minnie 171
Robert J 171
Walter 171
VAUGHN 96
Jesse 96
Jessie 96
VENITA 92
VERDIE V 142
W LEE 77
W R 113
WACHUBBY
Rhoda 88
Willie 88
WADE
Alemas H 198
(Illegible) 198
Lizzie 198
Mary 15
Matt 15
WAIT 142
Emely 141
Katie 139
Mary 139
WAITE
A R 141
Catherine....... 114, 126, 139, 140, 141
Della 159
Emely 141
Fred 139
Grace C 141
Katie 139
Leo E 141
Mary 139
Mary E 141

T F 139, 141
Thos 126
Thos F 114, 140, 141
Verdi V.. 141
Winifred 141
WALDEN
Thomas.. 170
WALDON
Bill Byrd...................................... 122
Ebelene.. 156
Hosea Thomas............................. 156
Hosey 156
Ja?cy 156
Jimmie 122
Joe 122
Lisa Maria 122
Maria 122
Sadie 156
Sina 156
Sophia 122
Sophie 156
Susie 156
Thomas.. 123
Thos 156
Tom 122
WALKER
Delia 111
Mary 111
Thomas.. 111
Thomas H.................................... 111
Thos 111
WALL
Malsie 182
WALNER
Ebb 124
Ed 125
Frank 124
J H 164
Jim 124
John 124
John H 163
Lena 124
Lula 164
Robert 124
Susan Carter................................ 112
Wm 112, 124, 164
WARREN
John 57
Ma? 57
Mary Catherine 57
Mary J 57
Nannie 58
Nannie C 57
R W 104
Reuben 57
Reubin 58
Ruth Bixby 57
William 58
William Byrd 57
William F 57
WASHINGTON
J R 76
John R 76
John Richard 76
M E 76
May Ellen.......................................76
Mollie 76
Russ 69
Sally 76
William Edward 76
Wm 33
WASSON
Abbie 100
Clark B..100
Emma Janette Chloe....................100
Joseph 100
Joseph J.......................................100
Nannie E 100
Victor B.......................................100
WATKINS
Betty 104
Bill 104
Edna 77
Elizabeth 77
Eugean 109
Eugine 109
Henry Patton 104
James 104
James Artie 104
Nora 104
R L 109
Susan 58
W R 77
W R, Jr 77

William Eugene 104
WEBB
Daisy Maude 50
Daisy N 50
Geo H 50
Geo W 50
George H 50
Guy L 50
Guy Laflore 50
Stella L 50
Stella Laflon 50
Susan S 50
WELCH
Alice 147
Mattie 147
WELLS
Benj 31
Maria J 31
WESTON
Harry 64
Ida 64
WHEATLEY
G W 106
Louisa 106
WHITE
Annie 177
J N 30
James 176
John 177
Willie 176
WHITEBEAD 91
WILL 113
WILLIAM
Charles 168
WILLIAMS 67
Allie 118
Alonza 118
Ben 68
Bill 48
Clara J 66
David S 118, 119
Elizabeth 155, 157
Eva 99
Fletcher 157
G M 99
I F 155
Jennie L 118
Kittie 118
Lelia 118
Missie 48
Orin 99
Sam 118
Sam, Jr 118
Samuel L 118, 119
Susan Elizabeth 118
Wade 118
WILLIE 66
WILLIFORD
Joe 92
Margaret 92
Nannie 92
Richard 92
WILLIS 180
Archie Leonard 48
Floradel 48
Frances 48
Francis 49
J Hamp 85
Jacob L 48
Johnson 179
Wm 54
WILSON
A T 135
Adeline 200
Alex 73
C A 134
Cicily A 73
Claude Allen 134
Emma B 135
Emme B 134
G W 63
George 200
J B 134, 135
Joseph B 134
Kate 200
Lem 200
Philip 134
Phillip 118
S E 134
Sue Ellen 134
Susan E 134
W A 147
WISDOM
Aaron 107

Birtha 107
Malinda 106
Manwell 106
Sampson 107
WITTEN
Charles F 146
Matilda 146
WOLF
A H 80
Bella 74
Carrie 80
Dewey 80
Frank 80
Jessie 80
May 80
Monroe 97
Murphy 98
Sarah 80
Susan 80
T J 80
WOLFE
Frances 17
Francis 18
Harriet 157
Harriett 17
Jim 18
Joe 157
Mattie 17
Moses 196
Susan 81, 144
Wolfe 81
WOLFENBARGER
Bert 105
Birdie 104
Garnett 104
James Hanson 104
Joseph 104
Launa 104
Lula 104
Rella 104
WOLFORD 77
WOOFENBARGER
James 105
Lorena 105
Reila 105
Zula 105
WORCESTER
Arlington T 12
Arlington Telle 12
Nicholas 12
WORLEY
C R 134
Martha 134
WORSHAM
Birdie 42
Birdie Guy 41
Farley 41
Jewel 41
John Farley 41
Loucrita 41
Lucretia 41
Martha 41
Mattie 41
Richard 41
Sam 42
Samuel 41
Tennie 42
WRAY
Daisy 99
David 99
William 99
WYNDOM
Lizzie 85
Wyatt 85
YARBROUGH
Jas 30
YOAKUM
Bertha B 174
Beulah Pearl 174
D H 175
Fannie 174, 175
George H 175
John J 174
Leonard 175
M B 175
M M 174, 175
Mary B 175
Minnie 174
Minnie A 174
Uana Lee 174
William 175
YOUNG
Adaline 82
Bettie May 82

Carrie 82
Carrie Lee...................................... 82
Granville W.................................. 82
Greenville...................................... 82
James Granville............................. 82
James L 82
Jos 82
Judy 82
Lizzie 82
Lizzie Bell..................................... 82
Lucy 82
Lucy Branferd 82
Mattie 82
Mattie Lou..................................... 82
Nancy 82
Nancy Colbert 82
Patsey 82
Z A 28

www.ingramcontent.com/pod-product-compliance
Lightning Source LLC
Chambersburg PA
CBHW030241030426
42336CB00009B/196
* 9 7 8 1 6 4 9 6 8 0 3 9 6 *